HARVARD UNIVERSITY PRESS

A HISTORY

Harvard University Press

A History

MAX HALL

HARVARD UNIVERSITY PRESS

Cambridge, Massachusetts, and London, England

Set in Linotron Sabon and designed by Marianne Perlak

Library of Congress Cataloging in Publication Data

Hall, Max.
Harvard University Press.

Bibliography: p.
Includes index.
1. Harvard University. Press—History. 2. Univer-
sity presses—Massachusetts—Cambridge—History.
3. Publishers and publishing—Massachusetts—Cambridge
—History. 4. Printing—Massachusetts—Cambridge—
History. I. Title.
Z473.H34H34   1986   070.5'94'097444   85–8736
ISBN 0–674–38080–0 (alk. paper) (cloth)
ISBN 0–674–38081–9 (paper)

To Judy, Nancy, and Clay

Contents

Introduction:
A University and Its Publishing House   1

1. Antecedents and Founding   4

2. First Steps under C. C. Lane, 1913–1919   25

3. The Murdock Years, 1920–1934   43

4. Malone and a Wider Audience, 1935–1943   66

5. Wartime Shock   86

6. Scaife and Survival, 1943–1947   105

7. Wilson and the Rise of the Press, 1947–1967   125

8. The Paperback Question, the Double Helix,
and Other Stories   156

9. Crisis and Reorganization, 1968–1972   176

Notes   205

Sources and Acknowledgments   241

Index   245

Illustrations

1. Birthplace 12
2. Edwin Gay 18
3. Donald Scott 18
4. A. Lawrence Lowell 21
5. Robert Bacon 21
6. C. C. Lane 26
7. George L. Kittredge 29
8. Keepsake of Randall Hall 34
9. W. A. Dwiggins 38
10. Harold Murdock 44
11. A Dwiggins book cover 53
12. A Bruce Rogers title page 55
13. Thirty-eight Quincy Street 59
14. Dumas Malone 67
15. *Great Chain of Being, Functions of the Executive,* and *Philosophy in a New Key* 74
16. Mott's magazine history 77
17. James B. Conant 87
18. David Pottinger 97
19. Warren Smith 101
20. Roger Scaife 106
21. *Dictionary of Music* 112
22. Scaife and his staff 118
23. Thomas J. Wilson 126
24. Jewett House 130
25. Kittredge Hall 130
26. *Eleanor of Aquitaine* 136
27. Waldron Belknap 139

28. *Poems of Emily Dickinson* 145
29. The Adams Papers 147
30. Wilson and President Kennedy 149
31. H. M. Jones and Nathan Pusey 151
32. *John Keats* 153
33. *The Browser* 154
34. Mark Carroll, Warren Smith, and Thomas Wilson 157
35. Joseph Elder, Maud Wilcox, Eleanor Kewer, and Max Hall 158
36. Burton Stratton, Grace Briggs, Loring Lincoln, and Mark Saxton 158
37. David Horne 160
38. Don Scott and Tom Wilson 170
39. *Reporting the News, City Politics, Process of Education,* and *Animal Species* 172
40. Mark Carroll 178
41. *Insect Societies* 179
42. The first ten Harvard Paperbacks 181
43. Brian Murphy 194
44. Oscar Handlin 200
45. Arthur Rosenthal and Derek Bok 202

HARVARD UNIVERSITY PRESS

A HISTORY

A University and Its Publishing House

A PUBLISHING HOUSE in a university is an agency of some importance to civilization, and it is also interesting for another reason—namely, that it is a rare and puzzling species, carrying within itself the question "Is it a business or isn't it?" To answer "It is both an educational institution and a business" does not necessarily settle the matter because at different times and places, and even at the same time and the same place, there can be wide disagreement over where to put the emphasis.

Notwithstanding the university press's intellectual influence and its self-contradictory nature, in the United States there has not been much examination of its antecedents, birth, development, and relations with the parent university. True, university presses as a group are very self-conscious and self-improving and have studied their own operations a lot. But there is room for another kind of attention: a historical account of the publishing activities of a major research university. Up to now, such an account has not been undertaken. At Harvard in the 1930s Samuel Eliot Morison could write a five-hundred-page book, *Three Centuries of Harvard,* with scarcely a mention of Harvard University Press or its long series of Harvard forerunners. Even at that time, this left a gap. Half a century later there is much more to be told.

The purpose of this book is to fill that gap—to tell the story of Harvard University Press, including its ancestry, founding, and evolution, its vividly contrasting leaders, its successes, failures, and troubles, all in the context of the university of which it is a department.

What kind of history is this? For one thing, obviously, it is Harvard history. Harvard presidents, vice-presidents, treasurers, professors, and alumni are leading characters, along with Press administrators, editors, authors, and others directly engaged in the enterprise. It is, in a way, intellectual history. It is also printing history, for Harvard has owned three printing offices. A printing press came into Harvard's possession nearly 350 years ago (a fact well known to printing historians and well described by Professor Morison in his *Founding of Harvard College*), and in 1802 Harvard established a printing shop actually named "the University Press" (a fact not at all well known). Conceivably, too, business historians will have some interest in the managerial and financial problems of the publishing house. The term I prefer for a book so consumed with the development and nature of a university press is "institutional history," though institutional history at its purest would contain penetrating generalizations about university presses, whereas I concentrate so hard on understanding what went on at Harvard that I make few comparisons with other campuses.

It is also fair to inform the reader that I was on the scene from 1960 to 1973 as the Press's first Editor for the Social Sciences. I hope this has helped rather than hindered my ability to see the Press whole.

Three main themes run through the Harvard story. They are accomplishment, struggle, and generosity.

1. ACCOMPLISHMENT   The Press has disseminated the results of investigation and analysis in more than six thousand books. Notwithstanding the organization's limitations and imperfections (which have sometimes been conspicuous), nothing can take away that fact. The accomplishment belongs more to the authors than to the Press, and it belongs in part to the distinguished Harvard departments that many of the books sprang from. But the Press has been the agency that has enabled the authors to have their say. Moreover, the Press has not been an inert conduit. It has originated, sought out, and encouraged important projects. It has consistently upheld standards of accuracy and clarity—qualities not always abundant even in academic environments. By editorial suggestions and graphic design it has helped authors to put their ideas across more effectively. In so serving the author it has also served the reader, who after all is the most important person in the whole publishing enterprise. Finally the Press has not only brought the scholar's findings to other scholars but has deliberately made itself into a bridge for scholars to reach a broader public. All these are scholarship-enhancing functions, and they can be epitomized in a phrase used by Press Director Dumas Malone in the 1930s: "scholarship plus."

2. STRUGGLE The organization has almost always seen a need to do more than its funds and facilities would allow. Wars and economic slumps, mistakes and misunderstandings, the disappointments of individuals, the clashing of personalities, and the varying attitudes of university administrators have interfered at times with the sense of accomplishment and with the accomplishment itself.

3. GENEROSITY Without the help of a long line of faculty members, alumni, and friends, who gave their time and advice (even occasionally money), the institution could have accomplished little and would not have survived.

The more one ponders the accomplishment, the struggle, and the generosity, the more clearly one sees that those very themes have pervaded the history of the university to which the Press belongs.

The proposal that I write this book came from Arthur J. Rosenthal in September 1973. At that time he had been Director of the Press for about a year, and he is still Director as the book goes to press. Much has happened in the first thirteen years of his stewardship. The Press has published some fifteen hundred books, many of them influential, has increased its annual sales receipts from $3.6 million to more than $12 million, and has tightened its organization and management. The history of the Rosenthal period will be an important part of the Press's story. But now is not the time to write it. The close-to-the-present sections of many institutional histories suffer from the inability of the authors to make the same sort of scholarly historical analysis that was possible for the earlier stages. Hence the decision to end this book with Rosenthal's appointment in 1972.

CHAPTER ONE

Antecedents and Founding

THE BOOK PUBLISHER known as Harvard University Press began life under that name in 1913, but publishing and printing at Harvard were already in full career. They had been going on in-termittently since the 1640s, for Harvard had owned and operated the first printing press in British North America. The event that took place in 1913 was more like turning up a gaslight than striking a match.

The Press of 1913 had its home in University Hall, a white granite edifice in the middle of Harvard Yard, designed by Charles Bulfinch a century before. President A. Lawrence Lowell, whose office was in the same building, had only to stroll across the hall to reach the lofty faculty room where he presided over the first meeting of the Press's governing body, the Board of Syndics. But Lowell's earliest prede-cessor, President Dunster, had had an even more convenient situation: the college press thumped in his own home. The story of how it got there gives Harvard a special position in the history of American printing.[1]

The First Press

In the summer of 1638 a well-to-do Puritan clergyman named Josse Glover sailed for Massachusetts with his family and with a locksmith named Stephen Day and *his* family.[2] On board there was also a print-ing press, with type and a large quantity of paper. Glover's intentions about the printing press are not known. He died on the voyage.

The ship docked at Charlestown at about the time young John Harvard of that place died and left some books, money, and his name to the little college just getting started in Cambridge. Glover's widow, Elizabeth, occupied one of Cambridge's largest houses and bought a smaller one for the Day family and the printing equipment. Stephen Day probably set up the apparatus, but his son Matthew, no more than eighteen at the time, probably did the first typesetting.[3] In this way Cambridge acquired a printing press thirty-seven years before Boston, forty-seven years before Philadelphia, and fifty-four years before New York.

The press's first offering consisted of a single paragraph, a freeman's oath, issued in late 1638 or in 1639. Its second was an almanac. Its third, issued in 1640, was *The Whole Booke of Psalmes Faithfully Translated into English Metre,* the first real book produced in the English colonies, later called the "Bay Psalm Book."

In August 1640 another English clergyman, Henry Dunster, thirty years old, arrived in Cambridge and promptly was appointed the first president of Harvard College. He also married Elizabeth Glover and moved into her house. In 1643 she died, after which Dunster took possession of the press, type, and paper; and so 1643 can be reasonably considered as the year in which Harvard became a printer. Dunster soon married again and moved into a house built for him in Harvard Yard, taking with him the five Glover children and the printing press. Very likely the press was operated by Matthew Day, who was also the college steward.[4]

When Matthew Day died in 1649 he was succeeded by Samuel Green, who ran Harvard's printing office for forty-three years and was the progenitor of a mighty printing family.[5] The printing office was moved into another building in Harvard Yard and continued under presidents Chauncy, Hoar, Oakes, Rogers, and Increase Mather. The shop more than satisfied Harvard's printing needs; mainly it printed books and pamphlets for clients outside the College. As time went on, Green operated very like an independent businessman, paying the College for the use of its press and types, and for proofreading.[6] Like other colonial printers, he almost certainly did some "publishing"—that is, at his own risk—but typically he did his work on behalf of others, including Boston booksellers. Booksellers were the first professional publishers separate from printers.[7]

The Cambridge shop was dispersed in 1692, and for more than a century, until 1800, Harvard sent its printing jobs to private firms in Boston.[8] Each time it did so, the College was, in a sense, a "publisher." In 1723, for example, Harvard published the first college library catalogue in the colonies, a book of 106 pages. Its first notable textbook was *A Grammar of the Hebrew Tongue* (1735), by Judah Monis, a Harvard instructor in Hebrew.[9] In 1763 the College published another

Hebrew grammar, adapted by Stephen Sewall from the works of two English scholars. Almost all college textbooks were still imported from Britain, but after the Revolutionary War there was a rising demand for academic books prepared in America, and moreover the Harvard faculty became more disposed to be authors or compilers. So the College's business with Boston printers quickened a bit. And in 1800, at just the right moment of this textbook boomlet, printing came back to Cambridge.

The First "University Press"

The man responsible was William Hilliard. He was only twenty-one at the time, just beginning a career as a powerful mover in the world of bookselling, publishing, and printing. He was innovative, ambitious, restless, prickly, civic-minded, and church-minded, and he achieved such a reputation that in 1824, when Thomas Jefferson was beginning a library for the University of Virginia, he turned to Hilliard to buy the books.

The little that has been written about this important man is fragmentary and often inaccurate.[10] He was born in Barnstable, on Cape Cod, where his father, Timothy, was the pastor before moving to Cambridge when William was five.[11] William's father, William's two brothers, and William's two sons all received M.A. degrees from Harvard; yet there is no record that William ever attended college.[12] Instead he became an apprentice in a printing house, presumably in Boston, and got his education in the book trade.

When Hilliard opened his shop, President Joseph Willard sent some printing his way, and two years later Harvard took a larger step. The chief governing body of Harvard University was—and still is—the "President and Fellows of Harvard College," consisting of the president, the treasurer, and five fellows. This board is known informally as the Harvard Corporation. On April 10, 1802, the Corporation voted to establish a printing office, the "University Press." Hilliard was engaged as the printer.

The responsibility for buying equipment, choosing the printer, and writing the Press's regulations was assigned to two men, President Willard and Eliphalet Pearson, an energetic faculty member with a special interest in publishing and an ambition to be president of Harvard. Pearson, nicknamed "Elephant" by the students, was the Hancock Professor of Hebrew and Other Oriental Languages and was also a member of the Corporation. Before joining Harvard he had been the first principal of Phillips Academy at Andover.[13] Pearson supervised the University Press and acted as a sort of publisher. Hilliard, as the college printer, used the University's printing press and types alongside his own.[14]

The action of 1802 meant that Harvard had begun its second venture in the printing field. It also meant that Harvard had founded the first "university press" in the United States, through which it issued textbooks and other works. The new institution, however, was not like the Harvard University Press of the twentieth century, with delegated authority to decide what to publish.

Two of the earliest books bearing the University Press imprint, issued in 1802, were textbooks prepared for publication by Eliphalet Pearson—an abridgment of Hugh Blair's *Lectures on Rhetoric,* a work widely known abroad, and a new and shorter version of the Hebrew grammar that Stephen Sewall had compiled.[15]

The "Regulations Respecting the University Press," composed by Willard and Pearson and approved by the Corporation on November 16, 1803, appear in the Corporation's minutes of that date. They specify, for example, that the Press was to be well supplied with types of the best quality at the expense of the University. Everything printed for the University was to be on good paper, executed in the best manner, and proofread by a University representative. The printer was permitted to do work for his own benefit, if he had time and if the Corporation approved each job, but he was not to use the term "University Press" on anything printed for his own benefit.

Hilliard's first contract provided for the University to receive 12½ percent of the income from all University Press work.[16] The University advanced him money for working capital, on which he paid interest of 6 percent. Later the arrangement gave way to one whereby Hilliard's firm paid a fixed rent on the equipment and office space and continued to borrow funds at interest. Around 1808 the firm became Hilliard & Metcalf, the partner being Eliab W. Metcalf, who had learned the printing trade in his hometown of Wrentham, Massachusetts, and now became an active citizen of Cambridge.[17] The shop continued to function as both University Press and commercial firm.

The University Press remained under Harvard ownership until 1827, twenty-five years in all. But after President Willard died in 1804 and Professor Pearson failed to be chosen as his successor and left Harvard, the Corporation gradually lost its enthusiasm for deciding the details of publication. The University Press continued to print a good many textbooks for use at Harvard and other institutions. The *publishing* function, however, shifted from the Corporation to booksellers, chiefly to Hilliard in his bookseller capacity. Some title pages named not only the University Press but also Cummings & Hilliard, a Boston bookselling firm that Hilliard had formed with Joseph Cummings.[18] Harvard firmly held title to the printing equipment.

Over the years there were many signs of mutual dissatisfaction between the Corporation and Hilliard. He asked for more type fonts, more furniture, more space, loans for working capital, and loans for personal use. Sometimes he got what he wanted, sometimes not. In 1813 he insisted that an investment of only eight or ten thousand dollars would turn the University Press into a source of profit to Harvard. He suggested the printing of the Greek and Roman classics and thereby anticipated Harvard's Loeb Classical Library. He also proposed Bible printing on the ground that this had brought considerable revenue to Oxford and Cambridge universities. This was exactly a century before the present Harvard University Press was founded with the presses of Oxford and Cambridge as models.[19]

But on September 28, 1827, when Harvard was in the midst of a financial crisis, the Corporation sold the printing establishment to Eliab Metcalf for $5,500.[20] Harvard retained ownership of a new building it had erected for the Press on Holyoke Street and leased it to Metcalf. The Corporation said that the University Press had been sold because it "had not been, as was expected, a source of income, but one of great expense."[21]

The printing company under private ownership became one of America's distinguished book printers. Though it never again was controlled by the University, it performed Harvard's printing for decades and appeared in Harvard's annual catalogues as "Printers to the University."[22] In 1865, when it was calling itself "University Press: Welch, Bigelow, & Company," it moved away from Harvard property and set up in a former hotel in Brattle Square. By 1880 it had more than three hundred employees and fifty-eight presses, and had printed original works by almost all of New England's greatest authors.[23] In 1895, going under the name "University Press: John Wilson & Son, Inc.," it erected still larger quarters on University Road near the Charles River. By that time the company was claiming—and may even have believed—that it had been founded in 1639 by Stephen Day.[24] Its actual founding by William Hilliard and Harvard had been lost in the mists of time.

The Printing Office of 1872

Harvard's third printing venture began on September 24, 1872, when the Corporation authorized President Charles William Eliot "to cause a printing office to be fitted up in the rooms over the Steward's office in Wadsworth House." This printing office has existed ever since. From 1913 to 1942 it served as the printing department of Harvard University Press.

The event of 1872 has led one writer, Madeleine B. Stern, to list Harvard University Press as the oldest continuously operating university press in the United States. In her book *Imprints on History* (1956), she supplied a chronological list of current American book publishers that had been founded before 1900. She reasoned that the Harvard University Press of 1913 was an outgrowth of the printing office, which she dated 1871 (a mistake for 1872).[25]

This raises interesting questions. How can we tell the age of a publishing house? Is continuity essential to a fair reckoning? Should we measure age by how long the organization has had the same name? Should we measure it by how long the organization has performed the publishing function, as contrasted with printing only? If so, how should we define the publishing function? Still other questions arise when one looks closely at the evolution of particular organizations.

The questions are not easy, and they have been answered in all sorts of ways. For example, Harvard University Press observed its fiftieth anniversary in 1963 on the ground that it had been organized under that name in 1913—though printing and even publishing of scholarly books and periodicals had taken place before that date. The Johns Hopkins University Press considers itself born in 1878 (when a Publication Agency came into being) and it observed its centennial in 1978.[26] That same year, Oxford University Press had a five-hundredth-anniversary celebration, though what happened in 1478 was the *first printing* at Oxford University, not the start of uninterrupted printing, and certainly not the founding of any institution with the name or function of Oxford University Press.[27] Cambridge University Press, which started its uninterrupted activity in 1584, chose that as its year of birth and celebrated its four-hundredth anniversary in 1984. Apparently it is the oldest continuous publishing house in the world, one year older than Oxford's press.[28]

The decision to establish a printing office at Harvard in 1872 sprang from dissatisfaction with commercial printers, particularly with the University Press. Some of the dissatisfaction was over prices, but even more of it was over examination questions. Written examinations came into vogue around the middle of that century. The exam questions were sent out to be printed, and this created opportunities for leakage. After several scandals the faculty became convinced that the skulduggery could be stopped only through a college shop with an impregnable safe.[29]

Harvard's new shop worked not only on examinations but also on circulars, envelopes, tickets, library catalogue cards, and the like. In 1883 the shop for the first time composed and printed the annual Harvard University catalogue, a book of 278 pages, taking the job away from the University Press. Around 1889 the operation moved to the basement of University Hall, where there was more room.[30]

The Publication Office of 1892

Harvard's catalogues and other official publications now were expanding so much that President Eliot decided to centralize their management. Moreover, official publishing was only part of the picture. Works of scholarship, too, steadily increased in importance and cried out for publication. The same idea was in the air at other leading universities. It had found its classic formulation in 1878 when Daniel Coit Gilman, first president of The Johns Hopkins University, declared: "It is one of the noblest duties of a university to advance knowledge, and to diffuse it not merely to those who can attend daily lectures—but far and wide."[31]

At Harvard from time to time various departments acquired publication funds through alumni gifts and bequests. The Annals of the Astronomical Observatory, crammed with new-found knowledge about the heavens, had been issued since 1856—huge books published approximately once a year by the Harvard Observatory and printed at commercial firms, mainly the University Press. In the 1860s and 1870s Harvard's rising museums, beginning with the Museum of Comparative Zoology, issued streams of scientific papers that have continued ever since. Other findings were issued by the Gray Herbarium and various laboratories. In 1886 appeared something new under the sun: the *Quarterly Journal of Economics,* or *QJE,* published for Harvard by George H. Ellis, a Boston firm, and financed from a gift to the Department of Political Economy by John Eliot Thayer.[32] In 1887 came another innovation: a group of law students began publishing the *Harvard Law Review,* the prototype of America's many student-edited legal journals.[33]

Famous professors, such as President Eliot, Henry Adams, Asa Gray, Dr. Oliver Wendell Holmes, James Russell Lowell, and William James, could command audiences through commercial publishers. But the fruits of research were not always so marketable. The scholarly monograph appeared on the scene, because the University had established a Graduate Department in 1872 and a Graduate School of Arts and Sciences in 1890.

Indeed, a burst of series publishing occurred around 1890. The Boston textbook firm Ginn & Company moved into the vacuum and began publishing three series on literature and language—all subsidized by Harvard departments. The first was the Harvard Studies in Classical Philology (1890), an annual instigated by Professor James B. Greenough and paid for by his Harvard class of 1856. Then came the magisterial Harvard Oriental Series (1891), founded by two men: the Sanskrit authority Charles R. Lanman, who was to be the general editor for forty-two years, and Henry Clarke Warren, who financed the books and himself contributed a distinguished volume, *Buddhism in Translations*.[34] In 1892 came Studies and Notes on Philology and Literature, whose guiding spirit was first Francis J. Child and then George Lyman Kittredge.

Harvard itself would eventually publish all those series and scores of others. But in 1890 the University had no central publisher.

The President and Fellows took a large step toward filling that gap in 1892. They voted on May 31 to employ a "publication agent," and on June 13 they appointed John Bertram Williams, a Harvard graduate with fifteen years' experience at the Riverside Press in Cambridge.[35] He opened the Publication Office in University Hall, just above the printing shop, and served for sixteen years. This Publication Office later became Harvard University Press.

The publication agent, said President Eliot in his Annual Report for 1891–92, "has charge of the printing and distribution of all the reports, announcements and other official documents which are issued in the name, or on behalf, of the University." He was responsible for editing the annual catalogue, directing the University's advertising, and arranging the publication and sale of the instructional aids which the teachers wrote for their classes. Finally, he "conducts the business relating to some of the various publications which are made by the aid of permanent funds belonging to the University."

Relations between the Publication Office and Printing Office may have been a bit hazy at first, but in 1896 the printing shop definitely came under Williams's control.[36] In the same year, Adam K. Wilson,

1. University Hall early in this century. The view is of its south end, where the Publication Office was transformed into Harvard University Press in 1913.

formerly of Edinburgh, was hired as foreman of the shop. For nearly fifty years thereafter, printing at Harvard was administratively subordinate to publishing. For thirty-five of those years Wilson ran the Printing Office. He was remembered as a man superbly trained in the technical aspects of bookmaking, "a man of dignified presence, recognized and highly respected in the University community and as a citizen of Cambridge."[37]

Publication agent Williams, broadly interpreting the president's instructions, worked with faculty members in academic undertakings. For example, in 1892 he published *State Papers and Speeches on the Tariff,* compiled by the economist Frank William Taussig, and some classroom guides by the historian Albert Bushnell Hart which evolved into sizable books. Meanwhile the volume of business gradually increased. In 1900 Williams took over the printing and distribution of the venerable Annals of the Astronomical Observatory and succeeded Ginn as publisher and printer of the Harvard Studies in Classical Philology. In that year the printing shop, occupying two rooms at the south end of the University Hall basement, had a work force of ten men. The typesetting was still done by hand (Monotype machines would be installed during the next decade).[38]

The operation supervised by Williams did not bear the name Harvard University Press, and it had no faculty governing board; but it was a good deal like many small enterprises that have called themselves university presses.

Castle in the Air

Nevertheless in that era neither Harvard nor the outside world considered that Harvard had a real university press. And the lack increasingly became a matter of regret among devotees of Harvard. In the first decade of the new century one of them decided to do something about it. This was James Loeb, class of 1888. His plan led to a strange episode.

Loeb, half-hearted financier and whole-hearted lover of literature, music, and art, had taken very early retirement from his father's firm, Kuhn, Loeb & Company. His happiest memories were of his Harvard years.[39] Around 1903 he conceived the idea of a Harvard press of the general character of the ones of Oxford and Cambridge. He took his benevolent scheme to Professor Emeritus Charles Eliot Norton, his beloved old teacher. Norton then brought into the picture Daniel Berkeley Updike, of Boston, founder and proprietor of the Merrymount Press, a scholarly entrepreneur, a perfectionist, strong-minded and thin-skinned.[40]

Loeb moved to Munich in 1905, never to live in the United States again. But Norton and Updike thought he was still interested in a Harvard press, and they enlisted H. Langford Warren, chairman of Harvard's Department of Architecture. In 1906 Warren designed a group of four buildings—a publishing headquarters, printing plant, power plant, and gatehouse.[41] Warren's fee was paid by a committee of twelve, all of them Harvard alumni except Updike, who had never attended college.[42] President Eliot made out a list of statues to be placed in the new institution and wrote inscriptions for them.[43] All this activity was a reflection of the spirit of the time, a period of cultural enthusiasm in which certain people on both sides of the Atlantic were trying to revive the aesthetic side of life to counteract materialism. The making of books was part of the movement; printing was held to be not just a technical trade but an art.[44]

Updike surely expected to be the director of the new press. Apparently nothing in the archives says this flatly, but the tone of the correspondence implies it, and Updike would scarcely have spent so much time and energy on the project for love of Harvard.

Supposedly the drawings traveled across the sea to James Loeb, but nothing happened. As late as March 1910, Updike told Eliot's successor, A. Lawrence Lowell, that he had nothing definite to report but thought some useful work had been done. Very likely he was then hoping for another benefactor. Only five months later, James Loeb wrote President Lowell that the suggestion had been made to him for an edition of Greek and Latin authors with translations.[45] Before 1910 was out, the Loeb Classical Library was under way, and the books began appearing around 1912. For the first quarter of a century Harvard was not involved. Harvard took over in 1934, and now there are more than 470 volumes.

John D. Rockefeller provided the young University of Chicago Press with its own building in 1902. Charles Scribner did the same for the young Princeton University Press in 1911. Most university presses have not started life so privileged. To this day Harvard University Press has never had a building that was designed for either publishing or printing. Besides its birthplace in University Hall it has occupied a former dining hall, a former residence, another former residence, and a former herbarium.

Centralization under C. C. Lane

When John Bertram Williams died in 1908 he was succeeded as publication agent by Charles Chester Lane, an ambitious man of twenty-four, described as earnest, conscientious, likable, and shy.[46] Lane had been born in Hingham, Massachusetts, on August 6, 1883. He had been a member of the Harvard class of 1904 but with typical impatience had earned his diploma in 1903 and had gone to work at Ginn & Company, where he had learned to set type and then had risen quickly to the double position of art editor and advertising manager.

President Eliot was near the end of his long regime when he hired Lane. Both men had in mind that a Harvard University Press would materialize when funds would be available.[47] Indeed, nearly half a century later Lane wrote that in his Cambridge years he had been "instrumental in starting the Harvard University Press."[48] And this was the simple truth. He was not the only instrument; the Press had no single founder. But probably no one deserves more credit than C. C. Lane.

Lane, however, had to be publication agent for nearly five years before he could be a press director. During that unwanted apprenticeship he bought two Miehle cylinder presses and some Monotype typesetting machines, compiled lists of Harvard publications and mailed them to booksellers and librarians, further centralized the University's monograph series and periodicals, published a number of new scholarly books outside those series, took over the publication of casebooks by Law School professors, and swelled the University's official literature with a profitable thirteen-hundred-page directory of alumni. Toward the end of 1912 he reported that more than eighty books and periodicals were being distributed from the Publication Office.[49]

By 1912 the basement shop supervised by Adam K. Wilson had become known as the Harvard University Printing Office and Lane was paying its expenses of about $50,000 a year by charges to the Harvard departments that used its services. Predictably, there was some controversy over the charges.[50]

In 1909, after a meeting of the editors of the University's publications, Lane became the publisher of the twenty-three-year-old *Quarterly Journal of Economics,* replacing George H. Ellis, and the one-year-old *Harvard Theological Review,* replacing the Macmillan Company.[51] Being the "publisher" of those quarterlies, however, meant little more than distributing them and receiving a "publishing commission"; and this remained true even into the 1970s, when they and Harvard University Press finally parted company without much regret. The Press has never been an important journal publisher, never in the same league with the University of Chicago Press, for example.

Much more fundamental to future operations was Lane's centralization of book series. In 1912 he took over two notable series that were owned by Harvard departments but were being handled by commercial publishers. These were the Harvard Historical Studies, founded in 1896 by the Department of History and Government, and the Harvard Economic Studies, founded in 1906 by the Department of Economics.[52] He also added two brand-new series to his list. One was the Harvard Studies in Comparative Literature, founded in 1910 by Professor William Henry Schofield, volume 1 being *Three Philosophical Poets* by Professor George Santayana. The other, in 1912, was the Harvard Semitic Series, which, oddly, started with volume 3—*Sumerian Tablets in the Harvard Semitic Museum*—because volumes 1 and 2 were delayed until 1924.

Perhaps even more interesting to Lane were the books he handled outside the various series. From 1908 to the end of 1912 he published about nine of these books and put into production still others which would bear the Harvard University Press imprint in 1913. Three of the nine deserve special mention:

1. *A Manual for Northern Woodsmen* (1909), by Austin Cary, who had recently been assistant professor of forestry at Harvard. He had submitted the book to several publishers; they declined to take the risk. After the manual was subsidized by the Harvard administration it was a financial success.[53]

2. *A Laboratory Course in Physiology* (1910), by Dr. Walter B. Cannon. He wrote the book mainly for his classes at the Harvard Medical School, but it became so widely known that it ultimately went through nine editions. According to Lane it had been declined by commercial publishers and could not have been published without a guarantee fund from the Medical School.[54]

3. *Applied Ethics* (1911), by Theodore Roosevelt. This book of fifty pages, bound in hard covers, was the forerunner of all those plums that have dropped into the hands of the modern Harvard University Press when celebrities have come to lecture. The former President's book had been a William Belden Noble Lecture in 1910.

Lane's takeover of legal casebooks in 1912 added twenty titles to the backlist. For four decades, under deans C. C. Langdell and James Barr Ames, the Law School professors had been teaching by the case method and had been publishing fat collections of judicial opinions in their special fields. The authors dealt directly with printers—or dealt through the *Harvard Law Review* staff—and owned the plates from which reprints could be made. Lane's office provided a central place where these tomes could be ordered. After 1913 the Press reprinted some of them and brought out some new ones. Eventually, as the market for casebooks grew, commercial law-book publishers took over the business.[55]

The Law School figured in another event of 1912 when the University, in the person of C. C. Lane, contracted to handle the student-published *Harvard Law Review*. Lane's office, in return for a commission of 10 percent of total receipts, took over the printed copies ready for sale, distributed them, kept the subscription list up to date, and tried rather unsuccessfully to sell advertising space. This collaboration went on for six years after the founding of Harvard University Press in 1913.[56]

Meanwhile Lane found many opportunities to talk up the idea of a "real" university press, a subsidized institution to publish works of high scholarship "that can never pay in dollars and cents."[57] The *Harvard Alumni Bulletin* of May 3, 1911, in an editorial remarkably similar to Lane's Annual Reports, called for immediate action, pointing out that the works of scholarship produced at Harvard would add not only to the University's prestige but also to the sum of human knowledge and "would be of incalculable value to scholars in all parts of the world." Many of these works were never issued, however, "because from their very nature they are not profitable ventures and the commercial publisher cannot afford to take them."

There was only one difficulty: Where was the money to come from? The truth is, this question was never really answered. But something that *seemed* an answer was worked out. And the process of working it out began with the Graduate School of Business Administration, better known as the Harvard Business School.

How Harvard University Press Was Born

The Society of Printers, in Boston, had been founded in 1905 for "the study and advancement of the art of printing." On January 4, 1910, the society heard an address by J. Horace McFarland, an unusual printing proprietor from Harrisburg, Pennsylvania. He proposed a university course for future printing executives, "a West Point for printers, at which officers for the army of working printers might be properly trained to perform well their duties." He had made the suggestion before—for example, he had tried hard to convince the president of Cornell University that the graphic arts were fully as good a university subject as dairy farming. But this was the first time his audience had included the dean of the Harvard Business School. Dean Edwin F. Gay was an innovative and decisive man who later had a hand in founding the National Bureau of Economic Research, the Council on Foreign Relations, and other solid institutions. One must suppose that his presence at the meeting was due to C. C. Lane, who was the society's secretary at the time. The Business School, just two years old, was then located in Harvard Yard, and Dean Gay's office was on the same floor as Lane's in University Hall.

The result was three Harvard courses in printing and publishing, given intermittently from 1910 to 1920. Dean Gay put C. C. Lane in charge of them, and Lane stayed in charge until 1918. The Society of Printers helped organize the courses. For the instruction Lane depended upon a parade of distinguished outside lecturers, including D. B. Updike, Bruce Rogers, and William A. Dwiggins, who

2. Edwin F. Gay, first dean of the Harvard Business School and one of the founding fathers of the Press.

3. Donald Scott early in his career. He was a young New York publisher when he helped establish the Press.

were to become perhaps the three most honored American book designers.[58]

Dean Gay appointed an equally distinguished Advisory Committee on Printing. One member of it was Donald Scott (class of 1900), treasurer of the Century Company, the New York publishing house. As a result of the courses, Scott got interested in the Publication Office and became one of the founders of Harvard University Press. (Decades later, when Scott was the director of Harvard's Peabody Museum of Archaeology and Ethnology—and also during his retirement years before his death in 1967—he was an influential member of the Press's Board of Directors.)

An important meeting of Dean Gay's Advisory Committee took place on April 3, 1912. The chief topic was a proposal to erect and equip "suitable buildings for a Harvard University Press." The committee did not go the whole way, favoring only an enlargement of the Printing Office.[59] Nevertheless, as Lane said later in an account of the Press's founding, the committee's action "marked the beginning of a systematic attempt to secure an endowment for the Press."[60]

Scott did not attend the April meeting but received a copy of the minutes and asked Dean Gay to send him all the literature he could about the "Harvard Press," saying he did not know it was so firmly established. Lane sent lists of publications and told Scott about some books that had got away. Professor F. W. Taussig's *Principles of Economics,* for example, had been offered to the University but declined for lack of funds. (It was published by Macmillan, and by 1953 volume 1 had sold more than 175,000 copies and volume 2 more than 125,000.)[61]

Donald Scott's files contain 126 letters about the future Press which he wrote or received during the eight months between April 22 and the end of 1912. Dean Gay encouraged Scott to form a committee. Edgar H. Wells, general secretary of the Harvard Alumni Association, joined the undertaking and gave advice and help from time to time.

Lane and Gay wrote a draft of a circular giving "reasons for the establishment of a Harvard University Press," and Lane sent it to Scott on June 25. Scott sent back a revised draft on August 15. He supplied a new beginning that he thought would make the writing more persuasive to the Harvard College alumni, "since we are going to try to use this document as a cork-screw to draw funds from them." Lane and Gay accepted the changes almost in toto and held the circular until the fund-raising campaign could be organized.

The amended version gave seven reasons for establishing a full-fledged press. One was that an adequately endowed publication center would add greatly to Harvard's reputation for scholarship. Another was that it could contribute materially to the advancement of knowledge. It would also increase the effectiveness of the instruction in printing offered at the Business School. The authors strongly made the point that a learned press "would not be in any sense a competitor to the commercial publishers since its chief function would be the issuing of books that would not be commercially profitable." Then they mentioned the recently established presses at the University of Chicago, Princeton, Yale, Columbia, and Johns Hopkins and argued that none of them maintained a printing plant comparable to the presses at Oxford and Cambridge—"and in that fact seems to lie the opportunity for Harvard University." They closed with some dollar amounts: "To equip properly and endow a University Press, the sum of $500,000 would be needed." But a beginning could be made with an endowment of $200,000.

Gay, Lane, and Scott enlarged their circle of allies during that summer of 1912. Dean Gay reported that Professor George Lyman Kittredge "was very much interested in the project and heartily approved it." Kittredge was influential—and later cut such a figure in the early governance of the Press that long after his death the Press's head-quarters was named after him. Scott thought that J. H. Sears, president of D. Appleton & Company, had more ideas than any other alumnus he approached.[62]

Much depended on the attitude of President Lowell. Dean Gay had already had a run-in with the president that same year over fund raising for the Business School.[63] Moreover, Lowell was already im-mersed in other fund raising—for a new library, new freshman dor-mitories, and other facilities. In September, however, with Widener Library promised and soon to be built, Lowell agreed to be on a Press fund-raising committee, and he entered the project with characteristic vim. On October 4 he presided over a meeting of interested people whom Lane and Gay had rounded up.[64]

Lowell's ideas about a university press, like his ideas on most other matters, were clear and definite. First, he wanted a university press very much, and that autumn, in his Annual Report for 1911–12, he urged its establishment, using the same arguments that were in the fund-raising circular and declaring that "there is a growing conviction that a great institution of learning cannot attain its full usefulness without a university press which can publish the writings of its scholars." Second, he did not want a press that would have to scratch for funds or would be a drain on the University. "An endowment is absolutely essential if it is to be established," he said in the Annual Report. Third, he did not favor trying to raise the endowment piecemeal, but wanted to find a single benefactor.[65]

Thus it was that the Press crusade became a search for a lone tycoon, whom Scott began calling "our Croesus"[66]—a counterpart of Mrs. George Dunton Widener, who had given the funds for Widener Library in honor of her drowned son, Harry Elkins Widener.

The participants in Lowell's meeting of October 4, 1912, asked Lowell, Kittredge, and Scott to "look over the ground and appoint an executive committee," in Lowell's words.[67] The resulting com-mittee consisted of seven men, with Scott as chairman. Publication agent Lane now printed the circular that had been written during the summer—printed it handsomely in three large pages on heavy paper with a big red initial letter and the headline A HARVARD UNIVERSITY PRESS—and listed the members of the new fund-raising committee at the end: A. Lawrence Lowell, Robert Bacon, G. L. Kittredge, W. L. R. Gifford, J. H. Sears, E. H. Wells, and Donald Scott.[68]

On this committee Kittredge represented the faculty, Wells the Alumni Association, and Sears and Scott the publishing industry. Gifford was librarian of the St. Louis Mercantile Library Association. The member who swung the most weight in Harvard's high command, aside from President Lowell himself, was Robert Bacon.

In that era few names of Harvard alumni were more illustrious than that of Robert Bacon. Since January 1912 he had been a member of the President and Fellows of Harvard College—that is, the Harvard Corporation. Before that he had been U.S. ambassador to France. Before *that*, in 1909, he had been Secretary of State during the last few months of the administration of Theodore Roosevelt, his Harvard classmate (1880). And before joining the government he had been a partner in J. P. Morgan & Company and had taken part in the formation of the United States Steel Corporation. At Harvard he had been a star athlete, president of the glee club, a high-ranking student, and chief marshal of his class.[69]

4. A. Lawrence Lowell early in his Harvard presidency. He agreed to start the Press despite his misgivings.

5. Robert Bacon as a government official sometime before 1912. His proposal led to the founding of the Press.

Before the end of 1912, events moved to a decision without an endowment from a Croesus. The mover was Robert Bacon. He suggested that the Corporation go ahead with a university press and make loans to it for the publication of books. He thought that the Press could repay the money after it got on its feet, and he also may have hoped that the arrangement would soon be obviated by a lump-sum benefaction. Meanwhile at the beginning somebody would guarantee the Corporation against loss. President Lowell, who had so recently insisted that an endowment was absolutely necessary, allowed himself to be persuaded. Probably the main reason he went along was that the person who would do the guaranteeing was Bacon himself.

Nobody, not even Lowell, seemed to know the extent of the guarantee. Mr. Bacon was not a man whom people questioned very sharply about money matters or his judgment. As will appear in the account of the Press's crisis of 1919, the guarantee turned out to be much smaller than expected. So it can be said with reason that the Press was founded upon a miscalculation on Bacon's part and a misunderstanding on everyone else's.

On the question of the expected loans, Lane, in his brief official history of the Press's founding, wrote: "Mr. Bacon suggested that in view of the need of establishing the Press immediately it might be possible for the President and Fellows to advance $15,000 to $20,000 a year for publication, provided they were guaranteed against loss."[70]

Donald Scott received a telephone message that led him to think the Corporation had voted an outright grant of $20,000 a year, and on December 20, 1912, he wrote his congratulations to Lowell, Bacon, Gay, and Lane. But there was no grant. Lowell quickly corrected Scott: "You must have been misinformed about a Corporation vote of funds for the press, for the Corporation has no funds which it could use. I only wish it had. It has merely been suggested that the Corporation might lend the money for the purpose, if the interest and any loss were guaranteed."[71]

Scott said in his letter to Dean Gay, "All the credit for this belongs with you and Lane, who have worked for it so steadily and unselfishly." The dean replied, "I am glad for Lane's sake that a start can be made. The credit belongs to him, not to me." Gay added a postscript in longhand, telling Scott: "If you start assigning credits, I think a large share comes to you. Your keen interest in the enterprise and the way you have taken hold has greatly impressed Lowell and Bacon."[72]

The five men just named—Robert Bacon, C. C. Lane, Donald Scott,

Dean Edwin Gay, and President Lowell—can be considered the founding fathers of the Press.

The formal action of the Harvard Corporation establishing the Press took place on January 13, 1913. The minutes of the meeting, making no reference to money, say that the Corporation appointed as "syndics" Robert Bacon, Charles H. Thurber, and five professors: George F. Moore, George L. Kittredge, Edwin F. Gay, Arthur E. Kennelly, and Walter B. Cannon. The Corporation also voted to appoint C. C. Lane as the Press Director.

The word "syndic" was used in the sense of a representative of a corporation. "Syndics" was the term used by Cambridge University Press for its governing body, and Harvard evidently preferred it to the term "delegates" used by Oxford University Press.[73]

The first Syndics of Harvard University Press were a strong-minded group. Robert Bacon had arrived at a relatively quiet moment between successes of the past and a war hero's role to come. Charles Herbert Thurber, a Ph.D. and former college teacher, was chief editor of Ginn & Company and had been Lane's superior there. George Foot Moore, the oldest Syndic at sixty-one, erudite and authoritative, was a theological historian in the Divinity School. George Lyman Kittredge was a giant of literature and already a Harvard legend. Edwin Francis Gay, an economic historian too busy to write books, was building America's first strictly graduate school of business. Arthur Edwin Kennelly was a professor of electrical engineering who as a young man had been the principal electrical assistant to Thomas A. Edison. Dr. Walter Bradford Cannon of the Medical School, the youngest member at forty-one, was the first Syndic to be a Harvard University Press author: the Press inherited his perennial textbook on physiology from the Publication Office.

This was the group created to support and govern C. C. Lane, who was not yet thirty. All except Bacon and Gay were still members when Lane left Harvard in 1919; and four of them—Kittredge, Thurber, Kennelly, and Cannon—served into the 1930s.

When the board held its first meeting on January 15, 1913, President Lowell, according to the minutes written by Lane, called the meeting to order and said that the Corporation, "having been guaranteed against loss," was prepared to advance money for the publication of books approved by the board. He appointed Bacon as chairman of the Syndics. Bacon explained that $10,000 to $20,000 a year would be advanced "with the expectation that it would be paid

back, in a few years, from the receipts from the books published."
The next passage in the minutes, however, says ringingly: "It was
agreed that the purpose of the Press is to be the publication of books
of a high scholarly character, and that the institution is not to become
a competitor of the commercial publisher."

A few days later Professor Kittredge wrote to congratulate President
Lowell on the "auspicious founding."[74] Said Kittredge: "Dr. Thurber
remarked, in the course of our general discussion, that this foundation
is, in his opinion, the most important step for the advancement of
scholarship in America that has been taken for many years. We all
agreed with him. Every one of us felt that we were present at the
birth of a great institution."

CHAPTER TWO

First Steps under C. C. Lane

1913–1919

*Inaugurated primarily for the publication of books of a high scholarly char-
acter the Harvard University Press aims to aid in the advancement of knowledge by making possible the wide distribution of the work of the foremost
scholars of the world. It will also help in promptly disseminating the results
of original research and investigation by printing a number of serial publications. It does not plan, however, to compete with the commercial publisher,
since its chief function will be the issuing of books that would not be commercially profitable.* —Harvard University catalogue, 1913–14

FROM JANUARY 1913 to the end of 1919 C. C. Lane directed
Harvard University Press, including the Printing Office. Those
seven years were perhaps the worst of times, certainly not the best of
times, in which to place a publishing house on a strong foundation.
The Great War hampered the undertaking even before the United
States entered the fighting. The financial squeeze due to unsettled
conditions and to an inherent weakness of structure worsened until
at last, during the Press's first crisis, the Syndics were accepting no
manuscript unless all its expenses had been guaranteed by the author
or some other provider. Nevertheless the Press under Lane seems to
have published 156 new scholarly books.[1]

Even before the imprint "Harvard University Press" began appearing in books, Lane was already offering 202 items for sale to the
public.[2] Of this backlist, about 180 were scholarly books. Lane could
be considered the "publisher" of some and the "agent" for others.
During the Press's first year the existence of the backlist and the
ambiguity of the word "publish" led to fluctuations in the Press's
announced statistics. For example, only five months after the founding, Lane announced that the Press "already publishes" 95 books.[3]
Later in 1913 he said in the University's annual catalogue that "the
publications of the Press" included approximately 150 volumes. But
in the whole calendar year 1913 the Harvard University Press imprint
appeared in only seven books.

6. No, not a movie actor. This is C. C. Lane, first Director of the Press.

Fourteen months after the founding, the Press issued an impressive publication entitled "The First Catalogue of the Harvard University Press." It had sixty-three pages and included not only the books taken over from the Publication Office and commercial publishers but also many books "in press" and "in preparation."

Books and Syndics

The first book to carry the Harvard University Press imprint was the collected writings of James Barr Ames, who had died in 1910 while dean of the Law School. It was entitled *Lectures on Legal History and Miscellaneous Legal Essays*. The publication date was February 28, 1913, about six weeks after the founding.[4] Lane as publication agent had put the book in type earlier, and the Syndics had approved the book in January.

The second book with the imprint was volume 18 of the Harvard Historical Studies. This was *The Government of the Ottoman Empire in the Time of Suleiman the Magnificent,* by Professor A. H. Lybyer of the University of Illinois. The book was full of new conclusions and created a stir among historians. Of the 156 new books issued during the Lane years, about 80 were series books, and the number of series increased from nine to eighteen.[5] Series books are seldom brisk sellers. Yet it is undeniable that specialized series fill gaps and cumulatively make a large contribution to the world's knowledge.

President Lowell felt that the Press should start with books "which will be recognized at once all over the world as worthy of the University."[6] He himself showed the way, allowing the Press to publish *The Governments of France, Italy, and Germany* in 1914, *Greater European Governments* in 1918, and four later books. Many Harvard professors joined the president on the list during the Lane years— Frederick Jackson Turner, F. W. Taussig, Thomas Nixon Carver, J. H. Beale, L. J. Henderson, Melvin T. Copeland, Charles H. Haskins, and others.

But the Press never confined itself to the Harvard faculty. The Lane list was diverse in origin, subject matter, and tone. It embraced bibliographies, textbooks, translations from ancient languages, even Robert S. Hillyer's first volume of poems. And it included the Harvard Health Talks, which were hardcover books of about fifty pages—sponsored by the Medical School and based on public lectures there—with such titles as *The Care and Feeding of Children*; *Preservatives and Other Chemicals in Foods: Their Use and Abuse*; *The Care of the Sick Room*; *An Adequate Diet*; and *How to Avoid Infection.*[7]

Five of the seven charter members of the Board of Syndics appeared on the Lane list. Even Robert Bacon, the least academic Syndic, saw his name on title pages. When the Press published eight volumes of the papers of Elihu Root, who had been Bacon's predecessor as Secretary of State, the editors were Robert Bacon and James Brown Scott. In later times the Press has excelled in multivolume collections of documents, such as Theodore Roosevelt's letters, Emerson's journals, and the Adams Papers. The Root volumes were its first undertaking of that sort. Documentary projects have to be subsidized. The angel in this case was close at hand: Mr. Bacon promised to make good any losses.[8]

But the Syndic who led all the rest as a Press author was George Lyman Kittredge. To begin with, the Press in 1914 acquired a Kittredge work of 1902, *Observations on the Language of Chaucer's*

Troilus, when Ginn & Company transferred to the Press the early volumes of Studies and Notes in Philology and Literature. The big event, however, came in 1915 when the Press published Kittredge's captivating *Chaucer and His Poetry.* No other book from the Lane era approached it in longevity. Its "Fifty-fifth Anniversary Edition," in 1970, was the fifteenth printing. Its sixteenth, in 1972, was number 26 in the Harvard Paperbacks. The book originated in six lectures given at Johns Hopkins. *Chaucer* was followed in 1916 by *A Study of Gawain and the Green Knight* and, almost simultaneously, by *Shakspere: An Address.*[9]

Probably the Press has never had a Syndic more difficult to ignore than the famous "Kitty," with his learning, his flamboyant performances in the classroom, his terrible temper, his Prince of Monaco cigars, and the full beard he had worn since his Harvard undergraduate years. It might be a mistake to say that Kittredge dominated the first group of Syndics, but he does seem to have been the most respected leader in the approval or disapproval of manuscripts.

Not far behind was George Foot Moore, a huge man noted for his humanity, scholarship, and teaching skill. Dean Edwin Gay was the Syndic most concerned with the Press's economic soundness and its future. Chairman Bacon, who lived in New York, was a father figure with a proprietary interest, but he apparently did not involve himself much in operations. Drawn away by affairs larger than those of Harvard University Press, he attended only half the meetings during the first two years and only one more meeting after that. Whenever he was absent, the Syndics elected a temporary chairman, and this was usually Moore or Kittredge. In February 1915, when the Press was two years old, President Lowell and the Harvard Corporation appointed a new man to the board, Archibald Cary Coolidge, a historian who was director of the University Library. He quickly became one of the most active members.

"No book can be accepted for publication which does not receive the endorsement of the board." This statement in the Press's first catalogue has been a basic principle ever since. For books in the major series, however, formal action was not required in the early decades. True, the Lybyer monograph already mentioned was formally accepted, "having been examined by Professor Moore," but in April 1913 the board gave blanket approval to the Harvard Historical Studies, Harvard Economic Studies, and Harvard Studies in Classical Philology, and the individual books in those series were no longer mentioned in the minutes. In discussing the question, though, the

7. George Lyman Kittredge. This pencil sketch was made in 1910 by Francis C. Walker, a graduate student, in Kittredge's house on Hilliard Street, Cambridge.

board laid down a principle still adhered to: that in all cases "the endorsement of some responsible person" would be required.

In the Press's "modern" period—since the creation of a Board of Directors in 1947—the Syndics' role has been confined to controlling the imprint and thus protecting the scholarly standards of the Press. The Syndics, representing major academic fields and appointed by the President and Fellows, guide the Press Director and editors on manuscripts, sometimes by reading them but usually by giving general advice on projects, suggesting the best referees for manuscripts, and evaluating the referees' evaluations. The Syndics meet regularly to consider the manuscripts that survive the Press's screening process. They usually approve these for publication. Occasionally they disapprove a manuscript, though rarely one that is recommended with enthusiasm by a Director armed with favorable reports from an inside editor and one or more respected scholars outside the Press.

The earliest Syndics performed the watchdog function, only more so. They also worried about non-editorial matters, including finances, sales agents, and, at the beginning, even type and paper. Concerning manuscripts, they did not leave it to Director Lane to make all the proposals. They were active in bringing books to the Press and in getting outside opinions. The Press had no "editors" in the modern sense.

Weaknesses

The advent of the Press was not applauded by everybody. A few blocks from Harvard Yard, there was grumbling on the premises of that other "University Press," the printing firm which Harvard had founded in 1802 and sold into private hands in 1827. This company, whose full name now was University Press: John Wilson & Son, not only was claiming to have been founded by Stephen Day in 1639 but also was exhibiting on its letterhead the Harvard shield with its three open books. It still did jobs for Harvard but it had lost its place as *the* printer to the University. And now its very name had been appropriated. Harvard University Press, on its part, felt entitled to the exclusive use of the name and the shield.[10] The Harvard Corporation consulted its lawyers, who doubted that either side could force the other to give up its name, though they felt that the words "University Press" as used by the commercial firm had "always deceived the public."[11] The commercial firm, annoyed by Harvard University Press advertisements, threatened to call Harvard's printing office to the attention of the tax assessors and even intimated that it would bring suit. Said President Lowell, "I suppose there is nothing to do but let them sue us if they want to." He said he wasn't much afraid of taxation on the Press, "from which we make no profit."[12] Apparently this ended the affair.

The real threat to Harvard University Press did not come from any rival organization. The Press badly needed a sounder business structure and a clearer relationship with the University. Dean Gay had already furnished Lane with an efficiency expert to reorganize the work of the printing plant.[13] Now he went further. At the Syndics meeting of March 1913 he moved that a committee be appointed to investigate "the state of the financial relations" in the publishing office and to recommend changes. The motion was carried, and Chairman Bacon appointed Gay as a committee of one.

Soon after this, Gay took a surprising step. He approached Daniel Berkeley Updike, who was completing his third year as chief lecturer in the Business School's basic course on printing, to discover whether that personage would be willing to take over the Press. The negotiations had the approval of Bacon and Donald Scott. Whether Lane approved is another question. Updike spelled out the conditions under which he would consider selling his Merrymount Press and "going with my employees to the Harvard University Press." One of the conditions was "if I am allowed to have a basically free hand" in the Press's "up-building and management."[14] Gay consulted Bacon and found him sympathetic but just about to leave on a 50,000-mile journey to Asia, Europe, and South America.[15]

Meanwhile in the summer of 1913 Scott set forth anew on the hunt for a Croesus.[16] At his urging, Lane had architectural plans drawn up for a building to house the Press. Scott wanted to show the drawings to philanthropists.[17] By October he was ready to call a meeting of the fund-raising committee which had been appointed a year before and had never met. But President Lowell said they should wait for Bacon's return. Lowell looked at the architect's drawings and squelched them, saying that he and Lane thought a building could wait until the Press was an established success.[18]

Bacon finally returned in December, and Scott arranged a committee meeting in Cambridge. There seems to exist no record of what went on among the founding fathers at the end of 1913. Nor is there further mention of Updike as a possible panjandrum of the Press. Thus another scheme involving Updike fell through, as in 1906 when James Loeb had been expected to put up the money.

Loeb, however, was not yet out of the picture. Oblivious in distant Munich, he now became the prime target of Scott and committee member J. H. Sears, who was planning a European trip in the spring of 1914. Scott, using data provided by Lane, wrote a prospectus entitled "The Needs of the Harvard University Press." The needs amounted to about $600,000.[19] Sears took a preliminary copy of the document to Europe, and when he returned he wrote Scott a sad letter:

"I saw Loeb in Munich and he is very seriously ill. I was with him only for fifteen minutes and, although I spoke of the Press, he told me he could not even think of reading the plan and that for the present he did not want to take up any other business or consider any business questions whatever. In fact, he spoke despairingly of his edition of the Classics and said he wished he had never begun it."[20]

The chase after a Croesus was all but over. The World War broke out in August, and in March 1915 Scott told Gay that the economy was in such a slough that "at present everyone has 'no' on their lips before you begin to speak, and I think quite rightly."[21]

Dean Gay, meanwhile, had worked strenuously at a different approach to financial soundness. He proposed a contractual relationship between the Press and the University. For working capital the Press would borrow money from the Corporation (without guarantees from benefactors) and would pay interest on it. The Printing Office, in its work for the University departments, would charge prices sufficient to cover its costs and would also do commercial work for outside customers at a profit—and under certain conditions the printing profits would be used for the publishing department.[22]

The Syndics spent much time considering the proposed contract. On April 1, 1914, they referred it to a committee on which Gay was joined by Robert Bacon and the Harvard treasurer, Charles Francis Adams III. Soon, Gay reported that this committee had fully accepted the principles of the agreement. The Syndics approved the document on May 20. But when it reached President Lowell the whole scheme went up in smoke. Lowell told Adams, "I do not see how the Corporation can make an agreement with its own agents, or give them an independence of action entirely beyond its own control." He said Lane "is our agent" and "responsible to us." Besides, said the president, "I doubt whether it would be wise to advance money to the Press as a loan, with the hope that the Press would pay interest. It seems to me we have got to look to gifts for the endowment of the Press."[23]

Of course the Corporation was already advancing money and the Press was paying interest on it, but everyone then thought that the Corporation was guaranteed against loss. The Press's cumulative debt to the University, as shown in the Treasurer's Statements, was about $15,000 in July 1914, $20,000 in 1915, and a bit less in 1916; but it had grown to $41,491 by July 1917. The interest in 1916–17 was over $1,000.

Operations

The most heartening event of the Lane administration was a move to new and more spacious quarters in 1916. The Press was allowed to leave University Hall and take over Randall Hall, an unusual red-brick structure on Divinity Avenue at the corner of Kirkland Street, about a block from Harvard Yard. This was to be the home of Harvard University Press for sixteen years and of the printing operation for nearly half a century. Today William James Hall stands on the site.

Randall Hall, originally a student dining facility, had a main room 90 by 60 feet and about 35 feet high, with tall windows. This room was occupied by the compositors (setting type by hand and by Monotype keyboard), the proofreaders, and foreman Adam K. Wilson. The presses were installed in a former serving room along the north side of the building. The basement was used for the Monotype casters, the heating plant, lunchrooms, toilets, and storage of electrotype plates and standing type. Space for the publication staff, including Lane, his sales department, and his accounting department, was obtained by building a balcony across the front part of the great hall, with a glass partition overlooking the composing room. On the main level under his balcony were stocks of books and paper. A room at one side of the front door became the shipping department, and a room at the other side became the classroom for the Business School's courses in printing and publishing.[24]

By now Lane had completed two years as president of the Society of Printers, having succeeded Updike in that rather exalted office. Besides directing the Press, he was on the faculty of the Business School, supervising the printing and publishing courses and helping to teach them. Soon after the Press's founding he became a first lieutenant in the Massachusetts Coast Artillery Corps. By 1917 a Reserve Officers Training Corps regiment was drilling at Harvard, and Lane

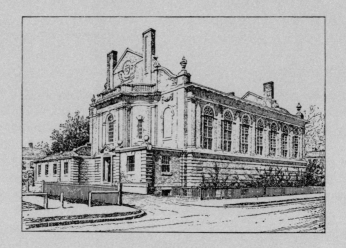

A Keepsake
printed on the occasion of the
first meeting in
Randall Hall
of the Syndics of the
Harvard University *Press*

October 30, 1916

8. Keepsake distributed in 1916, showing the second headquarters of Harvard University Press. Kirkland Street runs across the foreground.

served it as a tactical instructor, as a battalion commander, and as the regiment's adjutant.[25]

At the Press, Lane exerted himself to increase sales. After all, he had been advertising manager of the distinguished house of Ginn. Now he sent out streams of circular letters beginning, for example, "Dear Madam: Have you ever been in doubt as to the wisdom of adding some article of food to a child's diet?" and "Dear Sir: The student of economics will find much interesting material in four new books." He distributed printed notices, including little posters for libraries to put on their bulletin boards. He specialized in lists of books, the most elaborate being the Press's annual catalogues. To literary editors, Lane in 1914 sent an affable newsletter called *Literary Notes,* the forerunner of two livelier newsletters, *Book News* in the forties and *The Browser* in the sixties. The Press also advertised regularly in *The Nation* and irregularly in the *New Republic* and many other magazines, journals, and newspapers.[26]

But direct selling to bookstores was a different question. On the advice of a committee headed by Charles Thurber, the Syndics chose Baker & Taylor as the selling agent in New York and A. C. McClurg & Company in Chicago.[27] To visit bookstores was so expensive— and the Press's "trade books" so few—that regular personal solicitation of booksellers was infeasible. And this problem, common to university presses, brought some of them together in a collaboration, a very modest precursor of today's Association of American University Presses.

Toward the end of 1915 Lane reported that the presses of Harvard, Yale, and Princeton had formed a "University Press Association" to promote sales. It was hoped that eventually all of the important American university presses would join. The next move, instigated by Yale, was a Yale-Harvard sales office in New York City, opened in 1916. The collaboration fell apart in the early twenties. Since Yale had done much better from the arrangement than Harvard, it was felt in Cambridge that Yale books had been pushed harder. On the other hand, there is no doubt that Yale University Press had had more trade books to offer.[28]

Harvard University Press's total receipts from the sale of publications, as given in its Annual Reports, rose gradually from $61,000 in 1913–14 to $78,000 in 1916–17. Then they fell back, and the Annual Reports became vague about the receipts, but according to the Harvard Treasurer's Statement they were again down to $61,000 in 1918–19.[29] (Part of the income, of course, had to be transferred to University departments that had provided funds for publishing the books they owned.) Sales would probably have been better had it not been for the war's impact on market conditions, but this impact is difficult to measure.

War

The war wrought one kind of damage that was not in doubt: it picked off key individuals.

The first to go was the guarantor, Robert Bacon. From the war's beginning in August 1914, he was convinced that the United States must join in and had better get ready. He himself did not wait. Sailing to France, where he had recently been ambassador, he hired three automobiles and used them to transport wounded soldiers from the First Battle of the Marne. He took the lead in establishing an American military hospital, an American ambulance service, and a sanitary railroad train to carry casualties. With the collaboration of Sir William Osler in England, he arranged for an American surgical unit in a British military hospital. Back in the United States, he and others agitated for a training camp at Plattsburg, New York, after which he enlisted as a private and went through training there—at age fifty-five. In 1916 he came close to winning the Republican nomination for U.S. Senator from New York, campaigning ardently on the issue of military preparedness.[30] When the United States declared war in April 1917, he was commissioned a major on General Pershing's staff, sailed to France with Pershing, took charge of setting up the American military headquarters, became a lieutenant-colonel, and represented the U.S. Army at the British military headquarters.[31] Bacon resigned from the Harvard Corporation in 1918 but never did resign as chairman of the Board of Syndics, though he attended no meetings in 1915, only one in 1916, and none thereafter. He returned to New York in April 1919, thoroughly worn out. After a brief illness he was operated on for mastoiditis and died of blood poisoning.

At the end of 1917 the Press lost Dean Edwin F. Gay, another of its founding fathers. This inventive and energetic man spent a year and a half with war agencies in Washington, mainly the War Shipping Board, and went from there in 1919 to the presidency of the ailing *New York Evening Post*. He enlisted Donald Scott, first as New York representative of the Shipping Board and then as his right-hand man at the *Evening Post*. The newspaper under Gay acquired a brilliant editorial staff but lost huge sums, and in 1924 he returned to Harvard, not to the Business School or the Press but to his pre–Business School home in the Department of Economics.[32]

The Army took C. C. Lane in July 1918. As a major in the Adjutant General's Department, he had almost completed training for overseas duty when the November armistice arrived, but they kept him in uniform thirteen months in all. For the first ten the Acting Director of the Press, on a part-time basis for $83.33 a month, was the artist William A. Dwiggins, who stood it as long as he could.[33]

William Addison Dwiggins (1880–1956) was one of the most creative and versatile figures in the history of the graphic arts. Reared in Cambridge, Ohio, he spent his adult life in Hingham, Massachusetts (Lane's hometown), with a studio in Boston. By 1918, at age thirty-eight, he had distinguished himself in advertising layout, had performed many jobs involving hand lettering and ornament for Harvard University Press and for D. B. Updike, and for two years had taught the Harvard Business School's advanced course in printing and publishing. But his international reputation was still to come. Among the typefaces he designed, starting in 1929, were Metroblack, Electra, Caledonia, Eldorado, and Falcon. For Alfred A. Knopf alone he designed 280 books and parts of 55 others.[34]

Dwiggins's supervision of the Press was not one of his most satisfying experiences. His fellow artist Rudolph Ruzicka recalled that Dwiggins "hated the business of managing other people."[35] He also had no taste for negotiating with faculty luminaries. And Press operations were in a mess. Not only Lane but also his assistant had joined the military. A number of women on the staff had resigned to enter various kinds of war work. The bookkeeping fell behind, and the Press was subjected to severe criticism.[36] Parts of the burden of running the Press were assumed by Charles Barnes Blanchard and David Thomas Pottinger, both of whom had taken the Business School's basic printing and publishing course in 1916–17, and also to some extent by Walter Moreland Stone, on loan from the Business School.[37]

At the Syndics meeting of April 24, 1919, according to the minutes, Dwiggins asked to be relieved because of the pressure of his personal business. As Acting Director the Syndics chose Charles Blanchard.

By this time the Harvard administration and the Board of Syndics were growing very anxious about the Press's financial prospects. They had been edgy even before Lane's departure. For example, at a Harvard Corporation meeting in May 1918, the treasurer, C. F. Adams, had inquired about the Press's finances and had been told that Lane still expected Robert Bacon "to make up any reasonable deficit." He

9. William A. Dwiggins, en route to fame as typographer
and designer, shown at about the time he was Acting
Director of the Press in 1918-19.

was also told that for the duration of the war the Press was publishing
no books that were not backed up by adequate financial guarantees.[38]
The Syndics, for their part, were tired of declining good manuscripts
for lack of such guarantees. So it is not surprising that when Bacon
returned from Europe in April 1919 the Syndics resolved "that Mr.
Bacon be consulted in regard to the financial policy of the Press."

Lane, on a short military leave, attended the April meeting, and it
fell to him to write Bacon. In his letter he described the war-related
curtailment of activities and sales, recalled that Bacon had "made the
organization of the Press possible," mentioned the deficit, reminded
Bacon that he was still chairman of the board, and said the Syndics
"wanted me to ask you if it seemed to you that there was any opportunity of our securing an endowment at this time, or if you had
any suggestions to make as to what our future policy should be."[39]
Lane's letter, dated May 6, 1919, brought no response. Bacon died
May 29.

During that summer, a time of confusion in the affairs of the Press, President Lowell tried to discover exactly what Bacon had guaranteed. Lane reported he understood from Treasurer Adams that Adams had received "satisfactory guarantees" from Bacon, but added, "I never saw any formal agreement." Said Lane, "The plan under which we operated called for an expenditure of $15,000 the first year and $20,000 in each of the two succeeding years"—hence a total of $55,000— "with the understanding that at the end of five years any deficit was to be made up to the University by Mr. Bacon."[40]

In July the time bomb exploded. A letter from Bacon was found in Adams's files. It was dated January 15, 1913, the day of the first Syndics meeting, and it said in full:

> My Dear Sir:—
> In consideration of the establishment by Harvard College of a University press, I agree for a period of two years from such establishment to make good any annual loss up to the sum of five thousand dollars which the College may suffer, my total obligation being limited to ten thousand dollars.[41]

When Lane was asked for an explanation, he said he had never seen the letter and knew nothing about such an arrangement.[42]

In that month of July 1919 the Press's debt to the University was around $58,000 and Lane was still in the Army.[43] Kittredge told President Lowell that uncertainty over the time of Lane's return was "demoralizing" the Press, and Blanchard confirmed this. Many years later Kittredge recalled that the affairs of the Press in those months of 1919 "were in an almost chaotic condition." Lowell telegraphed Lane: "When do you return here. Press needs you very badly."[44] Lane finally returned in August and plunged into the tasks of cleaning up some of the problems, putting the best face on the situation, and arranging his own future.

On October first, Lane told the Syndics he intended to resign in order to become production manager of the *New York Evening Post* under Edwin Gay. In his formal letter of resignation, in November, Lane said he was not resigning because of any lack of faith in the Press's ultimate growth but because he wanted a bigger job.[45] He left the Harvard payroll on December 31. For the rest of his long career he worked on New York newspapers. He was promoted to business manager of the *Post* and later spent thirty years at the *New York Times* as assistant and associate business manager. He served terms as chairman of the New York Publishers' Association and president of the American Institute of Graphic Arts. He died on December 27, 1967, at age eighty-four.[46]

Hope

But there is more to tell about 1919. During the last few months of Lane's tenure, there were developments suggesting that the shaky Harvard University Press had a future after all.

In October the Board of Syndics arose as one man and protested the University's neglect of the Press.

At the Syndics meeting at October 1, the one at which Lane announced his departure, Archibald Cary Coolidge moved that Charles Thurber bring to the next meeting a draft of a memorial to the Corporation outlining the need for an endowed University Press. The Syndics discussed Thurber's draft, made some changes, had it printed, and sent it to the Corporation. The copy of record, dated October 22, is in the University Archives with the signatures of George F. Moore, George L. Kittredge, Archibald Cary Coolidge, Walter B. Cannon, Paul J. Sachs, C. H. Thurber, and A. E. Kennelly.[47] Apparently the document was not made public.

There was one new name in this list of Syndics: that of Paul Joseph Sachs, who had been appointed in September. In the 1940s Sachs was to be chairman of the Syndics during a great Press upheaval. In 1919 he was forty years old, an assistant professor of fine arts, associate director of the Fogg Art Museum, and former partner in the banking house of Goldman, Sachs & Company. Like James Loeb, he had studied fine arts at Harvard under the spell of Charles Eliot Norton and had left his family firm for the love of things aesthetic.

The Syndics said in their memorial, "Some of the best manuscripts offered have had to be declined for lack of funds." They informed the President and Fellows that businesses, especially publishers, must have working capital, for "in the nature of the case" the Press's books are "largely of a slow-selling kind." They concluded: "If the Harvard University Press is to be maintained at all, it should be maintained on a standard as high as that of any similar institution in this country and its worthy ambition should be to attain a rank comparable with that of the great university presses at Oxford and Cambridge, England. It is the belief of the Syndics that the University ought either to abandon the plan of maintaining a university press, or else support it to such an extent that it can perform its proper functions and be a creditable part of the University."

President Lowell soon demonstrated that he had no intention of abandoning the Press.

First, he quickly named Lane's successor, a man in whom he placed complete confidence. This was Harold Murdock, a vice-president of the National Shawmut Bank in Boston. On November 10, just two days after Lane's letter of resignation, the Harvard Corporation approved Murdock's appointment—as of January 1, 1920—not only as Director of the Press but also as chairman of the Board of Syndics.

Second, Lowell published a statement on the importance of a university press—one of his most eloquent on that subject. "We spend much upon the Library," he declared, "and it would be wise to spend more upon the Press."[48]

Finally, the income of the Press took a gratifying upturn, so that the picture looked better in December than it had in July. Just before leaving office, Lane reported to Lowell that the Press's gross business in the last six months of 1919 had exceeded $45,000. (It had been only $61,000 in the *twelve* months before that.) Lane said the Press's total deficit of $57,924 on June 30 had been reduced to $44,000. He attributed $3,603 of the reduction to the correction of errors in the accounts, the rest to a combination of "issuing no new books at the expense of the Press" and "vigorous pushing of the books already issued." Lane also pointed to two cash resources that would further reduce the debt. One was $22,145 from the Bacon estate, consisting of the original guarantee of $10,000 and the current deficit of $12,145 on the Elihu Root volumes, underwritten by Bacon. (Lowell had gently written to Bacon's widow asking if she was inclined to take up the two guarantees, and a check had arrived in mid-December.) The other was a "General Publication Fund," then at $11,866, which had begun in 1912 with a gift of $2,500 from Nelson Robinson and which Lane said "represents the profit on books already paid for by the Press." Lane told Lowell the sales increase "typifies, I think, the results that can be secured now that the war is over."[49]

The year 1919 was the time of demobilization, inflation, a "Red scare," race riots, a Boston police strike, and nationwide industrial unrest. Union printers in Boston won a large wage increase, and Harvard, which paid about $800 weekly to its thirty-five printers and proofreaders, went along with the increase even though its printing shop was not unionized.[50] The climbing cost of labor and materials led Lane to inform the Syndics in September that he was raising the price of a number of publications. Yet despite all the turbulence, business in the United States was good that summer and fall. People obviously were finding more money—not to create endowments, it appeared, but at least to buy books.

The Press needed more than favorable external conditions: it needed a stronger internal basis of operations. This came with its next Director.

CHAPTER THREE

The Murdock Years

1920–1934

HAROLD MURDOCK, banker, book collector, and author, headed Harvard University Press for about fourteen years, from the beginning of 1920 until his death in April 1934. He established financial stability by charging the University higher prices for printing, by printing for customers outside Harvard, and by using the printing profits to cover the publishing losses. He was able to do this because, being experienced at analyzing troubled businesses and being a friend of President Lowell's, he enjoyed the confidence of the Harvard administration more than any other Press Director until Thomas J. Wilson. Lowell appointed him not only to the Press but also to a three-man committee to reorganize the financial management of the University. Murdock at the Press, in the judgment of Professor Kittredge, "brought order out of chaos almost in the turn of a hand."[1]

In typography, the Murdock era was the Press's heyday, when the renowned Bruce Rogers was in and out of the shop and Harvard's reputation for book design stood higher than it ever has before or since. The Murdock years were also the time of David T. Pottinger's rise toward the Directorship, which, however, he never quite attained. And it was the time during which another Press mainstay, William Warren Smith, began his forty-three-year service in the organization. Murdock had special need of people like them because he had never been a publisher, never claimed to be one, passed parts of his days browsing about in the eighteenth century, and was absent for long stretches of illness in a hospital or at home. Even when healthy he customarily worked at the Press in the mornings only.[2]

During Murdock's tenure about 750 books and booklets appeared with the Press's imprint—an average of about 50 a year. The annual output climbed from about 20 to about 90.[3] Most of the books were owned by Harvard departments and other scholarly organizations—

10. Harold Murdock, second Director of the Press.

published by the Press for a commission which was typically 15 percent of the list price on all copies sold. Though they were excellent in scholarship, the great majority were too specialized for much of a sale. A paucity of working capital, as before, severely limited the publication of independent Press-owned books. Furthermore Murdock's administration, like Lane's, came into the path of an apocalyptic horseman—earlier the Great War, now the economic famine of the Great Depression. Receipts from the sale of books rose to $137,000 in 1927–28 but thereafter sank to $64,000 in 1932–33, when libraries and scholars were perhaps at their most threadbare. Sales were actually lower at the end of Murdock's administration in 1934 than in 1920.[4] In the academic year 1932–33 the Press published 85 books—but only 13 at its own risk.[5]

When Murdock became Press Director he was fifty-seven and had been a vice-president of the National Shawmut Bank for thirteen years. He was tall and slender, with a neat mustache. He impressed some people as being aloof in manner, even sometimes rude, others as being personally charming. He had no college degree, because he had gone to work in a banking firm at age eighteen. Murdock stayed in finance for forty years, but his heart was closer to the Club of Odd Volumes, a Boston organization dedicated to the world of books. In his twenties he began writing works of history in his spare time (published by Houghton Mifflin), went on to collect a celebrated private library, and in 1916 was awarded an honorary M.A. by Harvard.[6] Some of the books he wrote were designed at the Riverside Press by Bruce Rogers, and that was a fortunate thing for Harvard because Murdock brought his friend Rogers with him to the Press.

Finances

Two weeks before Murdock began his Directorship he made four recommendations for changes in the Press's status. President Lowell approved all four. The new plan was as follows, verbatim:

(1) So far as the University is concerned, the printing office and the publication end at the Press should be merged—the combination to comprise the Harvard University Press. The profits of the printing office should remain in the business instead of being withdrawn yearly as at present.

(2) The Press should conduct its own business, maintain its own bank account, paying for its own supplies, etc. Bills should be rendered to the University for work done for different departments and should be settled by check.

(3) For the year 1920, the Treasurer should extend to the Press a credit of, say, fifty thousand dollars to be furnished in round amounts as needed.

(4) The Press should be free to take on any outside printing or to publish any book that, in quality, commends itself to the Syndics.[7]

Of course the printing and publishing operations were already together in the sense that both were under the control of the Press Director. For financial purposes, however, the University had always treated them as separate organizations when listing their expenditures and receipts in the annual Treasurer's Statement. Printing receipts had averaged about 4 percent above cost, and this excess had been treated simply as University income.[8] Now the Press began setting the printing prices about 10 percent above cost and retaining the profits "in the business."

Moreover it greatly increased its printing for noncommercial clients outside Harvard.[9] In 1929–30 outside printing brought in about $87,000, which was 12 percent above cost as compared with a 9 percent profit on $96,000 of printing done for the University.[10]

Within the University, the issue of printing prices became more and more troublesome, and eventually, long after Murdock and Lowell had left the scene, it contributed to a storm of ill will in which the Press discarded the Printing Office and nearly lost its life. But in the 1920s, in the absence of an endowment (or even a campaign for an endowment) and in the absence of a direct annual subsidy from the University (which apparently was unthinkable), the revenues of the printing shop enabled the Press to survive.

Dean Edwin Gay had tried to move the Press toward more independence in 1914 but had been rebuffed. Murdock met with more success. The Press opened a bank account rather than continuing to handle its transactions through the University bursar's office, and its expenditures and receipts vanished from the Treasurer's Statements. Murdock installed a new bookkeeping system and hired a thirty-year-old accountant named Herbert E. Jacques (pronounced "Jakes") to supervise it.[11]

Fifty thousand dollars in one year was a marvel. But it was to be a loan, and Mr. Murdock knew all about loans—they were supposed to be paid back. He apparently did not borrow the full amount. Because of improved sales and other income (such as the payment from the Bacon estate), the Press's debt to the University actually decreased during the fiscal year 1919–20, that is, in Lane's last six months and Murdock's first six, and it amounted to $21,584 in June 1920. Then, during Murdock's first full fiscal year, 1920–21, it rose to $45,000 as he took advantage of his credit rating. Some of the cash went for badly needed equipment, including a third No. 2 Miehle cylinder press and much else.[12] But during the next twelve months, 1921–22, the debt balance of $45,000 turned into a credit balance of $10,000—and the Press no doubt had additional funds in its checking account. This turn-around must have been due to the rise in sales and the advent of printing profits.

Throughout the rest of the Murdock administration there were only two years in which the Treasurer's Statement showed a debit balance for the Press. The blessed solvency continued even after the bottom fell out of sales during the Depression. Even in 1931 the Harvard administration could assert with pleasure that "since Mr. Murdock has had charge of our press it has been making money."[13]

As for Murdock's declaration of the freedom to publish any Syndic-approved book, this can be best understood by remembering the rigid rule that had been in effect before he arrived—"issuing no new books at the expense of the Press," as Lane had put it. This constraint had driven the Syndics to something near rebellion. Now Murdock as Press Director and chairman of the Syndics was no longer bound by the rule. The Press did risk its own money many times, but the trend faltered because of the *new* rigid rule—to avoid deficits, or to snuff them out quickly when they occurred—and because of what the Depression did to the book business.

The Murdock plan of 1919–20 did not define the Press's legal status. That question was settled in 1926.

The Press had always copyrighted books and executed contracts simply in the name of "Harvard University Press." The contracts were made through an exchange of letters. In 1926 Murdock suggested to President Lowell that the Press be made a separate corporation like the presses at Yale and Princeton. Lowell replied that he had never been sure but he thought contracts had better be made in the University's name with the Press Director acting as agent.[14] Soon thereafter, on April 26, 1926, the Harvard Corporation voted that the contracts should be in its name—that is, in the name of "the President and Fellows of Harvard College."[15] Thus it came about that the Press, though it had the delegated authority to copyright books and execute contracts, did so forever after in the name of the President and Fellows. Officially it always was, and still is, a department of Harvard.

Governance

From time to time Murdock casually discussed the affairs of the Press with Harvard's president, treasurer, and comptroller.[16] He told very little in his Annual Reports to the president, other than listing the books published. He did take care, however, to keep the Board of Syndics abreast of the financial situation.

But the Syndics under Murdock exerted much less influence than before. They met less often and attendance was poor. Around 1923 Murdock began declining manuscripts and getting the board's approval later. Soon he went further and began accepting some manuscripts subject to confirmation by the board. He did, however, confer with individual Syndics between meetings.

Kittredge was more active than ever. The reduction in the board's influence and enthusiasm did not seem to apply to him. He attended more meetings than any other member except Murdock, kept his eye open for new books, read and revised manuscripts, and even improved advertisements.[17]

Only three Syndics served throughout the Murdock administration: Kittredge, Charles Thurber, and Paul Sachs. The man who had been writing the minutes, George Foot Moore, a pillar of the board since its beginning, stepped down in 1924 and was succeeded by another Divinity School professor, James Hardy Ropes, who served until 1932. Archibald Cary Coolidge died in 1928. Dr. Walter Cannon attended his last meeting in February 1929 (though at Murdock's insistence he remained a member until 1932) and A. E. Kennelly attended his last in June 1931. At the time of Murdock's death in 1934 the board consisted of Kittredge, Thurber, Sachs, Robert Pierpont Blake, John M. Maguire (the first Syndic from the Law School), Dr. Hans Zinsser, and William Scott Ferguson.

When the Harvard Board of Overseers provided the Press with a Visiting Committee in the year 1922–23, the first chairman was Henry James, lawyer, son of William James and nephew of Henry James the novelist. This turned out to be a far-reaching appointment, for James was a member of the Harvard Corporation during the Press's crisis of the forties. In May 1923 the Visiting Committee reported that the Press now was "upon a solid foundation" but wanted more "works of sound scholarship or literary quality that make a broader appeal."[18]

Henry James was succeeded by Thomas W. Slocum, a merchant of New York City, who remained chairman of the Visiting Committee for six years, from 1923–24 through 1928–29. After Slocum came Philip Stockton, a Boston financier, for three years. And in 1932–33, Allston Burr, another Boston financier, who took a great interest in the Press, began a five-year spell as chairman.

Books

The need for books of "broader appeal" was widely recognized. In 1924 the Harvard Alumni Bulletin said that in the Press's list, with some "notable exceptions," there was "an evident lack of books of general public interest" in comparison with the Yale and Princeton lists.[19]

Among the few Harvard books that had made a deep impression outside the academic world was a mighty work on typography, published in 1922. This was Daniel Berkeley Updike's two-volume *Print-*

ing Types: Their History, Forms, and Use, which he wrote, designed, and printed, but which was owned by the Press. Updike analyzed the typefaces and typographers that had been most important since the invention of printing and drew lessons for modern printers. After Updike died in 1941 Stanley Morison, the British typographer, wrote that the book's publication was "the most exciting event of a decade" and "to us at the time the book had a messianic quality."[20] *Printing Types* remained in print almost continuously for more than fifty years, had a steady though not spectacular sale of 12,500 in all, and was known as "the Printer's Bible."[21]

The road to publication was long and frustrating. The manuscript began to take shape in 1911 when Updike delivered his first series of twelve lectures at the Harvard Business School. In 1913 the Press announced that the lectures were "in press" and would be out in June 1914. This was wishful thinking: for years Updike continued to refine the text. When he thought he had the manuscript about ready, the embarrassed Press was too poor to publish it, and the Syndics voted in May 1918 and again in April 1919 that they would be glad to publish the work but could not. Even after acceptance in January 1920, about two and a half more years passed before Updike could satisfy himself with the manuscript and its 367 illustrations.[22]

Some of the other noteworthy nonseries books published during Murdock's administration are as follows: Charles H. Haskins's *The Renaissance of the Twelfth Century* (1927), still important enough in 1971 to be reissued as a Harvard Paperback; E. K. Rand's *Founders of the Middle Ages* (1928); G. L. Kittredge's *Witchcraft in Old and New England* (1929); George Foot Moore's *Judaism,* three volumes (1927 and 1930), a lively seller; the young Kenneth Murdock's *Increase Mather* (1925); and the young Perry Miller's *Orthodoxy in Massachusetts* (1933). The typical royalty was 10 percent of the list price, though as the Depression deepened the authors were lucky if they got any royalty at all.

Other faculty members who later became important to the Press showed up on the Murdock lists, examples being Harry A. Wolfson, Wilbur K. Jordan, Mason Hammond, Arthur H. Cole, Arthur N. Holcombe, and Ralph Barton Perry. The most constant habitués of the Murdock lists were Hyder E. Rollins of the English Department and Charles H. Grandgent, the Dante scholar. One or the other showed up almost every year.

The Press under Murdock was strongest in general literature and language (but not yet strong in American literature). It was also strong

in history, education, economics, art, and folk music. In art history
it started what was perhaps the Press's most persistently reappearing
book title, *A History of Spanish Painting*, by Chandler Rathfon Post,
published in fourteen volumes from 1930 to 1966.

The Harvard Historical Studies in this period included works by
the young scholars William L. Langer, Dexter Perkins, and Frederick
Merk. In 1932 the Department of History added a parallel series, the
Harvard Historical Monographs, little different in criteria but separately endowed. Number 1 was *Athenian Tribal Cycles in the Hel-
lenistic Age*, by William S. Ferguson, one of the new Syndics.

The Press's strength in economics derived mainly from the Harvard
Economic Studies, which poured out twenty-five volumes in the Murdock years. These included *The Theory of Monopolistic Competition*,
by Edward H. Chamberlin (ultimate sales 40,000); monographs by
other promising young men, among them Edward S. Mason and
Seymour Harris; and, in 1934, the first edition in English of Joseph
A. Schumpeter's *The Theory of Economic Development*.

The Press published books in the sciences, including the opening
volumes of *Check-List of Birds of the World*, by James L. Peters, and
early works by the physicist Percy Bridgman and the geologist Kirtley
Mather; but the number of scientific books decreased during Murdock's tenure. Most scientists had other outlets for their work. The
Press published little on government and politics, though a change
was signaled in 1930 when the Harvard Political Studies started with
J. F. Sly's *Town Government in Massachusetts (1620–1930)*.

The Press added thirty new series in the Murdock years, bringing
the total to more than forty. Of the 750 titles published in all, about
345 were in series, and the proportion was increasing. Nearly all of
the series books (and a great many nonseries ones) were owned outside
the Press and published on a commission basis. In 1924 the Press
became the American agent for the Publications of the Institute for
Comparative Research in Human Culture, which had its headquarters
in Oslo, Norway (many of these publications were in languages other
than English). Another distinguished and copious new series, begun
in 1932, was the Publications of the Harvard-Yenching Institute, printed
in China. Though the multiplying of specialized series during the
Murdock period did little for the Press's economic health, it did much
for world scholarship, to the credit of the Harvard departments that
conducted them. Among the other new subsidized series of enduring
importance were the Publications of the Wertheim Fellowship (1927),
which in 1954 became the Wertheim Publications in Industrial Re-

lations, presided over by John T. Dunlop; the Harvard City Planning Studies (1930); and the Harvard Studies in Business History (1931).

The two new series that promised the most books of broad appeal were the Godkin Lectures and the Norton Lectures. The authors were from outside Harvard—public figures, writers, artists, and musicians.

The Godkin Lectures had been founded in 1903 by friends of E. L. Godkin, magazine and newspaper editor. The lectures were on "The Essentials of Free Government and the Duties of the Citizen, or upon some part of the subject."[23] There was never any requirement that the lectures be published at Harvard. The Press did not tap this source until 1926, when it published *Congress: An Explanation,* by Congressman Robert Luce. Only two more Godkin volumes came out in the Murdock period, but in later decades the series blossomed.

The Norton Lectures *are* required to be published by Harvard. In 1925 Charles Chauncey Stillman, class of 1898, gave the University $200,000 to endow the Charles Eliot Norton Chair of Poetry. Each appointee would be in residence for one year and would deliver at least six lectures. "Poetry" in this case meant all forms of poetic communication—in language, music, or the fine arts.[24] The books at first were financed by income from the endowment and owned by the Harvard Corporation, but in later times the Press invested its own money and sometimes received a good return. The first Norton Professor, in 1926–27, was Gilbert Murray, professor of Greek at Oxford University. The Press published his lectures as *The Classical Tradition in Poetry* in 1927. By 1981 the Press had published twenty-five books in the Norton series. Some of the authors: T. S. Eliot, Sigfried Giedion, Igor Stravinsky, Aaron Copland, E. E. Cummings, Ben Shahn, Lionel Trilling, Octavio Paz, and Leonard Bernstein.

T. S. Eliot took part in another unusual Press undertaking—namely, the publication of phonograph records from 1933 to 1937. (This enterprise was the direct ancestor of *The Poet's Voice,* a packet of six tape cassettes that the Press would issue in 1978.) The discs of the 1930s were originated by Frederick C. Packard, Jr., an assistant professor of public speaking. As a part of a long-term voice-recording project which he called the Harvard Vocarium, he recorded Eliot reading two of his own poems ("Gerontion" and "The Hollow Men"), C. T. Copeland reading from the Book of Revelation, C. H. Grandgent reading from Dante, Fred N. Robinson reading passages of Chaucer, Bliss Perry talking about Emerson and Thackeray, and E. K. Rand reading from the Latin classics.[25] The Press marketed all those discs but was not really up to the business of phonograph records, and in

December 1938 the Syndics voted to transfer them to the Harvard Film Service.

Typography

At Murdock's death the *New York Times* said in a news story that he had raised the quality of the Press's work so that its books were "unsurpassed in this country in printing and design." Because the same wording appeared in other periodicals, the statement may have been put out by Harvard.[26] It is not a statement that can be proved, but it may have been near the truth. Bruce Rogers, D. B. Updike, David Pottinger—even W. A. Dwiggins to some extent—laid expert hands on the Press's output during the 1920s.

In the spring of 1923 the American Institute of Graphic Arts began its annual practice of choosing fifty of the country's best-designed and best-manufactured books for a traveling exhibition and awarded a medal for the most outstanding one of these sold in normal trade channels. The first medal went to Updike's 1922 classic, *Printing Types.* In 1924 the second medal went to another Harvard University Press book: *Doctor Johnson,* by Percy Hazen Houston. The designer of that book was Bruce Rogers. Harvard had five winners in the 1924 group of "Fifty Books"—more than any other publisher.[27] Rogers closely supervised their composition and printing. Twenty-four books published by Harvard from 1922 to 1934 were chosen for the annual exhibits. It seems impossible to identify the principal designer in every case, but here is an approximation: Rogers fifteen, Updike five, Pottinger three, and Melvin Loos one.[28]

Bruce Rogers (1870–1957), an urbane, scholarly, meticulous, ingenious, roving man from Indiana, who applied his arts for many publishers and printers on both sides of the Atlantic, is widely considered the first great professional book designer. Some think him the greatest ever.[29] Whether his influence was greater than that of Dwiggins, whose fame arrived much later, is a matter of definition and opinion.

When Murdock took over the Press, Rogers was forty-nine and had just returned from one of his sojourns in England, where he had been Printing Adviser to the Cambridge University Press and had put new typographical life into that ancient institution. At Murdock's request the Harvard Corporation created for Rogers the part-time position of Printing Adviser to Harvard University Press.[30] The connection lasted till 1936, but he served mainly in the eight years from 1920 to 1928. At the outset he spent two or three months helping to

11. *Modern Color* (1923), by Cutler and Pepper, designed by Bruce Rogers and William A. Dwiggins, two of America's leading graphic artists. Dwiggins did this front cover, stamped in black on a pale yellow binding.

reorganize the work of the Printing Office, and thereafter, for years, he was on hand for at least one spell a month. He designed some thirty books for the Press. He also made creative suggestions and generally improved the appearance of the Press's books and catalogues and of the ephemeral printing jobs performed for the University. His very presence in the shop was inspiring.[31]

As for Updike, he designed the Harvard books that his Merrymount Press printed. These included not only *Printing Types* but also two more that he himself wrote—*In the Day's Work* (1924), owned by the Press with a royalty to Updike, and *Notes on the Merrymount Press and Its Work* (1933), owned by Updike with a publishing commission to the Press.

Quantitatively, the principal designer of Press books in the twenties and thirties was David Thomas Pottinger. He was not in a class with Rogers and Updike but had been trained by them and deserved his reputation as a "workmanlike" designer—a "real craftsman," in Warren Smith's phrase. Pottinger had been deeply influenced by Updike's lectures and example. Rogers, in a 1938 letter, said Pottinger needed no advice from him and was doing a "splendid job" of designing at the Press.[32]

Pottinger and Smith

By the early 1920s David Pottinger was the main link between the publishing office and the printing shop. In 1926 the Society of Printers, in Boston, elected him president. By then he was making himself valuable to the Press not just as a typographer but as a publisher. He wrote and designed the Press's advertising. He visited bookstores to some extent, until he turned this activity over to Warren Smith. As the decade progressed, Pottinger took on various publishing decisions. Increasingly he negotiated with authors.

Pottinger was a small man with reddish hair, a squarish, ruddy face, and glasses. People who knew him have called him orderly, opinionated, irritable, witty, clever, *underrated*. He was born in Boston on Christmas Day 1884, and after graduating from Harvard in 1906 he taught English for a dozen years, brought out an edition of *Hamlet,* and did graduate work in English at Harvard. In 1916–17 he enrolled as a special student at the Business School to take the printing and publishing course supervised by C. C. Lane and featuring Updike. In 1917 Lane hired him at the Press.[33]

Pottinger had an immense capacity both for work and for outside

12. A title page designed by Bruce Rogers at the height of the Press's typographical reputation. The slim volume, with pages 8 ½ by 11 ½ inches, was printed throughout on light blue paper, befitting a book about Wedgwood.

activities. All his adult life he carried on a love affair with Cambridge; he used to say that he wanted never to live beyond the sound of the clock in Memorial Hall.[34] At the Press, Murdock depended heavily on him but questioned his administrative ability[35] and never was willing to clothe him with a title to reflect the de facto position he achieved as second in command.

William Warren Smith (the Press's future Business Manager), from Ogunquit, Maine, was sixteen years younger than Pottinger. In 1919, when Smith was a freshman at Harvard, Pottinger hired him to work on mailing lists for advertising circulars. In 1924 Pottinger gave him a full-time job, and he stayed at the Press until his retirement in 1967. At first he supervised the addressing of direct-mail ads and handled other odds and ends. Soon he began processing orders and visiting bookstores. All this took him into the shipping of books and, more important, into inventory control, which remained one of his most important responsibilities for the next forty years. Around 1927 he was made Sales Manager—the first Press employee with this title.[36]

Headaches

There is no limit to the number and variety of problems that can spring unexpected upon a university press. Two examples will do.

1. In 1921 a certain A. W. Ryder wrote several caustic letters about an increase in the price of a book in the Harvard Oriental Series. The book had been published in 1908 at $1.50. In 1921 the Press, having in the meantime taken over the series, charged Ryder $2.70. Ryder said this increase was shabby swindling and proceeded to publish a pamphlet entitled *A Correspondence with the Harvard University Press*. A sample of his prose: "The Harvard University Press, as conducted by its present Syndics, brings shame upon Harvard by charlatanism, profiteering, falsehood, and cowardly meanness."[37]

2. An archaeological tome by Professor George A. Reisner, entitled *Mycerinus: The Temples of the Third Pyramid of Giza,* became a sort of *cause célèbre.* This mammoth work was a report on the excavations in the pyramid of King Mycerinus, made jointly by Harvard and the Boston Museum of Fine Arts. The two institutions had agreed that Harvard would have the publication rights but had neglected to specify who would pay the publication costs. The Syndics accepted the book in 1925, and most of the manuscript was delivered in 1926. It was set in type, but the last chapter and the last two appendixes were not delivered until 1930, and publication did not take place until

1931. The cost of manufacture was $9,909.94. The Press, to its chagrin, wound up having to pay this and also lost a good deal of interest that could have been earned by the funds that were tied up so long during the production process. The total sales of the book: 209 copies.[38]

In addition to specific headaches, which occur in all periods, the closing years of Murdock's tenure brought a creeping ailment that threatened the Press with general disaster. The Printing Office, despite its high reputation, was deteriorating in efficiency. Early in 1930, Pottinger began discussing the situation with C. C. Lane, then business manager of the *New York Evening Post* and still a member of the Visiting Committee. And Lane discussed it with a New York printing salesman named Curtis E. Lakeman, who had been his Harvard classmate, vintage 1904. Lakeman worked for the George Grady Press, which did much of the printing for Columbia University and New York University. Lakeman suggested to Lane that his boss, George Grady, study the Harvard University Printing Office and recommend improvements, after which he (Lakeman) would consider an offer from Harvard.[39] Murdock commissioned the study.

Grady submitted his report on November 12, 1930. He congratulated the University on the general character of the plant but regretted to say that the superintendent, though a man of admirable knowledge and valuable service, "had long since passed the peak of his efficiency in the handling and supervision of men." Adam K. Wilson was then seventy-three. Grady also recommended that the printing and publishing departments be entirely separated and each placed under a competent and responsible head with full authority.[40]

Pottinger considered himself the appropriate man to be given full authority over the publishing department. Indeed, Pottinger told Lane that Grady had sketched out that job for him.[41] Presumably Grady had Lakeman in mind for the Printing Office. But Murdock rejected the plan, and in the spring of 1931 Pottinger's confidential letters to Lane grew more apprehensive. Faculty complaints about the Printing Office were increasingly severe.[42]

Finally Murdock, instead of hiring Lakeman or someone else from the outside, assigned Herbert Jacques, the accountant, to reorganize the Printing Office. Pottinger was dismayed.[43] Wilson retired on September 1, 1931. With Wilson gone and Jacques the manager of the plant, technical details of printing were supervised by a foreman, one of the veteran printers.[44] And in 1932 Murdock hired Horace Lane Arnold, a Harvard graduate twenty-nine years old, as purchasing agent for paper, engraving, binding, and miscellaneous supplies. Soon

Arnold also became the contact man between the Printing Office and its customers and prepared most of the estimates on the cost of jobs.[45]

Meanwhile, as the publishing program increased during the twenties, the Press again ran out of space. The stock of published books overflowed Randall Hall, and the publication offices on the balcony lost their charm.

In 1928 President Lowell allowed the Press to take over the nearby Rogers Building, or "old gymnasium," for book storage and shipping. Murdock also asked Lowell about an old factory building on the Charles River, then being used by Harvard's maintenance department. The President shot back: "The pioneers used to stake out claims in the wilderness in unoccupied lands, and the pioneers of the Press stake them out over buildings already occupied. Nevertheless, I will place on file your claim to a protectorate, or sphere of influence, over less civilized peoples."[46] The Press kept the old gymnasium less than two years, because the City of Cambridge wanted the site for a fire station (which was built and is still there). Most of the inventory was transferred to the riverfront factory Murdock had asked about earlier.[47]

In 1932 the Press fulfilled its desire for a better publishing office. On July 1 it moved its headquarters southward to 38 Quincy Street, a Harvard-owned frame house at the corner of Broadway, on a site later occupied by the Allston Burr Lecture Hall and still later by the Sackler Museum.

This was the third headquarters of the Press, and, like the second, it was the Press's address for sixteen years. The house was over eighty years old, was architecturally interesting, and had been lived in or visited by many well-known people.[48] It had not yet been visited by the wonders of electricity. The Press had to renovate the house with its own funds and had to pay rent, just as it did for Randall Hall. Murdock, Pottinger, Smith, and Murdock's two women assistants made a 38 Quincy Street population of five. Bookkeeping and shipping remained in Randall Hall along with the printing and proofreading; Jacques was left in charge of that building and almost all that went on there. The proof room was an exception.

The proof room in Randall Hall was not only a place for correcting typographical errors but also the nearest thing to an editorial department that the Press had. It was headed by an aggressive man named Joseph Tuckerman Day, a Harvard graduate in his early forties, who was a journalist and editor by profession and had worked at the *New York Times,* the Associated Press, and Ginn & Company.[49]

In that era, as in the previous century, proofreaders in book-print-

13. The Press's home from 1932 to 1948—an old yellow house at 38 Quincy Street, diagonally across from the northeast corner of Harvard Yard.

ing plants were apt to be well-educated persons who went beyond correcting printer's mistakes. Compared with proofreaders nowadays, they paid more attention to the writing itself and addressed more queries to the authors, both before and after the typesetting. Scholarly "correctors" sometimes had high reputations.

Day, joining the Press in 1929, had a mandate which he described thus: "to reorganize the proofreading department and to take over editorial duties of a miscellaneous nature," including "close contact with various authors from manuscript to printed sheets."[50] He supervised eight people and was directly responsible to Harold Murdock rather than to the authorities in the Printing Office.

In the United States by this time the editing of manuscripts had largely shifted from printing plants to publishing offices.[51] Harvard was late in making the shift. British university presses were even later. Throughout the nineteenth century the correcting and improving of the author's prose had been a printer's skill, and printers had elaborate style manuals to guide them. All this changed in the twentieth century.[52] Harvard's Press seems to have been slower than most in establishing an editorial department in the modern sense, possibly because its proof room was populous and versatile, possibly also because many of its books benefited from editing by the University departments or by Professor Kittredge.

Interregnum

During the last years of Murdock's life, two events outside the Press deeply affected the Press's future.

The first was the death of James Loeb, on May 29, 1933, at his Bavarian estate. He bequeathed the Loeb Classical Library to Harvard. He did not name Harvard University Press in his will, but the news of the legacy fired Pottinger and Smith with anticipatory excitement.

The second event was the accession of James B. Conant to the Harvard presidency. Kenneth B. Murdock, who was dean of the Faculty of Arts and Sciences (and son of Harold Murdock), had been widely considered Lowell's heir apparent, but he was passed over. Conant, a distinguished chemist on the faculty, forty years old, took office on September 1, 1933. Harold Murdock, by then in his seventies and in deteriorating health, had earlier shown signs of wanting to step down from the Press, but President Lowell had asked him to stay because he himself was going to retire and wanted his successor to pick the next Press Director.[53] Murdock attended his last Syndics meeting on October 19. Kittredge took the chair at the next meeting, December 7, and occupied it for two years. Murdock died on April 5, 1934.[54]

By that time President Conant had already begun his search for a Director. Meanwhile, the Press endured a two-year interregnum, from around December 1933, when Murdock had ceased to be active, until December 1, 1935, when the next Director took office.

Like Derek C. Bok in 1971, Conant came to the presidency believing that Harvard University Press was going to be a problem. Both of them were right.

During the interregnum, David Pottinger served as acting director, though the Corporation never dignified him with that title and the Press's Annual Reports for 1933–34 and 1934–35 were signed "G. L. Kittredge, Acting Chairman of the Syndics." Kittredge headed the decision making on manuscripts and attained the peak of his authority at the Press. As Pottinger assumed his heavier responsibilities, people turned increasingly to Warren Smith for various tasks. Herbert Jacques continued in charge of the Printing Office. On financial questions the Press depended heavily upon John Wilber Lowes, financial vice-president of the University, son of Professor John Livingston Lowes of the English Department. His position was a new one, created early in 1934.[55]

Later, in the 1940s, Conant became convinced that Harvard could get along without the Press; but in the 1930s, at the outset of his twenty-year administration, he made strenuous efforts to find the best possible Director. He wanted a leading figure from the world of commercial publishing, and he naturally sought the help of Harvard graduates who had achieved high positions in that world.

At first Conant thought of appointing Roger Livingston Scaife, class of 1897, a Boston publisher who had been on the Press Visiting Committee for the last nine years. Scaife, fifty-eight years old, resigned from Houghton Mifflin about this time after a long career there. He then joined Little, Brown & Company as a vice-president but still let Conant understand that he would accept the Press Directorship if it were offered.[56] Conant did give him the position—but not until nearly ten years later.

The Syndics put forward no candidate for Director, but they had strong feelings about the Press's future. Around the time of Murdock's death the Syndic Robert P. Blake, director of the University Library, wrote a memorandum suggesting that a Press endowment be sought in connection with Harvard's tercentenary coming up in 1936. The board revised this memorandum and made it their own. Kittredge sent it to the president on April 26, 1934.[57]

The Syndics informed Conant that the Press was able to publish only 20 percent of its output without subsidy and that the haphazard extraneous financing was "extremely disadvantageous for the orderly running of the business." They said two new publication funds were urgently needed: (1) a general endowment of $250,000, producing income that would guarantee the Press against loss in publishing "books of scholarly value and of lasting importance"; (2) a second sum of $250,000, with which the Syndics planned to undertake a new series of monographs, financed by the Press rather than by the departments, printed in a neat but not expensive manner, in editions of 600 copies.

Nothing came of this plan. No benefactor came forward with $500,000 for the Syndics' two purposes, and indeed Conant seems to have published no appeal for a Press endowment—not even in his Annual Reports. Instead of stalking a Croesus, he continued the hunt for a Director, carrying on a copious correspondence during 1934. In December he narrowed his list to four men: W. W. Norton, president of W. W. Norton & Company; Curtice Hitchcock, who was then establishing the new firm of Reynal & Hitchcock with Eugene Reynal after being a vice-president at the Century Company; Richard H. Thornton, president of Henry Holt & Company (where a future Press Director, Thomas J. Wilson, was climbing the ladder); and Allen S. Wilber, a vice-president of F. S. Crofts & Company. None of them had applied for the job. Conant chose Curtice Hitchcock and got the informal approval of the Harvard Corporation. But Hitchcock evidently declined, because in February 1935 the president said he was starting *de novo*.[58]

In the Conant Papers, under date of April 15, 1935, is a list of twenty-eight men under consideration for the Directorship. The one that came to interest the president the most was the poet Archibald MacLeish, who had served with distinction as an editor and writer on *Fortune* magazine. Conant negotiated with MacLeish, who was interested but was anxious to pursue his writing career. The Harvard Corporation voted to appoint MacLeish, and the Board of Overseers gave its consent, but MacLeish said no. Conant persisted, but MacLeish again declined.

The Loeb Classical Library

While all these appointments and disappointments were taking place, the Press under Pottinger and Kittredge exerted itself to keep the works of scholarship flowing. The Press was more humanistic than ever, its semiannual lists dominated by general literature and classics, art and archaeology, history and philosophy. The number of books and pamphlets stayed at about ninety a year.

Amid the uncertainties of the interregnum, the Press was strengthened by two transfusions from other publishers.

Ginn & Company, through its editor, the Syndic Charles Thurber, resumed its practice of giving the Press the rights to some of Ginn's Harvard-connected books. These books had no doubt passed their sales peaks, but they were far from dead. One was a standard reference work published in 1912, *Guide to the Study and Reading of American History,* by Edward Channing, Albert Bushnell Hart, and Frederick Jackson Turner, which was the second edition of Channing and Hart's *Guide to the Study of American History,* published in 1896. (Twenty years later the Press published a third edition under the title *Harvard Guide to American History.*)[60]

The other transfusion added nearly 300 volumes to the backlist. It took place when the Harvard Corporation involved the Press in the Loeb Classical Library. The awesome purpose of this series is to give access to all that is important in classical literature. Each pocket-sized volume contains a text in Greek or Latin and the best obtainable English translation, facing each other page by page. Greek volumes are bound in green, Latin volumes in red.

In 1933, when Loeb left the series to his alma mater, he threw in $300,000, a fund to be known as the Loeb Classical Library Foundation and to be used eventually for research in the classics. As it turned out, the vagueness of the will would contribute to an appalling tangle in the 1960s and 1970s. The will mentioned a goal of "about 375 volumes," and more than once the series has been declared complete.[61] But in the middle 1980s the number was above 470 and still climbing.

In 1933, however, this was not a worry. Pottinger went to London in January 1934 and stayed five weeks, arranging for the transfer of the Loeb Library to Harvard.[62] At that time the series had three editors: T. E. Page and W. H. D. Rouse, in England, and Edward Capps of Princeton. It was decided that the printing should still be done in England. The London publisher William Heinemann, Limited, continued to supervise the manufacturing and to distribute the books in Britain. In accordance with Loeb's will, the Harvard Corporation created a three-member board of trustees to administer the Loeb Classical Library Foundation. The first chairman, who served for thirty years until his death in 1964, was Arthur Stanley Pease, the Pope Professor of Latin at Harvard. Pottinger became secretary to the trustees. The Press officially took up its Loeb duties on July 1, 1934.

Whether the Press became the "publisher" of the whole Loeb Classical Library, or only the American publisher, or only a publishing agent, is a semantic question of little intrinsic importance. At any rate, the Press promptly placed on the cover of its autumn 1934 catalogue the words "Harvard University Press, Publishers of the Loeb Classical Library." As "fiscal agent" the Press was to "make all payments of any nature whatsoever." This included periodically balancing the accounts with Heinemann. As "publishing agent" the Press was to "keep in close touch" with Heinemann, the three editors, and the three trustees, and also acquire the U.S. sales territory. Editorial matters, including selection of the books to be newly published and the existing books to be revised, were put under the supervision of the trustees.[63] The Press took over a large stock of bound volumes from G. P. Putnam's Sons, which had been the American publisher. All later title pages bore the double imprint of Heinemann and the Press.

During the year ending April 30, 1936, receipts from Loeb sales in the United States were $27,405, about a quarter of the Press's total book receipts of $104,457. More than half of the Loeb revenue went to Harvard to build up the Loeb Classical Library Foundation. There was no thought of allowing any volume to go out of print; efforts were made to sell complete sets to libraries. New volumes arrived in batches—also reprintings and revisions of old ones—and eventually the Foundation, fed by sales receipts and interest, rose much higher than the original $300,000. The Press in those early times retained about 22 percent of the retail price of each volume sold. This could scarcely be called a profit, because it was probably more than eaten up by overhead expenses, but the Loeb operation was invigorating, and it heightened the reputation of the Press among the publishing houses of the world.

End of the Search

Meanwhile President Conant was planning his final attempt to find a Press Director from without before promoting Pottinger from within. In August 1935 he received a letter from Mark Antony DeWolfe Howe of the class of 1887, prolific author, former editor, sage of Beacon Hill, and member of the Harvard Board of Overseers. From that moment Pottinger's chances began to evaporate. For the Directorship, Howe recommended Dumas Malone, editor-in-chief of the *Dictionary of American Biography,* which was then nearing completion in Washington, D.C.[64]

Malone was forty-three years old, a Southerner and a Yale-trained historian. Howe, who was a major contributor to the multivolume biographical dictionary, wrote a persuasive letter. He enclosed a copy of Malone's entry in *Who's Who in America* and said he thought that few scholars in America knew more about publishing. Conant asked people about Malone, and the responses were glowing. Maxwell Perkins of Scribner's, the publishers of the *Dictionary of American Biography,* said it would be an excellent appointment.

Kittredge at this time was expressing the urgent need for "both a Director and a substantial endowment."[65] And Pottinger and Vice-President Lowes were eager for a housecleaning in the printing plant. Evidently it was felt that a reorganization ought to wait for the arrival of a Director; nevertheless Pottinger and Lowes took preliminary steps. Pottinger told Lowes about George Grady, the New York consultant who had studied the shop five years before. In the summer of 1935 Lowes commissioned Grady to make another study. Grady did so and recommended measures to reduce costs and increase efficiency.[66]

President Conant offered Dumas Malone the Press Directorship in November. Malone pointed out that he could not yet leave the *Dictionary of American Biography,* of which seventeen volumes had appeared and the other three were in final stages. Conant agreed that he could serve part-time at first. On November 18 the Corporation voted to appoint Malone as Director of the Press and chairman of the Syndics, effective December 1, 1935.[67]

Pottinger told Lowes that he wanted his own status clarified. The University, announcing Malone's appointment on December 4, said also that Pottinger would be Associate Director.[68] Pottinger wrote Malone a handsome letter of welcome, pledging his support and enclosing a list of fourteen people in the publishing department with their salaries and duties.[69] In a considerable understatement, he said the job "may seem, in the beginning at least, to have difficulties." He added, "but I can assure you that it also has its durable satisfactions." Neither the fifty-year-old Pottinger nor his younger superior could know that most of the satisfactions would come in the beginning of their relationship and most of the difficulties in its final years.

CHAPTER FOUR

Malone and a Wider Audience

1935–1943

THE FIRST three administrations of Harvard University Press were remarkably alike in structure. Each had two parts, a first part alive with hope and good feeling, a second part in which the institution was hit by external forces that laid bare its internal weaknesses. C. C. Lane's Press started bravely but fell apart in World War I. Harold Murdock's Press grew into an important agency for handling specialized works of scholarship but got caught in the Great Depression. Dumas Malone's Press brought the results of scholarship to a wider audience and greatly enhanced its reputation for publishing important books, but during World War II financial problems worsened and the University authorities turned against the Press.

Dumas Malone is best known as the author of *Jefferson and His Time*, a six-volume work that he wrote after leaving the Press. He was born in Mississippi on January 10, 1892, grew up in Georgia, graduated from Emory College, served as a Marine in World War I, and earned his Ph.D. at Yale in 1923. After rising quickly to a full professorship of history at the University of Virginia, he was called to the *Dictionary of American Biography* in 1929 as coeditor and became sole editor in 1931. When completed, the twenty volumes contained 13,633 articles by 2,243 contributors. The vast project had been made possible by a half-million-dollar grant from Adolph S. Ochs of the *New York Times,* just the sort of benefactor the Press had never been able to discover among Harvard alumni.[1]

Malone began his seven and a half years as Director of the Press on December 1, 1935, dividing his time between the *Dictionary* and the Press during the first six months or so. He was gracious, learned, articulate, strong-minded, and willing to make unpopular decisions. During the seven academic years beginning in July 1936, the Press published 541 titles, an average of 77 a year. The annual output

14. Dumas Malone, third Director of the Press.

gradually decreased from 95 to 61. At first the trend was hastened by a deliberate policy to discourage minor monographs subsidized by individuals.[2] Later the war cut the number of new books imported from overseas, including volumes of the Loeb Classical Library, printed in England, and the Publications of the Institute for Comparative Research in Human Culture, in Norway. And some of the monograph series from Harvard departments slowed or expired because of a shortage of authors and a shrinkage in departmental funds.[3] Unlike Murdock's time, the Malone years saw only a handful of new series.

There is never a sure correlation between the number of new books and the amount of money taken in. The Press's annual sales receipts more than doubled under Malone—from $104,500 to an unprecedented $217,700—despite the wartime loss of the foreign market. Malone attributed the rise primarily to the publication of books of greater intrinsic interest and to the building of a backlist of such works.[4]

Malone had no doubts about the nature of his mission. He was a "middleman of learning."[5] The Press existed not only to transfer the results of investigation from one scholar to another but also to serve as "a bridge between the whole group of scholars and the outside world." In January 1938, at a banquet celebrating the Press's twenty-fifth birthday, he called for books going beyond "barren displays of erudition" and labeled his policy "scholarship plus."[6]

The next month, in an address entitled "The Scholar and the Public," delivered at the American Philosophical Society in Philadelphia, he argued that academic publishers should be more rigorous in selection, not only for financial reasons but also for the sake of scholarship. No publishing house can perform its more important functions if swamped with dissertations and other "minor monographs." Publication is not justifiable as a means of contributing to professional advancement, and so universities must "devise less expensive tests of the intellectual calibre of prospective professors." But university presses ought to publish major works of scholarship even if the sales prospects are relatively discouraging.[7]

Along with those major works of scholarship, "I think we should encourage books, large or small, that seek to interpret scholarship and present its fruits to a larger audience." Important discoveries and ideas "should be shared with whatever portion of the public is capable of appreciating them." He had in mind "not the cheapening of scholarship, but the interpretation and more effective presentation of it at the bar of intelligent opinion. I am not thinking of books that are less than scholarly, but of works that are more than scholarly."[8]

Malone saw the Harvard University Press as an intellectual and educational institution with purposes like those of the University itself, rather than as a service agency or business firm. To him the Printing Office, which *was* a service agency, became a continuing headache, drawing down upon the Press the ill will of the departments and consuming his time and energy with administrative problems that he had not foreseen in accepting the Directorship.

One of Malone's first acts was to carry out the decisions regarding the Printing Office that had already been made. "I was a sort of lord high executioner," Malone recalled.[9] Herbert Jacques, the accountant who headed the printing operation, was discharged. So was J. Tuckerman Day, the editor who headed the proof room.[10] The man brought in to replace Jacques as manager of the Printing Office was, predictably, Curtis E. Lakeman. After about eight months he was succeeded by J. Albert Meyer, who had worked at five printing firms in three states. About this time the Press bought its first Linotype machines, three of them. All this reorganizing and equipping was supposed to expedite the work and reduce the prices charged to University departments.[11]

In financial affairs Jacques had held the title of treasurer, supervising the bookkeeping and records for both publishing and printing. To succeed him in that position the Press hired William Coolidge Rugg, a graduate of Harvard College and the Harvard Business School.[12]

Horace Arnold, who had been buying supplies and making estimates at the Printing Office, was moved to 38 Quincy Street as the publishing department's liaison with manufacturing. Thus, he was the Press's first full-time production man, and in that capacity he became Pottinger's protégé. Their alliance was to be an important factor in the dissensions of the early 1940s.

One of the biggest changes in the Press was the replacement of the Syndics. Never in the Press's history, before or since, has there been another such turnover in the board. It was done on the instructions of President Conant, who told Malone to "start from scratch."[13] All of the old members submitted their resignations, and the Harvard Corporation accepted them as of July 1, 1936. George Lyman Kittredge turned seventy-six that year. Conant thought he had been too long a power at the Press and indeed should retire from the faculty, and he privately asked Kittredge to do this. Kittredge complied.[14] The Press, which for twenty-three years had relied on Kittredge's services and authoritative presence, had to learn to do without him.

The Corporation immediately reappointed Paul Sachs, the former New York financier who was now chairman of the Department of Fine Arts; he was the only holdover. Later events showed that the president liked having him at the Press. Sachs was a forceful man, accustomed to having people defer to his judgment. The minutes of the Syndics show that in his first seventeen years on the board he usually had attended only one or two meetings each year, but after his reappointment he began attending regularly.

The Corporation had already appointed Malone as board chairman. Now, in addition to Sachs, it appointed the following faculty members chosen by Malone: Edward S. Mason, on his way to becoming one of Harvard's most distinguished economists and administrators; Thomas Barbour, naturalist, a vivid and anecdotal man who directed the Museum of Comparative Zoology; Zechariah Chafee, Jr., professor of law; A. Baird Hastings, professor of biological chemistry in the Medical School; James B. Munn, professor of English;

and Ralph Barton Perry, professor of philosophy and winner of a Pulitzer Prize for his biography of William James.

For the first time the appointments were for specified terms—two, four, or six years initially, but each man was renewed for six more years when his first term was up.[15] In 1938 one more faculty member was added, Malcolm P. McNair, professor of marketing at the Business School, a move that Malone soon regretted because McNair became one of his sharpest critics.[16]

That was Malone's board until 1942 when the Corporation deposed him as chairman and transformed the board's character. Until then, the Syndics and Malone worked well together. The Syndics backed Malone in policy changes, including a firmer attitude toward the other entities of the University. Invoking the Press's authority over its own imprint, he insisted that the Press control the printing, the typographical formats, and the editorial standards of all the books it published, even series books owned and financed by Harvard schools and departments.[17] Malone also began the practice of bringing series books before the Syndics along with other manuscripts.

Editing

In October 1936 Malone installed an editorial staff at 38 Quincy Street. The action was perfectly in line with his idea of "scholarship plus." "Surely," he wrote, "the Press has no more important function to perform than that of helping to make good books better."[18] To that end, he imported two manuscript editors from the completed *Dictionary of American Biography.*

The newcomers were Eleanor Dobson and Dorothy Greenwald. Both were earnest and meticulous, with high standards and no awe of important authors. Malone said all manuscripts, including those of series books, would pass through the hands of the editorial staff and that as soon as practicable all would be edited there.[19] At first the two editors did not fully realize the functional scope of the proof room. "Later we found," Dorothy Greenwald remembered, "that the really admirable proofreaders had for years done a wonderful job of catching inconsistencies and preventing errors, and I sometimes wondered whether we were achieving more."[20] But in time the editorial department became widely recognized for helping to make good books better.

Eleanor Robinette Dobson (after 1951 Eleanor Dobson Kewer) presided over the expanding editorial department for thirty years.

During her long career at Harvard she was wonderfully patient in solving problems of editors under her wing, firm in defending them against criticism, more absorbed with quality than with speedy movement of manuscripts, rigidly conscious of the practical problems of the printer, sometimes militant in battles with the production manager, and formal enough never to address the Press Director by his first name or to encourage the editorial staff to call her by hers.

At the Press in the 1930s, and for a long time after, the editorial department did not have the responsibility of finding good manuscripts and deciding what to publish. Those vital functions were performed by the Press Director and his assistant, with the aid of the Syndics. The editorial staff was composed of manuscript editors. Then and now, such a staff has been one of the chief characteristics of the Press. It is true that the manuscript editors have often done "first readings" of submitted works in order to recommend either rejection or further consideration. But their primary job is to take over manuscripts after acceptance, go through them sentence by sentence, smooth out snags, offer suggestions of all sorts, and in general obviate the ancient and costly practice of making improvements in proof. Manuscript editors at the Press take more responsibility for the manuscripts than do the typical "copy editors" of commercial houses. They deal directly with the authors and oversee all of the many stages of a manuscript's progress, from the time of its acceptance to the day bound books arrive.

Good manuscript editors are not easy to find or to train. Exactly what they do, and exactly how long they ought to take doing it, are rather controversial and mysterious questions, sometimes causing authors and even publishers to wonder. The amount of tinkering an editor does with a manuscript depends most of all on how much it *needs* (the ideal manuscript needs nothing except instructions to the printer). But, since "need" is not subject to scientific measurement, the amount of editing depends also on how much help the author wishes, on the book's importance, on the attitudes toward editing that prevail in a particular publishing house, and on the intellectual and psychological makeup of the editor. Editing is an art, requiring not only a solid grasp of the language but also an ample supply of empathy. Through empathy the editor can hope to understand what the author is trying to say and can get into the spirit of the author's style. Empathy with the book's future *readers* is even more important, for the editor must be able to see through a reader's eyes.

On May 26, 1937, eight months after the two editors had joined the staff, a new secretary reported for work at 38 Quincy Street. Although no one could know it at the time, this was a significant event, for the newcomer was Grace Alva Briggs, who would devote the next thirty-five years of her life to the Press. She had already spent eleven years at the *Journal of Education* in Boston. Malone hired her as secretary to Warren Smith and Horace Arnold (most of her work was for Smith), and she was soon handling some of the behind-the-scenes, time-devouring tasks that inevitably go with publishing. "Anything that was left over, I got," she recalled. Sales orders, book review files, Loeb Classical Library (both sales and administration), copyrights, permissions, translations, fund raising—these were some of her involvements at one time or another, mainly under Smith's direction, during a career in which she became Assistant to the Business Manager in the 1940s and Assistant Business Manager in the 1960s.

With the arrival of Grace Briggs the old yellow house on Quincy Street, with its fireplace in every room and its peeling wallpaper, had nine occupants, a small group compared to the typesetters, pressmen, proofreaders, bookkeepers, and shippers crowding Randall Hall. The nine were Malone, Pottinger, and their secretaries, on the first floor, and Smith, Arnold, Dobson, Greenwald, and Briggs, on the second. This was essentially the staff that published an average of seventy-seven books a year during Malone's administration.

Books and Authors

Among the influential works published in that period, two won Pulitzer Prizes and several have exceeded 100,000 in sales. Not until many years after Malone's departure was it fully realized how "big" these books were. In commercial publishing the success or failure of a book is apt to be obvious in the first year. When a university press publishes the scholarly equivalent of a best seller, the accomplishment may take shape in small increments over decades, during which the book demonstrates its enduring value.

The first of the Press's classics of the Malone administration was *The Great Chain of Being*, by Arthur O. Lovejoy. The book had been in the works for years before Malone came on the scene. It was published in 1936. Forty-eight years later, in 1984, sales were well above 100,000, consisting of 11,000 in the Press's hardcover, 60,000 in softcover as a Harper Torchbook, 32,000 as a Harvard Paperback, and at least 3,000 in foreign translations.[21] The book became a staple on college reading lists. When Harper bought the paperback rights in 1959, it paid the Press a $5,000 advance on a royalty of 7½ percent of the list price, saying this advance was "by a wide margin" the largest it had ever offered.[22] When the Press started its own paperback line in 1971, the Lovejoy was one of the first books it retrieved from other publishers.

Lovejoy was a professor of philosophy at Johns Hopkins. The book was based on the William James Lectures that he had delivered at Harvard in 1933, and the terms of this lectureship required publication by Harvard University Press. Lovejoy received no royalties on the first 500 copies, after which the royalty was 10 percent of the list price.[23]

The concept of the universe as a "great chain of being," composed of links ranging in hierarchical order from the lowest to the Absolute, had been accepted by most educated persons until late in the eighteenth century. But no one before Lovejoy had ever traced the concept through the ages and analyzed its implications. Previous intellectual histories were usually organized around a succession of great authors, and Lovejoy's method of following an *idea* had great influence on scholars.

For Harvard University, 1936 was the three-hundredth anniversary year, full of excitement. The climax of the celebrations came in September, with about seventy of the world's leading thinkers on hand to deliver papers and lectures. The result, for the Press, was five books in 1937—the Harvard Tercentenary Publications, financed by the University. One of these, *Factors Determining Human Behavior,* was the choice of the Scientific Book Club in February 1937.[24] And no wonder, for in that book Jean Piaget, C. G. Jung, Pierre Janet, and several other foreign luminaries became authors of the Press.

But the anniversary had an even greater publishing effect: it firmly linked the Press's name with that of the historian Samuel Eliot Morison. In June 1936 the Press published *Three Centuries of Harvard (1636–1936),* the last of his books on Harvard history. It was not meant to be the finale; Morison's narrative remains an unfinished symphony. His earlier titles on the subject were *The Founding of Harvard College, Harvard College in the Seventeenth Century* (two volumes), and *The Development of Harvard University, 1869–1929* (written by Morison and others). Those earlier works were parts of the official Tercentennial History, prepared by Morison as official Harvard historian and financed by the University. *Three Centuries of Harvard* was different; Morison threw the second half of it together "very hastily," he said, in order to publish in 1936, and it was never intended to be a complete reference book but was "written to be read and enjoyed," as he said in his preface. Morison planned two further volumes, covering the periods 1708–1805 and 1805–1869,[25] but projects for other publishers crowded them out. Some of his best work, though, remains between Harvard's crimson covers. Bernard Bailyn has said of the volumes on Harvard's founding and the rest of the seventeenth century that along with the later biography of Christopher Columbus (published elsewhere), "they are probably the finest products of Morison's pen."[26]

The Press in the Malone years continued to publish much about belles-lettres, but the books that drew the most notice and attained the largest sales were in other fields, including business, law, philosophy, and architecture. Especially striking was the Press's rise in the field of business. The Harvard Business School, the scene of intense intellectual ferment, took a central part in this rise, but the book that led the rest in circulation and influence was written by the president of the New Jersey Bell Telephone Company.

This was Chester I. Barnard, and his book was *The Functions of the Executive,* published in 1938 in a printing of 1,500. Barnard got no royalties on the first 1,200 (10 percent thereafter). Sales in the first six months were 932; this was good for a Press book, but it was followed by *annual* sales of 465, 307, and 242—obviously tapering off. Who could predict at that point that it was about to reverse direction and gather speed for the next four decades? Sales in the

15. Three classics first published in 1936, 1938, and 1942. Here they are in their cheerful paperback clothing of 1971.

forties averaged 870 a year, in the fifties 1,800 a year, in the sixties 3,000 a year, in the seventies 4,500 a year. By 1984 it had sold 115,000 copies in the English language—70,000 in hardcover and 45,000 in paperback. Besides, it had sold at least 9,000 in Japanese and about 5,000 in other languages. The Press, having refused all offers for the paperback rights, brought out its own paperback edition in 1971.

The Barnard book, like the Lovejoy, grew out of lectures, this time presented at the Lowell Institute, in Boston, a venerable center for adult education. Dumas Malone saw the announcement of the series, sought advice at the Business School, and went after the manuscript. Later, more than once, Barnard credited the success of *The Functions of the Executive* to Malone, who "incited" him to convert the lectures into a book.[27]

Barnard was a rare person (in his later career he was president of the Rockefeller Foundation and chairman of the National Science Foundation), but he was not an experienced book writer. After he rewrote his lectures, Malone and Eleanor Dobson found the second half of the manuscript "gorgeously interesting" (in her words) but the first half "hard going."[28] After three months they sent the manuscript to the author with a great many editorial suggestions. Barnard was stunned at first, but he produced a new version which the Press called a "magnificent" and "beautiful" job.[29]

Barnard's aim was to provide a comprehensive theory of cooperative behavior in formal organizations—not just business firms. He suspected that the search for universal characteristics of organizations had been obstructed by habits of thought concerning authority—as found in the state and in the church—and by an exaggerated notion of "economic man." He identified the essential elements of the organization as communication, the willingness of individuals to serve, and common purpose. And he concluded that the executive functions are not to "manage a group of persons" but rather to provide the system of communication, to promote the willingness to serve, and to formulate and define purpose. The elegance and coherence of his argument made the book one of the all-time basic works in the study of organization.[30]

In the literature of business administration F. J. Roethlisberger is in the same league with Barnard. Roethlisberger was a rising member of a group at the Harvard Business School that was establishing the importance of human relations in the management of enterprises. His first book, *Management and the Worker,* written with W. J. Dickson of the Western Electric Company and published by the Press in 1939, is considered a classic study of factory workers and has sold 35,000 copies in English (all in hardcover) and a few thousand in translations. His second book, a shorter one called *Management and Morale* (1941), has done even better —about 47,000 in English (again all in hard-cover) plus 21,000 in Japanese and at least 4,000 in other languages.

Management and the Worker was an analytical account of experiments that the Western Electric Company conducted at its Hawthorne plant in Chicago from 1924 to 1932. Company officials enlisted Business School professors to help them interpret their findings. The company's research began with varying the working conditions of small groups and ultimately generated data from half the plant's forty thousand workers. One of the observed phenomena—that workers seemed to be reacting more to the positive attention they were getting from the experimenters than to changes in physical conditions—became known as the "Hawthorne Effect."[31]

In these years the Press, thanks to the Business School, was in the forefront of a new discipline, business history.[32] Professor N. S. B. Gras, who had started the Harvard Studies in Business History in 1931, supervised volumes 2 through 7 while Malone was Press Director.

National recognition now began coming to the Press in the form of prizes. In 1938 *We Americans,* by Elin L. Anderson, won the John Anisfield Prize for the best work on "racial relationships," and Morison's unfinished history of Harvard brought him the Loubat Prize offered by Columbia University every five years for the best work on "the history, geography, archaeology, ethnology, philology, or numismatics of North America."[33]

The Press's first Pulitzer Prize came in 1939, for a work by Frank Luther Mott. He won the award in U.S. history for the second and third volumes of *A History of American Magazines* (1938).[34] Mott headed the journalism school at Iowa State and later at Missouri. His magazine history, both encyclopedic and readable, linked his name with the subject almost as firmly as the name Bartlett is linked to quotations.[35] Mott planned six volumes.[36] When he died in 1964 he was in the midst of volume 5, on the early twentieth century; the Press published that incomplete volume posthumously.

How the Press landed *A History of American Magazines* is a story of luck and initiative. In this episode Howard Mumford Jones performed the first of his many services for the Press. Volume 1 had been published in 1930 by D. Appleton & Company. When Mott finished the two thousand typed pages of volume 2, the Depression was far

16. The five lively volumes of Mott's *History of American Magazines.*

advanced and his publisher declined it. In 1936 Jones joined the
Harvard faculty. Having read the manuscript, he wrote Mott that
"this thing must be published" and that he was taking it up with
Malone.[37] The Syndics accepted the book. The Press acquired the
rights to Mott's first volume for $623.80. Meanwhile Mott finished
the manuscript of volume 3, and in November 1938 the Press put all
three volumes on sale under its own imprint. (Nineteen years passed
before publication of volume 4, which won a Bancroft Prize.)

The Press's second Pulitzer came in 1941, two years after the first.
The book was *The Atlantic Migration, 1607–1860,* published in 1940.
The author, Marcus Lee Hansen, never knew of his prize, not even
of the book's publication, for he died in 1938. Arthur M. Schlesinger
(Sr.) turned Hansen's rough draft into a polished manuscript and took
it to Malone. Schlesinger gave the following account in his autobiography: "Marcus Lee Hansen of the University of Illinois, dying when
but forty-five, had spent two decades gathering material, mostly in
Old World archives, on the social and economic background of em-
igrant groups to America from colonial days to the Civil War; and
in his last hours he expressed the wish that I put the manuscript into
final shape or that it be destroyed—an alternative which would have
entailed a grave loss to knowledge."[38]

Another pioneering work about immigrants, ahead of its time when published in 1941 but increasingly influential, was the first book by Oscar Handlin. It grew out of his doctoral dissertation under Professor Schlesinger and was published as number 50 in the Harvard Historical Studies under the title *Boston's Immigrants, 1790–1865*. Handlin was then twenty-six and just starting a long rise in the history profession and in the University, during which he was associated with the Press as author, Syndic, Acting Press Director, and chairman of the Board of Directors. His first book was a venture in urbanism and ethnicity, neither of which was yet thought of as a distinct field of historical inquiry. It brought Handlin the Dunning Prize of the American Historical Association. The book sold only 657 copies and went out of print in 1950. But the Press published a revised edition in 1959 under the title *Boston's Immigrants: A Study in Acculturation*, and by 1984 its sales had risen to about 60,000, of which 4,300 were in hardcover, 46,000 in an Atheneum paperback edition, and 9,800 in a Harvard Paperback.

Books on law were not very numerous in the Malone era, but three of them attracted much notice and each sold between eight and ten thousand before going off the market in the 1970s. These were:

Mr. Justice Holmes and the Supreme Court, by Felix Frankfurter, then of the Harvard Law School. This came out in October 1938, and its sales suffered not at all when Frankfurter himself was appointed to the Supreme Court three months later.[39]

Holmes-Pollock Letters: The Correspondence of Mr. Justice Holmes and Sir Frederick Pollock, published in 1941. The editor, Mark DeWolfe Howe, a son of Mark Antony DeWolfe Howe, was then the young dean of the University of Buffalo Law School.

Free Speech in the United States, by Zechariah Chafee, a professor at the Harvard Law School and a Press Syndic. Malone and the other Syndics asked him to write it, and they published it in 1941.

In science, as in law, the books were not numerous but some were of special importance. Members of the Syndics were helpful in bringing them to the Press, as shown in the Press's files. For example, in 1939 there was *Prehistoric Life,* by Professor Percy E. Raymond, whom Malone approached at the suggestion of the Syndic Thomas Barbour.[40] In 1940 there was *Why Smash Atoms?* by Arthur K. Solomon, a young Harvard research fellow who was steered to the Press by the Syndic Baird Hastings. In 1941 there was *The Nature of Thermodynamics,* by the future Nobelist Percy W. Bridgman.

Also in 1941 came *Benjamin Franklin's Experiments,* a definitive edition of Franklin's own account of his electrical work, edited by I. Bernard Cohen, then twenty-seven years old and a fellow of the Carnegie Institute. The book sold only 1,361 copies but made an important contribution to the history of science and started Cohen on his career in that field.[41] Obviously, the Franklin book did not meet Malone's criterion of broad appeal; rather it fell into his other category of "major works of scholarship" that a university press ought to publish even if the sales prospects were relatively discouraging.

And so did another book the Press published that same year, *The Structure of American Economy, 1919–1929: An Empirical Application of Equilibrium Analysis,* by Wassily W. Leontief, a young associate professor. Thirty years later Leontief was awarded a Nobel Prize for his "input-output" method of understanding the general interdependence of economic activities. The 1941 work, containing two huge folded input-output tables, was his first book on that subject, and it was one of the most significant contributions by Harvard economists in that era.[42] Only 614 copies were printed, and it took six years to dispose of them.

The truth is that the sales of the Cohen and the Leontief were fairly typical of the Press's books, most of which sold fewer then two thousand copies. In dazzling contrast, two other innovative books of that same time, philosophical and artistic in character, far exceeded 100,000 copies and were still flourishing in the 1980s. Their authors were Susanne K. Langer, a Radcliffe tutor, and Sigfried Giedion, a Swiss historian of art and architecture.

Susanne Langer's book, published in 1942, was *Philosophy in a New Key: A Study in the Symbolism of Reason, Rite, and Art.* She had written two previous books and was known as a logician but, at forty-six, had never held a professorial appointment. Women authors were not new to the Press; indeed the first had appeared on its list in 1913, the year of its founding.[43] But hardly anyone, woman or man, has ever written a Press book that attained a larger total sale than Susanne Langer's.

By 1984 *Philosophy in a New Key* had sold at least 545,000 copies. This figure included about 12,000 in the Press's hardcover; 447,000 as a low-priced commercial paperback (more on this in Chapter 6); 43,000 as a Harvard Paperback beginning in 1971; at least 32,000 in a Japanese translation; and about 11,000 in nine other translations. The book became required or recommended reading for students of semantics, general philosophy, English, aesthetics, music, and the dance.

The author took the manuscript to Malone in the summer of 1941, and he sent it to William Ernest Hocking of the Department of Philosophy for an opinion. Hocking, in the midst of reading it, impulsively wrote Malone that it was an important book and concluded, "I am prejudiced against books on philosophy by women: according to this prejudice no woman could write as good a book as she has written." Hocking wrote three letters in all. He pointed out that the "new key" of the title was the current interest in meaning and the symbols of meaning, a theme "in which logic, literature, art, and philosophy meet." The author, he said, "instructs the public, deluded by those bone-headed positivists who have deserved well for their industry and hell for their stupidity, that there are meanings in feeling, ritual, myth, music and other art-forms." Her book "will bring the discussion of 'semantics' into a wider general use than a criticism of word-meanings, bringing it to bear on the interpretation of ritual, myth, and art." In order to do this she "has brought out a theory of the origin of language in the symbolizing propensities of mankind, and has made a good case for it."[44]

Susanne Langer never claimed to strike the new key—others had been striking it—but "merely to demonstrate the unrecognized fact that it *is* a new key" and to show how it *"changes the questions of philosophy."*[45] Malone must have rejoiced at this perfect example of interpreting scholarship and sharing it with the public. Even so, given the Press's financial situation of 1941 he felt it advisable to exempt the first 500 copies from royalties. The book was not far beyond 500 when Malone left Harvard in 1943.

Sigfried Giedion, of Zurich, was the Charles Eliot Norton Professor for 1938–39, a small, excitable visitor who complained that Cambridge had no place to walk. His book was *Space, Time and Architecture: The Growth of a New Tradition.* Getting it out "caused more difficulty than a dozen ordinary books" (according to Warren Smith),[46] and when it appeared in 1941 it was already a Press legend. Forty-three years later it was even more legendary, for the Press had sold 129,000 copies, *all in hardcover.*[47] Many of the world's architects, art historians, city planners, and other readers consider the book a part of their upbringing.

The manuscript of Giedion's Norton Lectures at first bore the dull title "The Role of History Today" and was in such poor condition that Malone suggested he write it in his native German and have it translated.[48] Giedion had already done this for lecture purposes; now he devoted nearly a year to preparing another manuscript with the aid of two new translators. Then occurred a three-cornered struggle among author, designer, and Press to arrange 321 illustrations on what turned out to be 617 printed pages. The author was trying to direct traffic from Switzerland—at a time when Hitler was overrunning Europe and making communication difficult. Herbert Bayer, a freelance designer, sat in New York City, pasting up the proofs into a dummy and making adjustments right up to and beyond press time. At the Press, David Pottinger and Horace Arnold had to reconcile everything for the Printing Office. Furthermore there were partial reenactments of the experience after Pottinger and Arnold had gone; for the 1941 book was the first of five editions, each a considerable undertaking, and in the process the number of pages grew to 953 and the number of illustrations to 531.

In effect, architectural history and Giedion's book evolved together until death removed him from the march. The fifth edition came out in 1967, the year before he died, and has been a little best seller in itself, with sales over 44,000. Giedion's book is more than architectural history. He concentrated on the growth of the new tradition in architecture "for the purpose of showing its interrelations with other human activities and the similarity of methods that are in use today in architecture, construction, painting, city planning, and science."[49] Thus the Giedion book, like the Lovejoy and the Langer, bridged several disciplines.

Among the aspects of *Space, Time and Architecture* that make it remarkable in the Press's annals are its typography and its finances.

The physical design of the book departed vividly from the unpretentious, graceful style of nearly all of the Press's output up to that time. Giedion wanted something different. The "New Typography" had sprung up, and Herbert Bayer was one of its leading exponents.[50] Bayer and Giedion between them had the Press print on heavy slick paper in Bodoni type with wide outside margins, no running heads on the pages, and no paragraph indentions. The illustrations were displayed in a striking manner and bled off the pages in all directions. Very possibly the book's wide acceptance was due in part to its modernist look.

As for finances, the costs of producing the numerous editions and reprintings have been enormous by university press standards. If Giedion had not been a Norton Professor, the Press probably could not have published the book at all, certainly not without a large subsidy. Like other Norton books of that time, it was owned by the University, and Harvard's Norton Committee paid the costs and received the revenues except for the Press's commission. In 1947, however, after the Press had sold about 10,000 copies, the book was transferred to Press ownership. The Press has estimated that total production costs (including editing) during the period 1941–1984 were $358,000. Author's royalties were at least $162,000. Available records show an advertising expenditure of about $20,000. Total sales receipts were $791,000. That would seem to indicate a "profit" of about $250,000 before overhead—that is before taking into consideration salaries, rent, lights, equipment, and other expenses not attributed to specific books.

The Press was slow in beginning to count overhead as part of the cost of individual books, because it was understood until the early forties that the publishing overhead was to be carried by the joint organization—that is, by the printing plant. Consequently, according to Warren Smith, "practically all of our list prices were unjustifiably low." The unrealistic pricing, said Smith, was also encouraged by an early rule of thumb which said that a price higher than one cent per page would tend to price books out of the market, and by the widespread belief of university presses that they ought to charge low prices because they were nonprofit organizations and often subsidized—a view that libraries and professors shared "to the point of absurdity."[51] Apparently the first detailed study of the Press's publishing overhead was made in 1937 by the Press's treasurer, William Rugg, who calculated that actual overhead amounted to 45 percent of sales receipts.[52] But at that time this was not put into the prepublication estimate of the cost of a given book. Publishers vary in their methods of calculating overhead, and in recent decades Harvard University Press has used several methods. By the early 1980s it was calculating the overhead share of each book at 135 percent of its estimated manufacturing cost.

In the Malone era the Press continued active in the fine arts, and Malone deliberately set out to do more in music. The most impressive art production was the three-volume *Drawings in the Fogg Museum of Art,* by Agnes Mongan and Paul J. Sachs (1940). Examples of well-received books on music were *Music, History, and Ideas,* by Hugo Leichtentritt (1938), and *Choral Conducting,* by Archibald T. Davison (1940). Malone's greatest personal accomplishment in the music field was his encouragement, beginning in 1940, of a German refugee named Willi Apel, whose *Harvard Dictionary of Music* became one of the Press's best-known books. It came out in 1944, the year after Malone's departure.

Other authors of Malone's time included Ernest J. Simmons, whose

Pushkin was advertised as the finest biography in any language of Russia's greatest poet; B. Sprague Allen, whose *Tides in English Taste* provided a superb background for the study of literature; Crane Brinton, whose *Nietzsche* inaugurated a short-lived series called Makers of Modern Europe; William Brewster on birds; Bernard DeVoto on Mark Twain; John H. Finley, Jr., on Thucydides; George Sarton on the history of science; Wilbur K. Jordan on religious toleration in England; B. J. Whiting; George C. Homans; Richard W. Leopold; Daniel J. Boorstin; Charles Warren; Rudolf Carnap, and a string of Godkin Lecturers including Gunnar Myrdal, Roger Baldwin, and Robert Moses.

War Again

In the late spring of 1940, when France was going under and the British army was being driven toward Dunkirk, an estimated 200,000 copies of Loeb Classics rested in the London warehouse of J. Burn & Company. Up to that time shipments to the United States had been made in small lots as needed—500 copies of each new title, probably never more than two or three thousand books at a time. Now, Warren Smith, acting on his own, placed a huge order: 122,675 volumes were dispatched from England during the next few months. A ship bearing 9,643 volumes went to the bottom, but the other 113,032 volumes arrived safely.[53] On July 10, 1940, the Germans began their massive attempt to conquer Britain from the air. In the autumn, after Germany had lost the Battle of Britain, word arrived that a bomb had hit Burn's warehouse and destroyed nearly half of the Loeb books there at the time. In the renewed blitz of early 1941 another bomb struck the same spot, destroying all the rest of the Loeb stock.[54] James Loeb, having died in Germany eight years before, never knew what his adopted country did to his beloved classics.

Smith's transferral of the books was one of the most influential actions in the Press's history. After the bombings Heinemann, the British publisher of the series, was almost out of stock for the duration, but Harvard's sale of Loeb books actually increased during the war, and the Press's income from that source helped the institution to survive those troubled years. By 1946 it had run out of stock on 158 of the 369 volumes that had been published up to then.[55]

Books on international affairs became more noticeable on the Press's lists. And some war-related books were highly practical. An example was *Handbook of Health for Overseas Service,* a pocket-size manual for medical emergencies, printed in water-resistant ink on water-resistant paper. The principal author was Dr. George Cheever Shattuck, Clinical Professor of Tropical Medicine. The book sold more than 13,000 copies.

The Press's most important works inspired by the war, however, were a dozen dictionaries and textbooks for the study of Japanese and Chinese. They were published for the Harvard-Yenching Institute, then fourteen years old and directed by Serge Elisséeff at Harvard. Nine of these books were rushed out in 1942, the others soon after. New dictionaries could not have been compiled so fast; these were well-known works that had been published in Japan and China and now were reprinted without permission. As for the textbooks, the three main ones were compiled by Elisséeff and Edwin Oldfather Reischauer, a young language instructor who would one day be the U.S. ambassador to Japan and a grand master among Press authors. The first of their productions was *Elementary Japanese for University Students,* which the Press advertised as the only Japanese grammar that had ever been prepared specifically for university students in the United States. These Yenching books, widely used in the armed services, made a notable contribution to national defense.[56]

The dictionaries and textbooks fell naturally to the Press because it was already handling the Harvard-Yenching publications. Crammed with the ideographs used in both Japan and China, the books were "photolithographed" at the Murray Printing Company and other commercial printing houses—the Press's first major use of offset printing. (For the dictionaries the plates were made by photographing the earlier editions.) The sales were as astonishing as the speed of production. Because of the war-related nature of the enterprise, the books were sold almost at cost. But the Press's commissions mounted up, and so the Harvard-Yenching achievement did much for the financial health of the Press.

Two Chinese-English dictionaries stayed in print after the war and became Press fixtures. One was a revised edition of C. H. Fenn's *The 5,000 Character Dictionary,* a pocket-size book originally published at Peking in 1926. The Press by 1984 had sold 34,500 in cloth covers and 18,300 as a Harvard Paperback. The other was *Mathews' Chinese-English Dictionary,* a standard work that had been published at Shanghai in 1931. At Harvard it was revised and brought up to date. By 1984 the Press's sales had passed 45,000.

In the emotional atmosphere of the war effort, the Press on October 1, 1942, published two eloquent little books by Harvard leaders. One was *Our Fighting Faith,* by President James B. Conant, consisting mainly of talks he had given to undergraduates; the other was *Our Side Is Right,* by Ralph Barton Perry. The sales of both books were disappointing—Conant's about 3,500, Perry's about 2,000.

Our Fighting Faith was Conant's first book since he had become president nine years before. Hoping for a wide audience, he offered the manuscript to Roger L. Scaife of Little, Brown, who turned it over to Malone. The Press published it quickly. Malone's critics felt he mishandled the project.[57] An assistant to the president complained that he could not find *Our Fighting Faith* on display in Harvard Square, whereupon Warren Smith persuaded all the bookstores in the vicinity to put it in their windows. According to Smith's recollection many years later, nearly all those books were returned unsold.[58]

In 1944, when Malone had left the Press and *Our Fighting Faith* had sold about 3,000 copies, Conant learned that another publisher had just brought out a book with the same title. Conant took this to mean that the other publisher had never heard of his book. He said in a letter to Malone's successor, "I am afraid this is only one more bit of evidence to indicate that as the Press has been run one might just as well drop the book into the Atlantic Ocean as to have it published through that medium."[59]

What were the dreadful events that led the president of Harvard University to make such a remark? *Our Fighting Faith* was only one small part of it. The poisoning of relations between Press and University was long, complex, and agonizing.

CHAPTER FIVE

Wartime Shock

The man who coined the cliché that there is no business like show business overlooked or was ignorant of the tremendous possibilities for irrational, unpredictable, and zany behavior in the field of publishing: public taste which defies understanding; a fantastic market system that to a layman seems pure anarchy; accounting methods that drive the would-be analyst into the hands of another kind of analyst; authors who are more neurotic than opera tenors.

When you transfer this circus to the University you geometrically multiply the possibility for a type of behavior which can only be observed and never understood. This is because you bring several additional unpredictable elements into the equation—the president, two governing boards, alumni, professors acting as individual authors, and professors acting in groups as departments.

—Paul Herman Buck, Dean of the Faculty of Arts and Sciences, 1942–1953; Provost of the University, 1945–1953.

IN THE EARLY FORTIES Harvard University Press had a brush with extinction. Financially, and organizationally, 1942 was a year of alarm and shakeup. Printing and publishing went their separate ways, and so did the two top managers of the publishing operation. New authority figures moved in. One could imagine that the perennial difficulties of American university presses in the twentieth century—the scraping for funds, the personal animosities, the differing views of what a university press was supposed to be and what sort of person ought to be running it—had all somehow converged for a showdown in a single academic arena. The survival of the Press was not a certainty until the middle forties, long after the liberation of Dumas Malone into the world of Thomas Jefferson. Warnings of trouble had appeared before 1942.

At first the signs were scarcely noticed. The atmosphere was perhaps mellowest at the twenty-fifth anniversary in January 1938. President Conant, presiding over seventy banqueters, proposed a toast to "the future of the Harvard University Press—solvent, significant, successful."[1] The next day he congratulated Malone on his "scholarship plus" speech at the banquet and said the University was fortunate to have him.[2]

17. James Bryant Conant in 1933, the year he became Harvard's president.

The Director, however, had already been cautioning the Harvard administration about the financial outlook. The Press in its March 1937 study of overhead expenses not only found that publishing overhead amounted to 45 cents on each dollar of sales income but went on to explore the implications of this. For example, the Press was losing money on books owned by Harvard departments. The handling charge of 15 percent of the list price, according to the overhead report, covered only half the cost of publication and logically ought to be 30 percent. On Press-owned books, too, sales income was far from meeting expenses and could do so only by "long and steady growth" requiring the publication of more Press-owned books than the financial resources of 1937 would allow. With current sales and current overhead, an annual publishing deficit of $21,000 or so could be considered normal, the Press report said. Ever since 1920 such deficits had been covered by printing profits. Malone and his lieutenants believed that the Press, in order to expand the publication of good Press-owned books, needed more funds of its own; and the overhead report ended with the statement that "a direct subsidy of the Publishing Department may properly be considered as a possibility in the near, if not in the immediate future."[3] In April 1937, as a stopgap, Financial Vice-President J. W. Lowes authorized a drawing account on the University, not to exceed $50,000, to provide working capital for the publication of independent books. This enabled the Press to borrow funds at 4 percent interest.[4] The arrangement was about the same as Harold Murdock's in 1920.

Malone, like his predecessors, hoped for a Press endowment which would provide a direct subsidy, "such as practically all other university presses receive in one form or another."[5] In 1940, however, he fell back on a more modest money-raising scheme and turned to the Visiting Committee for help in carrying it out. At the same time he asked for and obtained as Visiting Committee chairman a man he knew and respected, Roy E. Larsen, class of 1921, president of Time Inc.[6] Malone's new idea for fund raising was "revolving publication funds"—gifts of $1,000 or more that would be invested directly in new books, whose proceeds would be reinvested in other books. Larsen took an interest in the plan, and another new member of the Visiting Committee, Maurice Smith, class of 1918, a New York lawyer, was downright enthusiastic.[7] Smith's enthusiasm did result in financial help—thirty-six years later!—when his widow bequeathed to the Press an endowment called the Maurice and Lula Bradley Smith Memorial Fund, which stood at $344,000 in 1984. But the scheme of 1940 never got very far.

Why is it that Harvard University Press in its first few decades had so little success in attracting philanthropy? Two reasons can be readily identified. The growing University always had a variety of more obvious needs, such as libraries, laboratories, athletic facilities, and endowed chairs, all of which not only promised more glory to benefactors but also made the University authorities reluctant to push fund-raising efforts for an agency that was, from one point of view, a business. The second reason was that the Press's most urgent quests for outside help were unfortunately timed—just as world wars were breaking out.

World War II made Conant a part-time president and disrupted Harvard. To keep the Press's crisis in perspective, one should realize that inside the University Conant had larger problems than the Press and that outside he was deeply involved in some of the largest problems of all, including the development of the atomic bomb. At Harvard in 1939, for example, a "faculty rebellion" of "angry men" (the words are Conant's) forced him to admit errors and alter procedures on promotions and tenure.[8] In 1940 President Roosevelt appointed him to the new National Defense Research Committee headed by Vannevar Bush, and Conant organized the nation's chemists for war research. In 1941 he succeeded Bush as chairman of that committee and became Bush's deputy director in a new parent agency, the Office of Scientific Research and Development. After the United States entered the war in December 1941 he spent several days a week in Washington.[9]

Even in Harvard Yard Conant's activities were largely war-connected. As he said in his autobiography—a seven-hundred-page book in which Harvard University Press is not discussed—Harvard became "primarily a university at war." There was an exodus of professors and graduate students, the undergraduate body shrank from 3,500 to 850, and training courses for military officers pervaded the University.[10]

The Divorce

The reorganization of the Printing Office in 1936 had not eliminated faculty displeasure with the Press. As early as November 1938 the office of the dean of the Faculty of Arts and Sciences presented evidence that the prices on certain jobs had risen surprisingly and were higher than estimates obtained from an outside printer.[11] Some Harvard departments abandoned the Press in favor of commercial publishers.[12] The Press protested, and the Corporation instructed the Syndics

to inquire into all Harvard-connected publishing and printing arrangements.[13] In November 1939 the Syndics recommended among
other things that no Harvard-sponsored materials should be published
by a commercial firm "unless express exception is granted by a committee to be appointed by this Board."[14] Thereupon Conant called a
meeting for January 1940, but it was postponed and apparently never
held. The minutes of the Syndics throw no further light on their report,
and the Corporation does not seem to have acted upon it.

The worrisome questions about the Press's finances and its function
in the University hung unresolved for another year or so. Meanwhile
the Press's reputation for good books continued upward, and as late
as May 1941 Conant told Malone: "The general history of the Press
for the past year is certainly one of which you may well be proud.
My congratulations and best wishes. Keep it up!"[15] But relations
between the Malone Press and the administration were never that
good again.

A crucial factor in the deterioration was the vanishing of John
Wilber Lowes, who went on active duty as a naval lieutenant in March
1941. While he was on leave, the administration discontinued his
position of financial vice-president and accepted his resignation from
Harvard.[16] The role of watchdog over the Press's business affairs was
taken over by the University treasurer, William H. Claflin, Jr.

Claflin was president of a sugar company and had been a partner
in a Boston brokerage firm. Harvard treasurers were not full-time
employees, but Claflin was much more active than most. He served
from 1938 to 1948, a difficult period in Harvard's history. In wartime
he ran the University's financial and business affairs with considerable
zest. Treasurers are ex officio members of the Harvard Corporation—
a distinction that vice-presidents do not hold. This circumstance, together with Conant's preoccupations elsewhere, gave Claflin a high
degree of authority.

From Claflin's point of view, it was his duty to guard the University's financial position in an abnormal time. He had no close knowledge of publishing problems and probably had little opportunity to
appreciate the importance of the books Malone was publishing. No
doubt he felt obligated to resist any Press defiance of Harvard University's well-known principle that every tub must sit on its own
bottom. Not being the most patient of men, he was not likely to go
about the matter in the gentlest of ways. (Yale was in a different
situation: the university treasurer, George Parmly Day, was also the
founder and president of Yale University Press.)

From Malone's point of view, Lowes had been "very fine, very understanding of the Press's problems." But "Claflin was different," a man who did not understand book publishing, who was "furious" when he belatedly discovered that Lowes had authorized a $50,000 loan account for working capital and that the Press had drawn $35,000 of it by June 1941, and who ordered that no more money be paid out of this fund. Malone believed that Conant did not have an adverse view of him as a publisher until after the president returned from one of his wartime absences and received a report from Claflin.[17]

In June 1941 Malone undertook to enlighten Claflin about the nature of the Press. He said the Press's status had long been "anomalous" and unless this could be clarified he was "distinctly doubtful of the future." He asked Claflin eight questions, one of them being: "If the publishing department of the Press (as compared with the printing department) renders an academic service, is it just that it should receive no direct financial aid from the University?"[18]

Immediately afterward President Conant appointed a committee of close associates, including Claflin, to look into matters of publication at Harvard.[19] The chairman was George Henry Chase, who had been dean of the Graduate School but had recently been given the unusual title "Dean of the University." In August Malone recommended to the Chase committee that all printing done for University departments be charged on the basis of actual cost, and "that the University provide for the use of the publishing department the equivalent of the printing profit that is thus surrendered." Finally, in October, with the concurrence of the Syndics, he went further and proposed that the Press be freed entirely from the printing function.[20] This arrangement was approved by the authorities and has been in effect ever since. The official date of the divorce was February 14, 1942. Forty years later, Malone told me he thought the separation of publishing and printing "was perhaps the best thing I ever did at the Press."

One of the factors in Malone's exasperation with the Printing Office was the mysterious disappearance of about $30,000 worth of type metal. The shortage was discovered in the summer of 1941 by a newly engaged auditing firm.[21] The mystery was never solved.[22]

The future of the Printing Office with its more than fifty employees was at first left up in the air. In January 1942 Claflin hired James W. McFarlane, a printer in Fulton, New York, with instructions to handle the details of the divorce. "I didn't necessarily expect to run the Printing Office," McFarlane recalled.[23] But Claflin was favorably impressed, and when the Corporation formally approved two separate organizations, McFarlane was chosen as director of the Printing Office.

Thus the Harvard University Printing Office was again a separate agency of Harvard, as it had been fifty years before. Harvard University Press instantly acquired the freedom to shop around for its printing and came to use outside suppliers more and more. James McFarlane remained director of the Printing Office for twenty-five years. In 1962 the Printing Office moved into a new building in the Allston section of Boston, and the University razed old Randall Hall to make way for the tall white tower of William James Hall.

Confusion and Uncertainty

For the Press itself, the separation in 1942 was a complicated affair. The accounts for publishing and printing had to be segregated. Some salaries had always been divided between the two functions, and now the Press had to assume the full salaries of the persons involved, including Malone, Pottinger, Horace Arnold, and several accounting employees. The Press also had to retain space in Randall Hall for its accounting and shipping staffs and pay for it month by month. The Press's independent checking account, so dear to Harold Murdock, was given up, and Press disbursements were again made through the University bursar, as they had been before 1920 and as they have been ever since.[24]

Difficulties of adjustment had been expected. An outcome that the Press did not anticipate—a shocker for Malone—was that the University did not offer any direct subsidy to compensate for the lost printing profits. Malone thought the administration had agreed that such help would be needed, and he had estimated the annual amount at slightly over $20,000, "approximately the salaries of a couple of professors."[25] At the time of the separation he met with President Conant and reported to the Syndics that "the Corporation recognizes that the publishing office will necessarily be carried on at a deficit."[26] Six months later the Syndic Zechariah Chafee wrote to the Syndic Paul Sachs, "It's as I feared when the severance was made. The University swallows the printing profit and then shudders at the publishing deficit."[27] Still later, Malone put it this way in his Annual Report to the president for 1941–42: "Although the University had assumed the responsibility for the publishing deficit which had previously been met from printing profits, the precise extent of the financial obligation was left undefined. Accordingly, a period of confusion and uncertainty in regard to personnel and finances ensued."

Treasurer Claflin was convinced that the Press should overcome its deficit by raising its commissions, by reducing its expenses, and, in general, by businesslike management. He had already ended the $1,600 annual rent on the Quincy Street house.[28] Now, as Malone recommended, he allowed the Press to increase its handling charge on books that it published but did not own. Malone negotiated new contracts with the University's departments and schools. The old commission of 15 percent of the list price was raised to 25 percent, a move taken calmly by some departments, angrily by others.[29]

But Malone had not said that a higher handling charge on Books Not Owned would enable the Press to break even, only that it would reduce the Press's losses on *those books*.[30] The prospect of a Press deficit remained. There now began a painful battle of the budget.

In previous years the Press had not prepared an exact budget, though there had been semiannual financial reports and an annual audit. But in the spring of 1942 Claflin wanted to see a budget for 1942–43, the first complete year in which the Press would be strictly a publishing organization. For months the Press, in the dark about the probable income from future Press-owned books, tried to frame a balanced budget. Finally Malone submitted a tentative document that presumably showed a deficit of about $20,000. The Syndics approved it unanimously. But Claflin did not approve it, and at the end of June the Harvard Corporation authorized him, pending establishment of a budget for the Press, to expend funds as he saw fit.[31]

By this time the budgetary situation had become further inflamed by news about the Press's current finances. While the Press was trying without success to come up with a break-even budget for the next year, it became known that for the current fiscal year, ending June 30, 1942, the Press would show a deficit of about $26,000. Malone explained that the year was abnormal and that the annual deficit in a normal year should be $20,000 or less.[32] But even $20,000 was unacceptable to Claflin. It was also unacceptable to Conant, who now lost what remained of his friendly feeling toward the Press.

The president and treasurer addressed the problem together, and Conant decided to arrange with some commercial firm to publish Harvard's books. In May the two men had lunch with Roger Scaife, who by then had been on the Press Visiting Committee for eighteen years. The next day Scaife wrote a memorandum to his Little, Brown colleagues, beginning thus: "President Conant wants to relieve the

University of the publishing department. He wants to turn it over to some publisher and I gathered that he would be delighted if Little Brown would take it on in some such fashion as the Atlantic. His idea is to retain only in Cambridge the Board of Syndics, together with an agent, who would at present be Dumas Malone."[33] Scaife went on to explain that the publishing firm would publish books recommended by the Syndics, some at its own financial risk and others at the risk of the University. The publisher would edit, manufacture, advertise, and sell all books. Scaife said it appeared that Conant was convinced that "publishing is not a part of a university's duties."

Little, Brown decided against the proposal. Scaife, reporting this to Conant, said he thought there was a "distinct place" for a university press at Harvard.[34]

Meanwhile, before Scaife's letter was received, Conant and Claflin met with Malone, expressed their doubts about the value of the Press, and unfolded their plan.[35] There is evidence that Conant asked Malone—either then or earlier—to explore commercial distribution and that Malone's failure to submit a report on that subject increased the president's hostility in the months that followed.[36] At any rate Malone considered resigning, and would have done so, he said later, if it had not been for the abnormalities of the times and his belief that his leaving would be injurious to the Press.[37]

Instead, Malone turned to the Syndics for support. In July he held a special meeting, told the Syndics something had to be done "and done quickly," and asked them to draw up a memorandum to Conant. He said Conant had indicated seven years previously that he wanted the Press run on an academic basis, and therefore "it should now be judged not from a commercial standpoint but for its contribution to intellectual and academic life."

The minutes of that rare midsummer meeting are the last ones written by Associate Director Pottinger. Writing them must have been a ticklish task, for communications between him and Malone had become very poor.[38]

That month of July 1942 was the time when Paul Sachs of Harvard's Fogg Art Museum emerged as a leading power at the Press. The Syndics voted that he serve on a committee to draft the memorandum that Malone had asked for. More important, Conant asked him to head a committee of Syndics who would meet privately and advise the president on what should be done.

Sachs called this the "Committee of the Press," or simply "the ad hoc committee." In writing to Conant he called it "your committee."

The Sachs archives make it clear that all the Syndics were invited to the meetings—except Malone. Soon, in practice, the Sachs committee became simply the Board of Syndics without its titular chairman, Malone, and its secretary, Pottinger.

The Syndics' memorandum was just about everything Malone could have hoped for. Whether the president ever saw it is unclear. What is certain is that the Sachs committee sent it to Claflin on July 20, invited him to dinner, and expressed confidence that they could quickly work things out with him.[39] Twice before, in 1919 and 1934, the Syndics had addressed urgent appeals to the administration. Now, in 1942, a different board (except for Sachs, who was a member on all three occasions) made the following points:

- The Press has lived up to its expectations for issuing quality books.
- The Syndics are prepared to examine finances and any other problems.
- The Printing Office is a service bureau and can be abolished if outside printing can be obtained less expensively.
- The Press is as deserving of support in wartime as in any other time.
- The Press should not be expected to end each year in the black and should be one of the small group of "deficit departments" along with the library.
- It is necessary for the Corporation to make a definite statement on its policy. The tentative status of the Press is "demoralizing, discouraging, and unfair from any point of view."
- To transfer the selling of the books to other hands would be "neither effective nor economical."

The dinner with Claflin was held at Shady Hill, the Sachs estate in Cambridge, on July 28. Five Syndics were there. Perhaps Claflin had been impressed by their written statement; at any rate he had some surprising words for the committee.

According to a memorandum that Sachs wrote for the record the next day, Claflin said the administration was willing to face deficits, if need be, "provided we all feel we are running the best possible kind of Press." Sachs said in his memorandum that "in the last analysis the discussion really came down to the competence of Malone for this particular kind of work and especially the competence of Pottinger."[40] This changed the picture, and the whole question was postponed until sometime in the fall.

During that summer Claflin pressed Malone hard to trim expenses. Malone hung back at first but finally accepted the need for cutting the staff. When the editor Dorothy Greenwald received a job offer from the Graduate School of Business at the University of Michigan, he felt unable to urge her to stay. Her departure reduced the editorial staff by half. As the next step, Malone planned to lay off Horace Arnold, the production manager and Pottinger's close associate. Pottinger didn't like that at all.

Suddenly in September Pottinger submitted his resignation—apparently in a daring gamble that the University would decline it and make him Director.

Pottinger had served the Press for twenty-five years, most of the time in a position of heavy responsibility. Under Harold Murdock he had carried the main burden of running the organization but had not received the title or recognition he deserved. After Murdock's death he had been the acting director, with reasonable hopes of becoming Director, but at the last minute had been passed over. Under Malone he continued to have a heavy work load and felt more and more put upon, and came to resent Malone's devoting some of his time to historical writing and lecturing.[41]

When Malone had become Director in 1935 he had not had the privilege of choosing his second-in-command. Until around 1939 he and Pottinger had seemed to work well together. But the relationship had deteriorated to the point where Eleanor Dobson believed that Pottinger and Arnold were "not anxious to make Mr. Malone look good." In retrospect Malone came to the opinion that Pottinger's activities, along with Claflin's financial pressure, helped create "the crisis that finally led me to resign."[42]

Pottinger wrote two letters to Claflin, both dated September 25, 1942. One of them simply offered his resignation on the ground that he could not "work effectively at the Press under the present management." In the other he asked Claflin's advice on whether he could still be of assistance to the University by conferring with Professor Sachs. The same day he asked Sachs for an appointment "at Mr. Claflin's request."[43]

It must have been obvious to Claflin and Sachs that Pottinger did not want his resignation to be accepted. The most direct evidence of his intention comes in the testimony of Warren Smith. Pottinger told him he had been advised by an important University officer that if he resigned his resignation would be declined and would be used as a wedge to get rid of Malone and elevate Pottinger to the Directorship.[44]

18. David T. Pottinger around 1942 after twenty-five years at the Press.

Pottinger was summoned to a special meeting of the Sachs committee, at which all the Syndics were present except Malone. According to the notes taken at the meeting, Pottinger pictured Malone as a man who had not contributed any forward-looking ideas to the Press and who knew nothing about the principles of book construction. When Malone was away on trips there was no discipline in the office. Costs in the editorial department were too high. On the severance of printing from publishing, Pottinger said Claflin had done only what Pottinger himself had been recommending for years. When asked why he resigned, he said recent events had precipitated long-standing doubts as to Malone's efficiency, and he went on to air a number of grievances.[45]

Pottinger's testimony was not answered by Malone, for it was not communicated to him. The Sachs committee unanimously recommended to Conant that the University accept Pottinger's resignation and grant him a paid leave of absence for the rest of the academic year.[46] On October 19 the Harvard Corporation so voted. Those who remained at the Press now had a heavier work load, and the plan to discharge Arnold was abandoned.

About a year later, after Malone's departure, Pottinger offered to return to the Press either as Director or in some other capacity, but the Syndics voted to decline the offer.[47] He then joined D. C. Heath as coordinator of production and later became an editor in their college department. He retired in 1951 and died in 1958. Only a few months before his death the Press published his book *The French Book Trade in the Ancien Régime, 1500–1791.*

Syndics in Control

In the autumn of 1942 Malone still had the University authorities to contend with. If there was to be a Press, he seemed less and less likely to remain its Director.

For that position, Roger Scaife apparently had a candidate in mind. Himself. This experienced book publisher gave more and more generously of his time and advice. In September he suggested to Claflin that the Board of Syndics be enlarged or revised to include a number of practical-minded literary and publishing men.[48]

Claflin and Conant liked Scaife's idea of packing the Board of Syndics. On the recommendation of the Sachs committee, the Corporation appointed Scaife and three other publishers—Roy Larsen of Time Inc.; George Stevens of J. B. Lippincott Company; and Curtice Hitchcock of Reynal & Hitchcock.[49]

The appointment of Syndics from outside the Harvard faculty was not unprecedented, for the original Syndics in 1913 had been headed by Robert Bacon and had included Charles Thurber of Ginn & Company. As it turned out, the main effect of the 1942 appointments was to get Scaife inside the tent. He attended forty of the next forty-three regular meetings of the board, many more than the out-of-towners.

The Board of Syndics not only acquired new faces but rose in stature. The Harvard Corporation endowed it with the powers of a board of directors and appointed a new chairman in place of Malone. The Sachs committee recommended these actions on November 6, and the Corporation carried them out on November 23. In the interim between those two dates, Sachs and his colleagues were busy.

First, Sachs's committee made it clear to Malone that the Directorship was "a full-time administrative job," that both Malone and the Syndics were "on the spot," and that "there are still very serious questions of organization which if not solved promptly and effectively might easily lead to the closing up of the Press by the administration."[50]

Second, the committee began a search for someone to fill a powerful new position to be known as Business Manager, "on a par with the Director."[51]

Roy Larsen and Roger Scaife thought that David W. Bailey might be a good man for this job. Bailey, a former newspaperman and a longtime friend of Pottinger's, was at that time the University's publication agent (publisher of Harvard's official publications) and hence a major customer of the Printing Office. He did not volunteer for a role in the Press. He told Scaife he would be interested only (1) if Conant expressed himself unmistakably in favor of maintaining the Press, (2) if Malone's connection with the Press were severed, and (3) if a way were found to take advantage once more of Pottinger's ability and experience.[52] Bailey told the Sachs committee that there was no future for the Press under Malone. Armed with statistics on Press editorial costs (obtained from Horace Arnold), he repeated many of the same criticisms that Pottinger had made. In my judgment Bailey's testimony against Malone made a deep impression on some of the Syndics, including the new member Roy Larsen, Bailey's Harvard classmate and friend. Larsen did not attend the meeting at which Bailey appeared, but Bailey wrote him a long letter giving an account of his testimony.[53]

It was obvious that Bailey's three conditions could not be met, and he told Conant that he was not interested in the Press job. Conant told him he believed that Harvard should not be in the business of book publishing.[54] (Bailey later became Secretary to the Corporation.)

The Corporation's new regulations of November 23 concerning the Syndics were brief and clear. The board "shall have general authority in all matters relating to operations of the Press subject to the President and Fellows of Harvard College." The Press Director was to report to the board. The budget drawn by the Director was to be subject to review and modification by the board. The board chairman was to report periodically to the President and Fellows on the condition of the Press.

Who would be the new chairman of the Syndics? Sachs urged Conant to appoint Roger Scaife, but Conant decided that Sachs himself should be chairman. The Corporation appointed Sachs to serve from November 23, 1942, to July 1, 1944. Malone did not protest. He wrote Conant that the arrangement under which the Syndics became a real governing board seemed to him the best possible setup.[55]

At 38 Quincy Street, the overloaded staff continued to produce scholarly books and had little solid information about the high-level struggles. Even Malone did not know what went on in the Sachs committee. Warren Smith recalled that in the information vacuum the conviction grew that Conant had washed his hands of the Press and had assigned Sachs to be offensive not only to Malone but to "everybody at the Press" so that the staff would leave and the Press would expire. Smith thought that Sachs, who was widely esteemed as a genial and kindly man, was anguished by his role and that his health was affected by it.[56]

Documents seem to show that Sachs, instead of wanting the Press to expire, was trying in his own way to save it. Starting in December 1942 his way was to take up arms against Malone. It can be assumed that when Sachs sought to learn Conant's attitude, the president had nothing complimentary to say about the Director. In addition, the new head of the Printing Office, James McFarlane, expressed to Sachs a number of grievances against the Press, especially the editorial department, and held Malone to blame.[57] Around the same time Sachs declared that he was beginning to be "fed up" with the position he had drifted into, namely that of "protecting, if not actually whitewashing, Dumas." Sachs made a list of criticisms of Malone that had come to him.[58]

Meanwhile the hunt for a Business Manager made no progress. In March 1943 Sachs appointed a search committee consisting of Larsen, Scaife, Hastings, and himself. Malone urged them to hurry, for the situation was "almost intolerable."[59]

On April 5 the Syndics held an extraordinary meeting at the River Club in New York City, with Roy Larsen presiding as host, and unanimously appointed Warren Smith as Business Manager, with the responsibility of taking charge—under the Director—of "the general administration of the Press."[60] The idea of placing the Business Manager on a par with the director had been abandoned, but the new position was a responsible one indeed. Malone, putting on paper the duties of the office, told Smith he would be the executive business officer of the Press, in charge of production, promotion, sales, shipping, accounting, the physical plant, and the stock of books. He would advise the Director on the feasibility of publishing the manuscripts approved by the Syndics, pass upon the financial arrangements made with authors, and prepare financial statements.[61]

In retrospect, the River Club meeting seems to have been a sort of turning point for the Press. The minutes, written by Professor Chafee, reflect new confidence among the Syndics. Warren Smith, stocky, mustached, calm and deliberate in manner, had been with the Press for nineteen years and seemed to provide continuity in the midst of uncertainty. The Syndics had not immediately hit upon him for the job, but the idea had grown on them. If Smith had not stuck it out at the Press during its recent ordeal, the administration very likely would have had less hesitation about putting an end to the enterprise. Also, sales continued to gain. Malone reported to the River Club gathering that the 1942–43 deficit would be less than $10,000, and

19. W. Warren Smith about the time he was made Business Manager in 1943.

it was the sense of the meeting that the Corporation should be willing to face an average annual deficit of $25,000 (even more than Malone had said would be the average), since the sales of the Japanese dictionaries might not keep up.

The board also voted to give Smith an assistant for business matters and two other assistants for promotion and sales, and to give Horace Arnold a pay raise and the formal title of Production Manager. Arnold, however, soon left the Press. Always out of tune with Malone, he had pleaded with Sachs and other Syndics to keep Pottinger. Smith quickly chose a replacement for him—Alfred V. Jules, Boston sales representative of the Colonial Press, who served as Production Manager for the next five years. In 1944 Arnold became assistant director of the Printing Office under McFarlane.

Exit of a Director

All this time Malone himself was a sort of lame-duck leader, working to develop the *Harvard Dictionary of Music* and other books, still interested in publishing good things but taking little joy in the details of the job, feeling unwelcome at Harvard, wishing to be a full-time scholar, apprehensive over the Press's fate, not knowing what would happen to the Press and to his personal finances if he quit. He stayed longer than he should have, as he later acknowledged.[62]

In January 1943 he proposed to the Syndics that both his salary and his routine tasks be reduced; in April the Syndics agreed. In May he made the same offer to President Conant, suggesting that he devote himself to what he was best at—the editorial sphere and the realm of academic, personal, and public relations—while Warren Smith managed the business end.[63]

Conant responded by asking Sachs to poll the Syndics on whether they had confidence in Malone as Director. Conant said Malone had proposed in effect "that he abdicate as Director and become literary editor" with considerable time for his own scholarly and literary activities. This was not Conant's conception of the position to which the Corporation had appointed Malone.[64]

Thus, Conant and Malone differed about the nature of Malone's mission, and each thought the other was trying to change the rules and break the original agreement. Conant looked upon the Press as a business enterprise that happened to belong to an academic institution. Malone looked upon it as an essential academic program that happened to sell its products in the marketplace.

As for the Syndics' poll of May 1943, the outcome could not have been in doubt. The president asked the board, in voting on whether they had confidence in Malone, to consider the position of Press Director thus: "the head of a publishing house involving administrative responsibility, wise editorial judgment, and publishing acumen." Most people would consider those to be reasonable requirements. The Syndics well knew that Conant, Claflin, and Sachs had made up their minds that Malone did not qualify for the job as so defined. They also were aware of Malone's desire to escape administrative responsibility. Even Syndics who liked Malone and admired his accomplishments might well have doubted his future effectiveness in these circumstances. One more thing: Conant orally requested Sachs to tell the Syndics that if the result was a vote of no confidence, Malone would be given the utmost consideration and would be paid his full salary for one year. After the poll, Sachs told the president that a very large majority had voted no.[65]

Conant met with Malone in June. Conant may have had this meeting in mind when he told me thirty years later: "I remember having a session with him and he suggested that we'd better call it quits. He was thinking around that time of a better basis for his work on Jefferson. I think it was a sort of mutual decision. For all I know, Dumas might say that his departure was—accelerated."[66]

Malone submitted his letter of resignation on July 17. In it, he said he could not be happy in a position "where the major criteria by which my work is judged differ materially from those applied to the academic departments of the University." He said he had no desire to head an organization that approximated a commercial establishment. He said he dared believe that during the last seven years the scholarly and literary standards of the Press had measurably improved, that it had served the cause of learning with increased effectiveness, and that it had reflected credit on the University.

The Corporation promptly accepted the resignation, effective retroactively to June 30. At their next meeting they voted him a year's pay. The University issued a news release saying that Malone had resigned to devote himself to his Jefferson biography and that Roger Scaife would be Acting Director until a new Director was appointed.[67]

Malone moved to Charlottesville, Virginia, and worked on Jefferson during the twelve months covered by his Harvard salary. In 1945 he joined the faculty of Columbia University. *Jefferson the Virginian,* volume 1 of his epic, came out three years later. This event must have pleased Scaife, because it was he who had signed Malone to a Little, Brown contract in 1938.

The Press in 1943 was not yet safe and the question of survival had not yet been settled, but Malone's administration had ended. His departure did not lack irony: in 1942–43, the final academic year of his administration and the very year for which he had struggled unsuccessfully to prepare a balanced budget, the Press almost broke even. The loss was only $5,197.10, and there would have been a small *profit* had it not been for $5,836.58 paid to Pottinger in salary during his terminal "leave of absence." This unexpected showing was reported by Scaife in the Press's Annual Report for Malone's last twelve months, a report in which Malone's name is nowhere to be found.

For thirty-eight years Malone had almost no communication with the Press and nearly succeeded in blocking the Harvard experience out of his mind. In July 1981, when he was eighty-nine and much in the public eye because volume 6 of *Jefferson and His Time* had just appeared, one of the messages he valued most was a telegram that read: "Undoubtedly one of the great moments in human events is the publication of the last volume of your Thomas Jefferson biography. Warmest congratulations from the Harvard University Press to its distinguished former director."

CHAPTER SIX

Scaife and Survival

1943–1947

THE HEADMEN of the Press have come from different molds. Harvard presidents, when confronted with the task of choosing a Press Director, have been governed by the needs and circumstances of the hour. C. C. Lane was an ambitious young production man who was conveniently on the scene—indeed, one of the Press's founders. Harold Murdock was a banker and bibliophile. Dumas Malone was a scholar and editor. Roger Scaife was a commercial publisher with a flair for promotion. The talents of all these men were needed in their own times.

Roger Livingston Scaife was a skilled publicity person, an "idea man," an "authors' man." He contributed a pugnacious determination to put the Press on the map, a resolution not at all compatible with the notion of a dying organization. He was always considered only temporary, but he had no intention of presiding over the dissolution of his little empire. He was sixty-eight when he took charge and seventy-two when he left, balding, graying, often ill, shuffling a bit when he walked. A Harvard graduate of 1897, he had gone to work for Houghton Mifflin in 1898 and switched to Little, Brown in 1934. He told *Who's Who in America* he was the author of these anonymous books: *The Confessions of a Debutante, Muvver and Me, What Daddies Do, The Land of the Great Outdoors,* and *Cape Coddities.*

The special requirements of academic publishing perplexed Scaife a good deal, notwithstanding his aggressiveness. For example, in 1945 he said President Conant had once told him that one reason he wanted to dispose of the Press was that the University was not in business. Later, however, Scaife discovered that members of the Corporation and others were very pleased over Press profits—and this, he said, was "an indication, at least to some, that we are in business."[1]

Scaife's vanity sometimes prevented his being taken seriously. People who knew him called him a "character," a promoter in the best sense of the word, funny, stubborn, hell on wheels, competent, vainglorious, a demanding man who hurt people's feelings and nagged the staff and used the "servants' bells" to summon them.

Despite these peculiarities, Scaife should not be written off as an insignificant figure. The personnel, including bookkeepers and shippers, had grown to twenty before he took over. He doubled it to more than forty, held regular staff meetings, taught Warren Smith to be more hard-boiled and Eleanor Dobson to assign work to others, and brought an atmosphere of energy to 38 Quincy Street. This does not mean that the staff was yet a highly professional one. William Bentinck-Smith, who was at the Press for a while in the mid-1940s, remembered it as a rather "shabby, poverty-stricken, depressing" place

20. Roger L. Scaife, fourth Director of the Press.

with low budgets and a staff on which the standout was Eleanor Dobson. Nevertheless, Donald Scott, who reappeared in Press affairs during this period after a thirty-year absence, wrote that although Scaife was incredibly ignorant of the practical aspects of publishing—from printing to accounting—he "brought a spark of fire to the Press."[2] Scaife, with Smith as factotum and stabilizer, kept the organization going, and growing, in a war-and-postwar period in which manufacturing services and paper were maddeningly scarce.[3] They held the fort while Conant gradually recovered from his spell of hostility and while a search committee found the next Director.

In the first fiscal year of Scaife's administration, 1943–44, the country's miserable publishing conditions caused the annual number of Press titles to drop from 61 to 41; then it rose to 42, 48, and finally up to 68 as the coming of peace allowed the importation of 15 titles from Norway and Sweden. Under Scaife and Smith the annual sales receipts more than doubled, from $218,000 to $443,000—an increase due partly to inflation, partly to greater promotion and sales efforts, and perhaps most of all to the presence of some good sellers on the list.[4] These included works published under Malone, such as the oriental dictionaries, the Lovejoy, the Barnard, the two Roethlisberger books, and the Giedion. They also included new books. The Press showed a profit in each of Scaife's four years, and although the University put $50,000 at his disposal to finance deficits, he did not draw upon any of it. True, he suggested to Treasurer Claflin that part of the $50,000 be earmarked as a revolving fund to finance scholarly books that would not pay for themselves, but Claflin did not agree.[5]

Defense of the Press

In 1943 the partisans of the Press were acutely conscious of the danger from above. When Malone resigned, Warren Smith was already running the organization from his position as Business Manager, and he continued to do so. But there was no Director to represent the Press vis-à-vis the University. Conant's last search for a Director had taken two years, and now he was one of the civilian leaders in a national war effort that was still far from victory. So when Scaife offered to be part-time Acting Director, without compensation, the Syndics quickly accepted the offer on July 27 and Scaife began dividing his time between the Press and Little, Brown. Chairman Sachs recommended in September that the Corporation agree to this arrangement until

December 31, when a "permanent Director" would be chosen, and the Corporation obliged—but without promising a permanent Director. Beyond the four-month grace period, all was uncertain.[6]

Now began a campaign to educate the war leader on the subject of university presses. Syndics acting as individuals made their views known. As a body, they adopted a strategy of buying time by asking that the Press be continued for three years beginning January 1, 1944, with Scaife as full-time Director armed with adequate funds. They instructed Scaife to appoint a committee of three, including himself, to draw up a statement of the Press's purposes and appropriate fields of activity.[7] Zechariah Chafee and Ralph Barton Perry, among the stalwarts of the faculty and by now veterans of the Press's battlefields, joined Scaife in that crucial assignment. The trio's handiwork, dated November 18, 1943, was probably the most influential message ever to proceed from the Syndics to the seat of Harvard's governance.[8]

The committee emphasized Harvard's intellectual leadership and the Press's function of reaching a large audience. They defined university press books in such a way as to suggest the need for a wide net to collect authors. That is, they sorted such books into eight overlapping groups: books (fiction excepted) on any subject, well written with scholarly thoroughness and contributing to the knowledge of both scholar and layman; specialized books contributing to any branch of scholarship; books of timely interest that may stimulate public opinion; reprints of books with permanent value; reference books; "books, the result of research, which contribute new information"; books by Harvard faculty members (to be considered with special care); and textbooks (to be considered later when funds were at hand).

The committee said some of those books might well yield a handsome profit, but they excluded the objective of profit making as such. "We do not believe that the Press can be operated at an annual profit and at the same time undertake the publication of scholarly books for which it was originally intended," they declared. "Nor do we find that the other university presses strive for a profit, but rather to serve scholarship." They said the University should plan for a loss not exceeding $50,000 a year. The Press was "understaffed from top to bottom" and needed better quarters when possible. Warren Smith had become "indispensable." The Press deserved the support of the administration and the faculty.

Scaife then had a highly important conversation with the president. They discussed reasons for continuing the Press with adequate funds and with Scaife at its head. The Acting Director left Conant some literature dating from the Press's beginnings, probably the fund-raising circular of 1912 entitled "A Harvard University Press." He followed this meeting with a letter to Conant in which he listed twenty-two other university presses and said he had been told that they did not make money but served simply to publish, in book form, the results of scholarship. Then Scaife introduced an argument that was bound to give any president pause. He said abandonment of the Press "would be interpreted as a confession of weakness which might have distressing results, especially since the Press has future publishing commitments, both in and out of the University, which carry distinct obligations."[9]

Conant offered Scaife the Directorship for three years. He told Scaife, however, not to seek a bright young man as successor until the Corporation had taken "one more look at the fundamental problems." Sometime before June 1 the Corporation would "decide whether to cut bait or go ashore."[10] The president then asked two members of the Corporation, Henry James and Grenville Clark, both New Yorkers, to study the question. James had headed the Press's first Visiting Committee twenty years before. Clark was a well-known lawyer and later a Press author.

Though Conant did not feel ready to promise the Press a long life, one can look back today and see that he was tired of the struggle. When he appointed James to the two-man committee he knew that James favored continuance of the Press.[11] And his letter to James contained this extraordinary statement: "Much as I feel if we were honest and brave, we would give up the Press, we cannot undertake the gruesome slaughter. The death agonies would drag out for many years because of the nature of our contracts and many commitments." Conant acknowledged that if left to himself he "might well be the executioner of the Harvard University Press."[12]

James and Clark began their deliberations, and the Syndics asked Ralph Barton Perry to write a statement for circulation around the Press and the Corporation. In January 1944 Perry sent a three-thousand-word memorandum to James entitled "Should There Be a UNIVERSITY PRESS?"[13] The document is a classic manifesto in the history of the university press movement.

"A university exists for the joint purpose of scholarship and education, or for the purpose of creating, conceiving, and imparting knowledge." But why should any university do its own publishing? Because it has peculiar publishing assets. Through its faculty members it has connections with the whole world of scholars. It has the treasures of its libraries. Above all, it "holds in its hands and can apply a seal of scholarly honesty and accuracy"—its name is a "certificate of quality." *What* should the university publish? Not only new works of scholarship but books for public education. Furthermore, because of the growing tendency in higher education to substitute "readings" for textbooks, popular works of scholarship serve as implements of teaching.

A university press is not "in business," Perry said. It does not publish for the sake of profits. But there is no reason why the public it serves should not pay for the service or why the Press should not use the profits from a work of popular scholarship for the enlargement of its usefulness.

To be successful, Perry said, a university press must have personnel who enjoy the sense of rendering an important service, and the importance of that service must be recognized by the university as a whole, for "a press that is obliged to be apologetic, and which is regarded as of dubious value, or as a stop-gap, or as an inferior substitute for something else, will be a poor press—even if it be deemed necessary to have it."

James and Clark made their report to the Corporation the following month. Revisions in their document were proposed and accepted, and the Corporation discussed the Press at several meetings. Some time in March or April an understanding was reached that the Press would be continued. The details remained to be worked out, but apparently the main issue had been settled.[14] The president circulated to all faculty members a letter by Scaife seeking their support.[15] On May 22 the Corporation laid down new rules for the organization of the Syndics— rules that were still in effect in the middle 1980s. Under this decree the board consists of the Press Director, ex officio, serving as chairman (thus, Scaife replaced Sachs in the chair), and not fewer than nine nor more than twelve members appointed by the Corporation, three each year, for four-year terms (instead of six as before). On June 28, 1944, the Corporation went the whole way. They adopted a six-point resolution drafted by Henry James which began: "1. As a matter of University policy, the Corporation considers it appropriate to continue operating the University Press."

The rest of the document was mainly a ratification of current practices. The Director and Syndics were to be responsible for the executive management of the Press. To be accepted by the Press a manuscript had to be recommended by the Director and approved by a majority of the Syndics at any meeting or by a subcommittee appointed to pass on manuscripts. An exception was made for series books—the Syndics did not need to consider each manuscript—but five months later, after Conant had questioned whether certain departmental books really should have been published by the Press, the Syndics decided that no book, whether in a series or not, would be accepted without a formal vote of the board, and this became the rule from then on.[16]

Books

Of the books published during Scaife's administration, the most notable were the *Harvard Dictionary of Music,* by Willi Apel; *General Education in a Free Society,* by a faculty committee headed by Paul H. Buck; *The Letters and Private Papers of William Makepeace Thackeray,* edited by Gordon N. Ray; and the opening volumes of the American Foreign Policy Library, a series begun and owned by the Press rather than by an academic department.

Willi Apel, pianist and musicologist, departed *presto vivace* from Nazi Germany in 1936, when he was forty-three, and this turned out to be a momentous event for the Press. In Cambridge, he joined the Longy School of Music, was appointed a lecturer at Harvard and Radcliffe, and worked strenuously on manuscripts he hoped the Press would publish. Dumas Malone was especially impressed with one of the projects, a dictionary of musical terms. Eleanor Dobson surveyed the existing musical dictionaries, thought most of them superficial, and commended Apel's efforts. Malone, with the backing of the Syndics, reached an understanding with the author in April 1940 under which the Press would pay a royalty of 10 percent of the list price on the first 5,000 copies and 15 percent thereafter. This was long before the manuscript was completed. Apel was not a wealthy man, and, as the years passed, Malone authorized $350 in outright grants for expense money and $500 in advances on royalties.[17]

Scaife was Director when the manuscript became ready for editing, and in February 1944 he and Apel signed a formal contract on the same terms Malone had offered four years earlier. Meanwhile the heap of paper resting on a table at 38 Quincy Street stimulated the expansion of the editorial department.

At that time Eleanor Dobson was working with only a recent Radcliffe graduate as assistant. Scaife insisted that she take on Marion Hawkes, who had been a proofreader in the Printing Office, and give

21. Willi Apel's magnum opus, which was published in 1944 and which appeared twenty-five years later in this enlarged second edition.

her the Apel manuscript to edit. When Scaife left office in 1947 the editorial department had a secretary and four assistant editors.[18] One of them was another recent Radcliffe graduate, Phoebe Rous Donald, who a few years later married Scaife's successor, Thomas J. Wilson.

The *Harvard Dictionary of Music,* a landmark of culture in a world still at war, was published on November 15, 1944. It had 834 pages and the price was only $6.00, which was too low to break even and was soon raised to $7.50.[19] The first edition sold 155,000 copies. The second edition, enlarged to 953 pages and published in 1969, was up to about 200,000 at the end of 1984 (retail price then $25), bringing the total hardcover sales to about 355,000.

That is not all. In 1950, long after Malone and Scaife had departed, Apel signed a Harvard contract with Director Thomas Wilson for a condensed version. Ten years later the Press published *The Harvard Brief Dictionary of Music,* in which Apel was assisted by Ralph T. Daniel. In the next two decades, sales of the hardcover edition approached 50,000.

Even before publication of the hardcover, Wilson sold the world paperback rights to Pocket Books, and in 1961 a paperback edition, priced at 60 cents, began flooding the country under the imprint of

Washington Square Press, a division of Pocket Books.[20] Remarkably, Wilson granted the paperback publisher the rights "without limit of time."[21] Nearly always, paperback rights are sold for a specified number of years, after which the agreement continues year by year at the discretion of the original publisher; but in the case of the *Brief Dictionary* the Press was forever prohibited from retrieving the rights. Even more remarkably, in the period 1961 to 1984 Pocket Books sold 892,000 copies.

Moreover, in the late sixties and early seventies the AMSCO Music Publishing Company sold about 13,000 copies of a large-format paperback edition of the *Brief Dictionary,* published by special arrangement with Pocket Books and Harvard.

All these sales meant that by 1984 Apel's dictionary in its various versions had achieved a towering total of about 1,300,000 copies, and it was still in demand.[22] It is the only Press book to have sold more than a million copies.

General Education in a Free Society, with an introduction by President Conant, came out in 1945. The Press published it on commission, not with its own funds. The book was an immediate hit, to the Press's surprise, and eventually sold 56,390 copies.

This project had its origin in 1942, soon after Paul Buck became dean of the Faculty of Arts and Sciences. He and Conant asked each other why the professors remaining at Harvard in wartime could not devote themselves to planning education for the postwar world. The next year, Conant appointed a committee of twelve with Buck as chairman, and the Corporation gave it a generous expense account. The result was an important document in Harvard's history, leading to the adoption of a General Education program as part of the curriculum of the College. The book stimulated Thomas W. Lamont to give $1,500,000 for the construction of the undergraduate library that he and library director Keyes Metcalf had been discussing for six years. But only one of the chapters was specifically about Harvard. The book attracted wide interest.[23]

Buck's General Education Committee owned the book, paid the bills, received the revenues, and published a separate paperback edition of 3,500 copies for free distribution. Scaife was displeased about these free copies, and he expected to sell no more than 5,000 of the hardcover version, even at the low price of two dollars. Ten months after publication there had been ten printings, none more than 5,000 though the General Education Committee had urged bigger printings to save on manufacturing costs.[24]

Publication of *The Letters and Private Papers of William Make-peace Thackeray* had been approved by the Syndics in 1940, when Dumas Malone was Director, just before the editor, Gordon Ray, got his Harvard Ph.D. But the editorial work, financing, and printing ran into nearly all varieties of publishing difficulty. Howard Mumford Jones took responsibility for the proofreading and editorial decisions while young Ray was earning seven battle stars in the Pacific theater. To help finance the project, foundations put up $5,000, and in 1943, immediately after Scaife succeeded Malone, the Syndic Roy Larsen added $5,000 on the ground that the Press under Scaife's leadership needed help at a critical time[25] (as though it had not needed help before). The printing was done in Randall Hall, and the friction between the divorced Press and Printing Office was unpleasant.[26] (Indeed, relations between Scaife and the Printing Office were never smooth.) The four volumes finally came out in 1945 and 1946 and were enthusiastically received.

Another large project of the Scaife years was the American Foreign Policy Library, which is still alive in the 1980s. This is the series whose volumes are usually entitled "The United States and," followed by the name of a country or region. Though Scaife could not claim to be the originator of the music dictionary or the report on general education or the Thackerary letters, he could be proud of launching the foreign policy series, and he was.

The suggestion came from Bessie Zaban Jones, who in wartime felt a need for brief informative books on the various countries in the news, books that would give the history of each country and an account of its relations with the United States. Her husband, Howard Mumford Jones, passed the idea along to the Board of Syndics, and Scaife instantly saw this as a great publishing opportunity.[27] Sumner Welles, who had recently resigned as U.S. Under Secretary of State, consented to become the editor. Donald C. McKay of the Department of History was appointed associate editor.[28]

Contrary to the Press's usual procedure, the books of the American Foreign Policy Library were commissioned—that is, the topic was set and the right author was selected, pursued, and if possible hooked to a contract. Then a long and profound silence might ensue, because few scholars can accurately predict a delivery date for a manuscript. Though the Press in announcing the Foreign Policy Library listed seven books "planned for publication in 1945,"[29] only two had appeared when Scaife left office in 1947. But what he had set in motion was very soon to prosper. In the first thirty-seven years of the American

Foreign Policy Library about thirty titles were published; some of these were brought up to date again and again.

The foreign policy series was not the only expansive scheme that Scaife seized upon in order to put the Press on the map. Another was a series to be called the John Harvard Library. This was an idea before its time. Scaife thought the label wonderfully appropriate because John Harvard had bequeathed his own library to the College in 1638— but appropriate for what?

Apparently the name was first suggested by David McCord, then editor of the *Harvard Alumni Bulletin*. In March 1944 the Syndics considered his proposal for a John Harvard Library consisting of small books by Harvard professors about their investigations.[30] Scaife began pushing the idea hard in 1946, except that he leaned toward the republication of standard works by such authors as Montaigne, Rousseau, Adam Smith, Tocqueville, Darwin, and Ruskin. He won the approval of the Syndics and sought a Corporation grant of $25,000, but his plan was too nebulous. Lawrence P. Belden, who was hired as Assistant to the Director in the fall of 1946, recalled that his first assignment was to figure out what should be published in the series; he thought that neither he nor anyone else found the answer.[31]

Meanwhile, Howard Mumford Jones made a different approach. He wanted the Press to rescue and republish books that had influenced American culture and history, putting them into permanent form for library shelves. But Scaife was aiming at books with more sales appeal and, according to Jones, never quite understood Jones's proposal.[32] The series that Jones had in mind was inaugurated under the John Harvard Library label fourteen years later.

It is not surprising that the publication plans of university presses sometimes have to be abandoned. Even before the Scaife administration Harvard University Press had experienced its share of disappointments. Most of them could be traced to the uneasy coexistence of abundant Harvard brains and insufficient Press funds. An example of a disappointment *not* linked to finances occurred when the said David McCord in 1938 suggested that the Press publish a Harvard anthology of verse to be edited by Robert Frost. A contract was signed, but Frost never produced the book. Said McCord later, "I probably should have offered to help him."[33] It was not the first time Frost had let the Press down; he was also one of the very few Norton lecturers who never put their lectures in shape for publication.

In 1944 Scaife and the Syndics went pretty far with a "Dictionary of American Invention," suggested by Paul Buck, but after one year of discussion the project was tabled for lack of funds. In 1945 a plan to issue the complete works of Melville collapsed for the same reason. In 1946 the Syndics favored a proposal to acquire from P. F. Collier & Son the rights to the fifty volumes of the Harvard Classics—"President Eliot's Five-Foot Shelf."[34] This plan, too, came to nothing. But the Scaife enterprise that floated the highest and fell to earth with the most disconcerting crash was the great "Harvard Atlas of History and Literature."

Scaife hired as the editor of this atlas the Harvard historian William L. Langer, who was already the editor of Houghton Mifflin's *Encyclopedia of World History*. Langer and a geographer, Arthur H. Robinson, laid plans for about 300 maps, ancient, medieval, and modern. The Syndics expected a large initial sale and a profitable life of many years, and the Harvard Corporation authorized $100,000 for the undertaking.[35] But after the war Langer took on other assignments, cost estimates on the atlas kept rising, and Langer came to believe that the Press's plan to finish the job in three years was "entirely visionary." Eventually the contract was canceled with no evident hard feelings in any quarter. Only a few thousand dollars had been spent. Thirty years later, Langer declared that the need for such an atlas had become even greater; he was convinced that some foundation ought to provide several million dollars for it, and he was astonished that the need had continued to be overlooked.[36]

An additional sampling of titles published under Scaife includes: *Ideas in America* and *Education and World Tragedy,* the first two of Howard Mumford Jones's eight Harvard University Press books; *Jonathan Draws the Long Bow,* the first of Richard M. Dorson's four Press books on folklore; *Philo: Foundations of Religious Philosophy in Judaism, Christianity and Islam,* the third of Harry A. Wolfson's nine prodigious feats of scholarship for the Press; and *The Navaho* and *Children of the People,* by Clyde Kluckhohn and Dorothea C. Leighton.

During the Scaife years the Press was unexpectedly drawn into one of its earliest and most important roles in the paperback movement. The book in question was Susanne Langer's *Philosophy in a New Key,* which had come out in 1942.

In the forties the American book industry was experiencing a revolution in mass marketing. The growth of book clubs was part of the story; another part was the coming of 25-cent paperback reprints. Penguin Books had already become established in Britain. Pocket Books met with huge success in the American market in 1939, followed by Bantam and others. Penguin Books, Incorporated, a U.S. company with ties to British Penguin, appeared in 1942 and planned a large postwar nonfiction series under the name Pelican Books. Very few university presses stood a chance in this new arena. Scholarly paperback series were still in the future. But in September 1945 Penguin Books, Incorporated, offered Harvard University Press a $750 advance on royalties for the right to publish a 25-cent edition of *Philosophy in a New Key*. Penguin offered a royalty of 4 percent (a penny a copy) on the first 150,000 copies sold, and 6 percent thereafter.[37]

But what would this do to the hardcover edition, then selling at $3.50? Nobody knew. Warren Smith, after consulting the author, accepted the offer; but, because of the uncertainty, the hardcover book went out of print—after sales of about 1,500—and remained out for six years.

As it happened, the paperback edition, which the Press expected month by month, did not appear until February 1948, and then at a price higher than planned: 35 cents. The imprint at first was Pelican Books, but around that time the New American Library entered the picture, becoming the publisher of Penguin Signet Books and Pelican Mentor Books (later dropping the words Penguin and Pelican); and soon *Philosophy in a New Key* bore the words "A Mentor Book." By 1951 the New American Library had printed more than 110,000 copies. That same year, pressure from the author and book buyers convinced the Press that a market for the hardcover existed after all; so the hardcover came back into print and stayed there. Meanwhile the Mentor Book achieved a steady sales volume, typically around 17,000 a year worldwide, and by the 1980s exceeded 400,000. The New American Library gave Susanne Langer a larger reputation and a much greater intellectual influence on her times than the Press could have given her in hardcover. Such considerations would enter into the Press's great paperback debate of the sixties.

People

Arrangements for editing, designing, promoting, and selling the books of the Scaife period moved a little closer to what should be expected of a modern, professional publishing house.

The expansion of the editorial department has already been mentioned. The Press also acquired its first full-time designer. This was Burton J. Jones, who joined the staff in October 1945 and stayed more than twenty years. He had formerly been director of the adult art program of the New York City Board of Education.

New attention was paid to promotion activities. Before the forties, there had been very little "promotion" in the modern sense—what Warren Smith called "the smart work that gets word-of-mouth publicity going."[38] The Press's first full-time Promotion Manager was Catherine S. Scott, hired by Smith in July 1943 just before Scaife took office; she stayed for fifteen months before moving to Columbia University Press at a higher salary. Various other people worked on promotion from time to time, including Francesca Copley Morgan,

22. Roger Scaife and most of his staff on the steps of 38 Quincy Street, probably in the spring of 1947. Scaife looms in the second row, second from left, flanked by Warren Smith and Eleanor Dobson. Behind her is Loring Lincoln. Standing at extreme right is Burton Jones, and third from the right in that row is Grace Briggs in a white blouse. Standing at the left is Alfred Jules. Directly in front of Scaife, left to right, are Francesca Morgan (in plaid dress), Marion Hawkes, and Lawrence Belden.

who had majored in philosophy at Radcliffe and had earned a degree in retailing at Simmons College.[39]

Scaife also brought in reinforcements from the *Harvard Alumni Bulletin*. In particular, he recruited the managing editor, William Bentinck-Smith, to take charge of the Press's promotion in October 1945. At Scaife's suggestion Bentinck-Smith wrote a newsletter called *Book News*, which helped bring the Press to the attention of booksellers, reviewers, and faculty members. Scaife had steered Bentinck-Smith from the *Boston Globe* to the *Bulletin* five years before. While at the Press, Bentinck-Smith remained in his *Bulletin* job, and he left the Press after nine months to become editor of that periodical.[40]

Warren Smith continued to be Sales Manager as well as Business Manager. His assistant, Grace Briggs, headed the order department. As for the visiting of bookstores, any improvement had to be gradual. In most regions of the country the Press used commission agents who also represented other publishers. Smith himself called upon major bookstores in the Boston area and in New York. And in the summer of 1945 Smith hired the Press's first full-time salesman, Loring B. Lincoln, a man with a variety of experience, though not in publishing. Grace Briggs taught him to write up orders; then he began calling on bookstores under Smith's guidance. Later he served as Sales Manager for seventeen years.[41]

The Press also acquired new faces in its higher councils.

In March 1945 President Conant created a brand-new Harvard office, that of vice-president for administration, and filled it with Edward Reynolds, a successful businessman. The birth of the new position was a weighty event in the Press's history. Conant needed an authoritative person to oversee the University's housekeeping arrangements—its nonacademic services such as buildings and grounds, personnel, dining facilities, housing, health, police, printing, government contracts, and so on.[42] The Press, unlike the libraries, was put in this domain, no doubt because of the Press's "business" aspect.[43]

Reynolds claimed no knowledge of publishing. To get a better grasp of the subject, he asked an assistant, N. Preston Breed, a graduate of the Harvard Business School, to study the Press. In September 1946 Breed produced a lengthy report. "The Press is badly misunderstood," he said, "and the faculty opinions regarding its shortcomings are completely contradictory." The situation of university presses in general "forces the conclusions that certain difficulties are inherent rather than the result of poor management, and hence that drastic change can be expected only if extraordinarily competent management is secured and given good sustained university support . . . Nearly all presses are directly or indirectly subsidized and probably few know their true costs."[44] (In 1947 Reynolds installed Breed as secretary of the Press's first Board of Directors.)

Another new figure was Frederick Lewis Allen of the Board of Overseers, editor of *Harper's* magazine and author of *Only Yesterday* and other books. He succeeded Roy Larsen as chairman of the Press Visiting Committee in 1946 and took an immediate interest in trying to raise funds for the Press.[45] At the war's end the Visiting Committee had brought back and elaborated Malone's idea of seeking donations for particular books. Scaife worked with committee members Maurice Smith and Larsen on a "Guarantee Plan" under which "Friends of the Press" would pledge certain sums for projected books—the funds to be called for if necessary.[46] The new chairman, Allen, carried this forward until December 1946, when Conant told him the time was inappropriate and Allen put the project "on ice."[47]

Scaife was much upset when the Guarantee Plan was tabled. Like Malone, he repeatedly let the authorities know how badly a publisher needs working capital. The fact is that Scaife did not really expect to break even in all years. In his first Annual Report (for 1942–43) he said "it will seldom be found that the Press can show a profit," and he suggested that any profits made by the Printing Office be applied to a revolving fund for the publishing of books. In 1945 he complained that whenever he had consulted the administration on raising a Press endowment, he had been told "that it would be just as well not to approach any individual or concern which might provide an endowment for the Press since that might in turn prevent the University as a whole from securing a larger sum."[48]

The membership of the Board of Syndics was gradually transformed during Scaife's administration. When Scaife began to clean out his desk in 1947 he and Larsen were the only Syndics who had been members at the beginning of his administration—and by then Larsen was not very active.

Three new Syndics appointed in May 1944 were especially notable. One was Howard Mumford Jones, who had always been an abettor of the Press. Another was the historian Wilbur K. Jordan, the new president of Radcliffe College.[49] The third was Donald Scott, then nearing retirement from the directorship of the Peabody Museum of Archaeology and Ethnology. Long before becoming an anthropologist he had been one of the founders of the Press; during the last twenty-three years of his life, he would be one of its leading governors.

Paul Sachs left the Syndics in 1944, after twenty-five years on the board; this was longer than any other Syndic has ever served or is likely to serve. All those who had been installed in 1936 when Malone had taken office—Perry, Chafee, and the rest—were gone by the end of 1946.

Among the new appointments to the Syndics, that of Keyes DeWitt Metcalf was one of the most interesting. A professional librarian, he held the double position of director of the University Library and Librarian of Harvard College, having been hired away from the New York Public Library in 1937. Before becoming a Syndic in 1946 Metcalf had already been drawn into several connections with the Press. For example, he permitted it to keep a large part of its book inventory in the basement of Widener Library, free of charge. More important, he was chief of the head-hunting party that brought home the next Press Director.

Saviors

The Harvard Corporation's resolution of June 1944 seemed to assure the Press's survival. Or did it? Everyone knew that Scaife was a stopgap, perhaps a sort of experiment, until the end of 1946. Were the Press to falter under Scaife's leadership, or were Conant to become fed up with his frequent suggestions and the running warfare between Press and Printing Office, what then?[50]

In the fall of 1945 the president took the crucial step of creating a committee to search for Scaife's successor. Ten years before, he had tried to do it all himself, and he did not want to make that mistake again. He asked Metcalf to head the search committee. Metcalf and Donald Scott were the most active members. Even then, uneasiness persisted. Metcalf's impression was that "if we hadn't got Tom Wilson," Conant would still have been ready to drop the Press.[51] The choosing took more than a year.

Scaife urged Metcalf to name someone at Harvard, such as Warren Smith.[52] But the search committee, with Conant's encouragement, looked for people with experience at other university presses. The man they selected, Thomas J. Wilson, had never been at Harvard. He was director of the University of North Carolina Press. Wilson had taken over at North Carolina in January 1946 and did not feel he could leave there any sooner than mid-1947. The committee unanimously recommended him on December 2, 1946. On the same day, Metcalf told Conant in a personal letter that the committee had interested itself in the Press's finances and "we all believe that it will need financial backing in order to do its work satisfactorily." He said that Wilson, if offered the job, would want to talk with Conant, before accepting, about an endowment or a large sum for working capital.[53]

On December 16 the Corporation voted to offer the Directorship to Wilson as of July 1, 1947, and extended Scaife's appointment until that date. Wilson conferred with Conant in January 1947, after which he wrote Conant a candid letter. "I fear," said Wilson, "that the position does not have in the minds of the Administration the importance it actually possesses." He thought this might be explained by Harvard's ill fortune with the Press, "but a well-run, effective Press at Harvard can be much more than a mere 'service' organization: it can be a genuinely creative department of your university." If Harvard wanted him as Director, it "must assure me that the remedies to be tried will be my remedies until I have had a fair trial at working matters out."[54]

Wilson was speaking for himself, but he might have been speaking for the whole line of Press Directors before him—Lane, Murdock, Malone, and Scaife. This time the administration understood better what was at stake. The assurances about finances and other matters were evidently sufficient, and Wilson accepted the job in February. There was a little trouble about salary, but Metcalf and Scott persuaded the administration to meet Wilson's figure. The Corporation made Wilson a Syndic during the interim in the first half of 1947. His appointment as Director was announced in a press release April 11.

That same week, on April 7, 1947, the Corporation created the Board of Directors, to begin operating July 1. Vice-President Reynolds was named chairman. The other charter members were Thomas Wilson, Keyes Metcalf, Donald Scott, Dean Donald K. David of the Business School, and Henry A. Wood, Jr., Harvard's deputy treasurer.

The Corporation decreed that the Board of Directors "shall be responsible for the business management of the Press" and asked the board to frame its own bylaws and submit them for approval. These bylaws, as approved by the Corporation on May 20, gave the board "general supervision of the business affairs of the Press, including specifically matters of finance, accounting, purchasing, contracting, etc., and all other matters of business procedure and policy." (This language was still in effect in the 1980s.) The 1947 vote of the Corporation thus ended the Syndics' general authority over the Press—

conferred five years before—and confined them to questions of what to publish.

The bylaws set the membership of the Board of Directors at three to seven and provided that the Harvard Corporation would designate the chairman. An amendment in 1955, initiated by Donald Scott, made it mandatory for the administrative vice-president to be chairman—a rule that continued until the board was reorganized in the 1970s. The 1955 amendment put the membership at seven, always including three ex officio members, namely the administrative vice-president, the Press Director, and the director of the University Library. The other four members were appointed for staggered four-year terms; two had to be faculty members, and the other two could be either Harvard people or outsiders.[55]

The solid core of the Board of Directors for a long time consisted of Scott, Wilson, Metcalf, and Reynolds. Scott's term as a Syndic expired just as the Board of Directors came into existence; he moved to the new board and stayed there until his death twenty years later. Wilson served even more than twenty. Metcalf was on *both* boards in 1947–48, and he was on the Board of Directors ten more years. Vice-President Reynolds was chairman for thirteen.

With Wilson in the fold and the Board of Directors established, there was no longer any doubt in people's minds that the Press had been saved. The saving, like the founding, was a group affair. In the lore of the Press, Ralph Barton Perry holds a special place. Other members of the Syndics were not far behind. Henry James and Grenville Clark of the Corporation certainly played a part. Concerning Roger Scaife, one must agree with this judgment by William Bentinck-Smith: "Scaife felt that he saved the Press, and he did."[56] But so did Warren Smith, who kept the Press functioning even before Scaife became Director. Thomas Wilson believed that Smith had been primarily responsible for holding the organization together during its leanest years and that Grace Briggs and Eleanor Dobson deserved "to share with him the credit for our survival as an operating unit."[57] Also among the saviors were Keyes Metcalf and Donald Scott, who snared Wilson and influenced the administration to appoint him on his terms. It can also be argued that Wilson himself rescued the Press, or at least put it beyond peril. Many years later Conant said, "Everything went so well under Tom Wilson that it seemed to prove that those who wanted to continue the Press were right."[58]

About four years after Wilson took over, Conant had an opportunity to reassure him that all was well. Wilson heard something that bothered him and consulted Conant about it. Whatever the problem was, the president put it before the Corporation, after which he wrote Wilson, "I know that I speak for the Board as a whole when I say that they regard the Press as being as important as any other part of the University." And the president added, "So far as I myself am concerned, any question as to the logical and useful place of the Press in the life of the University is a closed chapter."[59]

CHAPTER SEVEN

Wilson and the Rise of the Press
1947–1967

THOMAS JAMES WILSON, a tall, tough, courtly, convivial man from North Carolina, Oxford University, and New York City, injected into the Press an enthusiastic philosophy of expansion. Right away he became known as the man who said, "A university press exists to publish as many good scholarly books as possible short of bankruptcy."[1] At first he was sharply conscious of the dangers of overextension, but those dangers faded. In the favorable conditions of the postwar world and with the aid of financial windfalls from outside the University, the Press under his leadership had the means to put the philosophy into practice. It grew large in output and reputation, publishing about 2,300 titles including an abundance of important works.

During Wilson's long administration, from the middle of 1947 to the end of 1967, the annual number of titles increased from 68 to 144, the annual sales receipts from $443,000 to about $3,000,000, and the staff from about 40 to about 115. He took the Harvard job with the understanding that it was "not the purpose of the Press to make money but to render a service to the university without losing money"; yet in the fifties and sixties the profits mounted so fast that in 1967 the Press had a balance of $312,000 even after building a $300,000 warehouse.[2]

In his final year Wilson and his chief adviser and supporter, Donald Scott, fearing that the University would impose artificial limits on the Press's "natural growth," crusaded for a continuing increase in output, personnel, and space during the next four years—an aim of 200 books annually.[3] In this they went too far, not foreseeing the new circumstances after their departure. It now seems clear that the Wilson Press, hugely successful in its own time, was overextended and unprepared for a future time.

23. Thomas J. Wilson, fifth Director of the Press.

Wilson's place in the Press's history derives from much more than quantitative increase. Among other things, he raised the Press's public relations to a height never approached under previous Directors. He defined public relations as relations with the Harvard faculty, with authors whether or not at Harvard, and with the alumni and friends of the University. He saw the handling of such relations as one of the two ever-present problems of university presses, the other being finances. Wilson looked on a university press as a university enterprise—an ambiguous part of a university composed of people who are professional publishers but who have a "primary and overriding obligation" to serve the parent institution. He was the first Press Director to be made a Harvard faculty member, and he worked always to bring Press and faculty into accord.[4]

While raising the prestige of the Press at Harvard, Wilson also raised it in the publishing world. Certainly it would never have been said of any of his predecessors, as it was said of him, that he was a true spokesman of American university presses. Moreover he brought to the Press another wholly new phenomenon: close ties with the commercial publishing houses of New York.

Wilson and His Times

Before becoming a publisher, and even in his several publishing jobs, Wilson always breathed an academic atmosphere. He was at home with professors and they with him. Wilson was born on October 25, 1902, in Chapel Hill, where his father for a long time was registrar and dean of admissions at the University of North Carolina. The younger Wilson graduated there before he was nineteen and went on to an M.A. in French literature. He won a Rhodes Scholarship and spent the years 1924–1927 at Oxford, receiving a D.Phil in the same subject. Then he taught French at the University of North Carolina for three years, got excited by the idea of publishing educational books, and moved to New York in 1930. At Henry Holt & Company, after being foreign-language editor, he became manager of the college department. At Reynal & Hitchcock he spent two years in the same capacity. In both houses he was a vice-president and a director. His book *The Correspondence of Romain Rolland and Malwida von Meysenbug*, a translation from the French, came out in 1933. Wilson entered the Navy as a lieutenant in 1942, served a year on the carrier *Enterprise* as a hangar deck officer, and attained the rank of commander before being released in 1945. Then he returned yet again to Chapel Hill, this time as director of the University of North Carolina Press, and that was where Harvard found him.[5]

"A big, friendly aficionado of ideas"—that was Wilson, according to the Harvard historian John K. Fairbank, who added, "His imagination and enthusiasm could be quickly aroused by a readable manuscript on a new frontier."[6] Wilson was indeed an enthusiast. Like Dumas Malone, he was capable of stimulation of the scholarly field and companionship with it. Wilson was an optimist, and success increased his optimism. He was a superb politician, in the sense that he used the Board of Syndics, the Board of Directors, and the Visiting Committee with great skill, usually getting his own way (his and Donald Scott's) on major matters, especially during the second half of his regime. The members of those boards tended to be his loyal admirers. Part of it was a triumph of style; Wilson was elegantly effective at presiding over meetings. He was less brilliant in managing the Press staff than in managing the faculty boards; at least there was a good deal of internal friction and poor coordination which he did not prevent. But he respected his editors' judgment and stood behind them in their decisions.

Wilson was soft-hearted—reluctant to fire people, for example. Yet he could get terribly angry, sometimes even at a Harvard faculty member. His famous arguments with the production manager could be heard far down the corridor. His desk always bore large piles of letters waiting to be answered. Nathan M. Pusey, who succeeded Conant as Harvard's president in 1953, once wrote that Wilson "combined Carolinian charm and courtesy with Yankee frugality and horse sense."[7] There is no doubt about the charm and courtesy. But the Press's prosperity did not spring from frugality.

Several sets of circumstances contributed to the intellectual and financial flourishing of the Wilson Press:

The University's new attitude. The Press, later than many other university presses, had finally been accepted by its mother. Apparently nobody panicked when Wilson ran deficits for the first four years, because the new Board of Directors was in on the decisions. More important, the administration recognized at last that a publishing enterprise must have plenty of working capital. To put it simply, you have to pay the printer (and salaries and other costs) before you sell the books. The more books you publish, the more cash in advance you need. After Wilson arrived, the Press was allowed to draw such cash from the University, interest free. This permanent loan for working capital was quite separate from the Press's profit-and-loss balance. The loan was secured by the Press's net worth, mainly its book inventories. In 1958, when this debt was approaching $575,000, the Corporation sanctioned its continuation but stipulated that the Press would pay interest on all over $500,000. This had been recommended by the Board of Directors. The total reached $1,000,000 in July 1963 and fluctuated above and below that level for the rest of the Wilson era.[8]

External conditions. The wartime shortages of paper, printing, and binding had ended. This made it easier not only to publish new books but to reprint old ones—for example, the volumes of the Loeb Classical Library that had sold out or been destroyed in the conflict. Authors who had engaged in war work were writing again. And buyers of scholarly books were fast on the increase. From 1948 to 1968, approximately the period of Wilson's stewardship, faculty members in institutions of higher education tripled in number, degree-credit enrollments increased from 2.4 million to 6.9 million, resident graduate students increased from 174,000 to 808,000, and the conferring of doctorates increased almost sixfold. In the same period the income which institutions of higher education received annually from the federal government swelled from $526 million to $3,348 million, and their expenditures on libraries from $44 million to $493 million.[9]

Ford Foundation. The Press received $290,000 from the Ford Foundation in outright grants during a seven-year period beginning in 1957. The annual payments in most years were $39,500, and they enabled the Press to publish many books in the humanities and social sciences which could not be expected to pay their own way through sales. The Ford grants went to thirty-five U.S. university presses, $2,725,000 in all.[10]

The Belknap bequests. The Ford payments, though magnanimous, were dwarfed by another outside source of help. Two individuals named Belknap, dying ten years apart, left the Press a fortune.

New Quarters, New People

During most of its history the Press has been running out of space. Roger Scaife fretted over the flaws of 38 Quincy Street and the scattering of the ever-growing stock of books, but nothing could be done about it then. Under Wilson, however, the Press moved to larger quarters twice, in 1948 and 1956. Each time, the quarters soon became crowded.

First the organization moved several blocks north to the Jewett House, a red-brick mansion at 44 Francis Avenue, across the street from the Divinity School. The move was completed in February 1948, and the whole Press was under one roof at last, except for the shipping department and the books. The main stock from Randall Hall was carted to the basement of the Divinity School's Andover Hall. The rest of the inventory had to stay in the depths of Widener Library and in a graduate dormitory. By 1955 there was no room in the Jewett House for new employees, and besides, the Divinity School needed the house.[11]

Vice-President Edward Reynolds then came up with a fireproof red-brick building recently vacated by the Gray Herbarium about three fourths of a mile northwest of Harvard Yard. The Press occupied it in July 1956. This is still the Press's headquarters in the mid-1980s. Its address is 79 Garden Street, but its front door, flanked by two Japanese maples on a little knoll, faces southeast onto Fernald Drive.

24. The Jewett House at 44 Francis Avenue, home of the Press from 1948 to 1956. It had belonged to James R. Jewett, a wealthy professor of Arabic.

25. Kittredge Hall at 79 Garden Street, home of the Press since 1956. The building had been the Gray Herbarium, named after the botanist Asa Gray.

The building was constructed between 1909 and 1915 on the site of the residence of Asa Gray, the leading American botanist of the nineteenth century. The herbarium stood amid the Botanical Garden, a famous old field station where living plants were studied—and where now stands a Harvard-owned housing development also named Botanical Garden.[12]

In honor of George Lyman Kittredge, "Kittredge Hall" was carved above the door of this building.[13] With the shipping department in the basement, it was the best publishing facility the Press had yet occupied; yet lack of space remained a serious problem. The Smithsonian Astrophysical Observatory was entrenched in part of the old herbarium. Furthermore, the basement was not large enough for the whole stock of books, and when Widener Library reclaimed its own basement around 1958 the Press had to rent warehouse space at the Riverside Press. The office problem at Kittredge Hall was temporarily eased when the Smithsonian people moved out in the early sixties. The storage problem was eased in 1963 when the Press built its own warehouse across the Charles River, adjoining the new Harvard University Printing Office.[14]

When Wilson arrived in 1947 he saw an immediate need for two major new positions—a Sales and Promotion Manager and a Science Editor. He filled both jobs in 1948. That same year, the Production Manager resigned and was replaced by a man with a higher reputation.

Wilson's first Sales and Promotion Manager was Lynn Justus "Judd" Carrel, who had done well in the same capacity at the University of Oklahoma Press. In 1952, still in his forties, Carrel died of cancer.[15]

To succeed him, Wilson brought in Mark Saxton, a novelist and editor, who stayed at the Press during the remaining fifteen years of Wilson's administration. Saxton had graduated from Harvard in 1936, had published his first novel in 1939, and later had worked as an editor in New York publishing houses until he approached Wilson seeking an editorial position and was hired as Sales and Promotion Manager.[16] With him to the Press came his wife, Josephine, also a New York editor, who was Wilson's executive secretary until her death in 1967. In a reorganization of 1957, promotion and sales were split into two departments, with Saxton as Promotion Manager and Loring Lincoln as Sales Manager. There was little coordination between the promotion department and editorial department during most of Wilson's administration.

The first Science Editor was Joseph D. Elder. He moved to the Press from Wabash College in Indiana, where he had been teaching physics and serving as assistant editor of the *American Journal of Physics*. From 1948 until he retired in 1972, Elder was a gentle and important presence in the editorial department. He edited manuscripts in the sciences (sometimes other subjects) and helped the other editors in many ways, teaching them, for example, how to organize statistical tables.

Having a Science Editor was part of an effort by Wilson and the Syndics to publish more scientific books. For a number of reasons, university presses have usually done better in the humanities and social sciences than they have in the "hard" sciences. During the postwar boom in science, commercial publishers dominated scientific publishing. The Press, seeking its share, began issuing two new series in 1950, the Harvard Monographs in Applied Science and the Harvard Case Histories in Experimental Science. The principal scholar involved in the case histories was James Bryant Conant, just before and after he left the presidency. But the greatest infusion of scientific books came from an outside institution, the Commonwealth Fund, of New York, which for thirty years had been publishing scholarly works in medicine, medical education, and public health. In 1951 the Press accepted an offer to take over the Fund's entire book inventory of some 60 titles (the Syndics pronounced them all acceptable) and to handle the manufacture and distribution of Commonwealth Fund books from then on. The Press issued well over a hundred Commonwealth Fund books from then until 1983, when the arrangement was terminated. In 1952 the Press acquired another important scientific series, the Harvard Books on Astronomy, edited by Harlow Shapley and Bart J. Bok. This series had been started in 1940 by a commercial publisher, the Blakiston Company, which now offered it to the Press. The books have been remarkably enduring in their influence.[17]

The new Production Manager in 1948 was Burton L. Stratton, succeeding Alfred Jules. Stratton had been production chief at Henry Holt & Company. He was highly competent at the technical aspects of his position, was active in Massachusetts printing circles, and was elected president of the Society of Printers. At the Press he clashed sometimes with the editorial department and even with Wilson and with Warren Smith. The designer Burton Jones worked under Stratton for nearly eighteen years, but their relations were always cool.[18]

In the 1950s the continual increase of manuscripts forced some changes in the editorial department, not only the hiring of more editors but the appointment in 1958 of an Executive Editor to be in charge of schedules, assigning manuscripts, and day-to-day departmental management.

This was Maud Eckert Wilcox, the future Editor-in-Chief of the Press. She had graduated summa cum laude from Smith College, earned a master's degree at Harvard, taught English at Harvard, Smith, and Wellesley, and found her true vocation of book publishing in 1957. That summer, she took the Radcliffe Publishing Procedures Course, where Eleanor Dobson (by then Eleanor Dobson Kewer) taught editing and proofreading. This led to a job at the Press as secretary to Mrs. Kewer's editorial department.[19] The next year, Wilson discovered Maud Wilcox and promoted her. He later told the Board of Directors that Mrs. Kewer was an extraordinarily talented editor and teacher but that conditions had changed and her department had fallen behind others in efficiency.[20] The position of Executive Editor was his idea. For the next eight years, Eleanor Kewer and Maud Wilcox shared the responsibility for hiring new people and supervising the department. In time, Wilson came to feel that a real reorganization of the editorial department was needed.

The manuscript congestion at the Press also made life difficult in the front office. Wilson was in effect the Press's only "acquisitions editor," and during his first few years he read many manuscripts. He also accepted membership on various national committees, and his out-of-town commitments increased. He fell behind in his work (a condition from which he never recovered), and in 1950, when he was about to begin two years as president of the Association of American University Presses, he created the position of Assistant to the Director.[21] To that position he promoted Lawrence Belden, who was handling direct-mail advertising. In 1955 Belden gave way to Peter Davison, who soon left to join the Atlantic Monthly Press. In September 1956, just after the Press moved to Kittredge Hall, the job was taken over by a thirty-two-year-old Harvard graduate who for several years had been promotion manager of Yale University Press—namely, Mark Sullivan Carroll.

Meanwhile Warren Smith, throughout the first half of Wilson's Directorship, continued to be the reliable and respected number 2 man of the organization, though he was not recognized as such by title until 1954. In that year, Smith was awarded the title of Associate Director and Business Manager.[22] Besides supervising the inventories, the bookkeeping, the physical plant, and other traditional business matters, Smith was overseer of the ever-growing Loeb Classical Library and made trips to England, where he arranged for the press to be the American publisher of many British books. Among these imports were three literary series, the Reynard Library, the Muses' Library, and the Arden Editions of the Works of William Shakespeare. Smith was Acting Director when Wilson traveled in the Far East for five months in 1957 on a grant from the Rockefeller Foundation (Paul Buck acted as chairman of the Syndics). Smith conferred with Wilson on the financial arrangements for new books and countersigned the contracts.

But in Wilson's second decade, Smith's "scope and influence became gradually somewhat more localized, essentially confined to the specific departments for which he had supervisory responsibility," as Wilson put it.[23] One reason was that Wilson felt a need to develop younger talent (Smith was a year and a half older than Wilson). Another reason was that the two men were very different types of publisher. Smith, a deliberate man, advised caution many times when Wilson wanted to go full steam ahead, and Smith's advice often prevailed. Smith was not so expansion-minded as Wilson, or so optimistic in deciding how many copies of a book to print. Wilson became increasingly impatient and unwilling to listen. It seemed to members of the staff that Warren Smith retired little by little behind the closed door of his office during the years before he officially retired on June 30, 1967.

The turning point occurred at the beginning of 1959. Mark Carroll had been Assistant to the Director a little over two years, sifting Wilson's mail, doing research for him, procuring readers for manuscripts, and in general making himself useful to the overburdened and grateful Director. In 1959 he was given the title Associate Director.[24] Smith retained the title Associate Director and Business Manager. Wilson said Carroll would share with him and Smith "the responsibility for the direction and general management of the Press." Among other things, Carroll was given supervision over editorial operations.[25]

Books

The Wilson Press drew national attention to itself early. The first big season was the autumn of 1948. Five titles on that autumn list made the front page of the *New York Times Book Review*.[26] Among them was *The United States and China,* by John King Fairbank. This book put the Press and its American Foreign Policy Library on the map in a way that must have elated Roger Scaife, who had signed the contract with Fairbank in 1946. By 1984 the book had been revised several times, had grown from 398 pages to 664, and had sold about 378,000 copies. This total includes 50,000 in hardcover, 167,000 in a Viking paperback of the second edition, 149,000 in a Harvard Paperback of the third and fourth editions, and more than 12,000 in a Japanese edition. The book is a readable, illuminating, multidisciplinary survey of Chinese history and its relation to current events and to U.S. policy.[27]

The early, exhilarating Wilson years also brought forth *Foundations of Economic Analysis* (1947), by Paul A. Samuelson, a classic in the Harvard Economic Studies; *The Young Henry Adams* (1948), by Ernest Samuels of Northwestern University, a work which later rose in importance when the author added two more volumes to the Henry Adams life story; *This Was America* (1949), Oscar Handlin's collection of travel accounts, for which Scaife had signed Handlin to a contract in 1944; *A Theory of Price Control* (1952, new edition 1980), by John Kenneth Galbraith; *The Harvard Book: Selections from Three Centuries* (1953, new edition 1982), edited by William Bentinck-Smith; and *Guide to American Literature and Its Backgrounds since 1890* (1953, new editions 1959, 1964, and 1972), by Howard Mumford Jones.

The author in that period who brought the most joy to the Press staff was not a Harvard professor but a seventy-year-old woman who had been headmistress at a girls' school and a teacher of English composition at Wellesley College. Her name was Amy Kelly. She called her manuscript *Eleanor of Aquitaine and the Four Kings*. The Press received it without enthusiasm at the beginning of 1948 and came close to declining it, but she put up a cash subsidy of $2,500 and when the book finally came out in April 1950 it had such a hearty bookstore sale that it made the best-seller lists and stayed there for months.[28] The four kings were Eleanor's husbands, Louis VII of France and Henry II of England, and her sons, Richard the Lion-Hearted and King John. The Press and the Franklin Spier advertising agency publicized Eleanor as "the most glamorous Frenchwoman of all time."[29] At the last count the book has sold about 179,000 and is still selling. This total consists of 37,000 in hardcover, 110,000 in a Vintage paperback (1959–1971), and 32,000 in a Harvard Paperback starting in 1971.

Several policy questions were dealt with early in the Wilson era.

Author subsidies. The $2,500 paid by Amy Kelly must have been one of the last cash subsidies the Press collected from authors. Under Malone the Press had frowned on such payments. Now under Wilson it flatly ruled them out, and Wilson later called them "a bad and dangerous thing."[30]

Readers' fees. Time was when Harvard professors evaluated Press

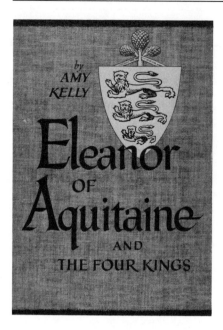

26. The stirring tale that put the
Press on best-seller lists in 1950.

manuscripts free, as a service to scholarship. By authority of the Syndics, Scaife had paid $10 to $25, or had given Press books. At the start of the Wilson regime in 1947 the Harvard Corporation, on recommendation of the Board of Directors, ruled that up to $20 could be paid to faculty members except those on the Press's two governing boards, who could be paid nothing. Over the years the maximum was raised several times and in the seventies and early eighties was $100.[31]

Festschrift volumes. In 1950 and 1954 the Syndics took a stand against festschriften.[32] Since then, the Press on rare occasions has published collections of essays that had originated as tributes to individuals, but the rule was that a book must stand on its own feet and neither be called a festschrift nor bear the conspicuous trappings of one.

Textbooks. The Press had never been quite sure what to do about textbooks. The Syndics settled the question in 1950. They voted that the Press would not start a textbook department and ordinarily would not consider textbooks for school and college courses whose needs were being met by commercial publishers.[33] In other words, they decided against entering the highly competitive, large-adoption, big-money business of textbooks synthesized from secondary sources. The Syndics, however, said they would consider textbooks that commercial publishers would not undertake, also "textbooks or books that may be used as texts for advanced instruction at the college or university level."[34] Thus the Press, in ruling out a drive for large-scale textbook markets, had no thought of ruling out books that could be used in teaching.

In 1950, the year of *Eleanor,* the Press published *The United States and Japan,* by Edwin O. Reischauer. In that year Reischauer attained the age of forty and a full professorship in Far Eastern languages. As Japan swiftly changed during and after the American occupation, Reischauer produced a second edition (1957) while he was director of the Harvard-Yenching Institute and a third edition (1965) while he was U.S. ambassador to Japan. The sales have been about 172,000. This total consists of 26,000 in hardcover, 88,000 in a Viking paperback, and an estimated 58,000 in editions published in Japan.

By means of the Fairbank, the Reischauer, and other volumes in the American Foreign Policy Library (on Mexico, India, Italy, and so on), the Press influenced American understanding of foreign peoples to an extent seldom achieved by a book publisher. And this contribution was enhanced in the postwar years when a quartet of major centers for foreign studies took root in the Faculty of Arts and Sciences. The first of these was the Russian Research Center in 1948, followed by the Center for Middle Eastern Studies, the East Asian Research Center, and the Center for International Affairs. They all went in strongly for book writing, and the Press was their publisher.

The Russian Research Center Studies began in 1950 with *Public Opinion in the Soviet Union,* by Alex Inkeles. Number 37—*The Soviet Bloc,* by Zbigniew Brzezinski, published in 1960—was also the first book in the series of the Center for International Affairs. But probably the most influential book from the Russian Research Center, deeply impressing generation after generation of students, was *How Russia Is Ruled,* by Merle Fainsod, professor of government and Syndic of the Press.

How Russia Is Ruled, like the Fairbank and Reischauer books, is one of the classics of the Press. The first edition appeared in 1953, the second in 1963 when Fainsod was director of the Russian Research Center and about to become director of the University Library. The two editions sold 76,000—all in hardcover because sales were so steady that Wilson never allowed the book to go to a paperback reprint house. Fainsod died in 1972 without having found the time to make a further revision. (In 1979 the Press brought out a revision by Jerry F. Hough, bearing the by-lines Hough and Fainsod and entitled *How the Soviet Union Is Governed.*)

The Harvard East Asian Series, presided over by John Fairbank, began in 1959. It had thirty-one volumes by the end of the Wilson administration and three times that many by 1980. Not noted for best sellers or "classics," the series itself is a classic. "In the new field of Modern China," according to Fairbank, "we needed a monographic foundation for historical thinking." The East Asian Research Center was "an institution that could help dissertations become books." This is not the kind of publishing that usually excites publishers, but it excites innovative scholars. The Center got into the field ahead of other universities and for a time had the pick of the country in China manuscripts. Fairbank felt that "the essential thing was editing." He set up a large staff of editors headed by Elizabeth M. Matheson. From outside sources, mainly the Ford Foundation, came the necessary funding, including money paid to the Press as subsidies for the individual books.[35]

During the early fifties, while the Press was establishing itself in foreign affairs, it became the vehicle for some unusual dashes in other directions.

In the social sciences, there was *Toward a General Theory of Action* (1951), edited by Talcott Parsons and Edward A. Shils. Much of it was difficult to read, but it became famous as a synthesis of sociology, anthropology, and social psychology. It stayed in print thirty years and the Press sold 11,000 copies.

In American history, there was *The Letters of Theodore Roosevelt,* published with fanfare in eight volumes from 1951 to 1954. The letters themselves had been given to the Harvard College Library.[36] The project editor, Elting E. Morison, and the associate editor, John M. Blum, were in the history department of the Massachusetts Institute of Technology. Blum also wrote a short book for the Press, *The Republican Roosevelt* (1954). The *Letters* and the Blum book caused a wave of new interest in Theodore Roosevelt.

In 1953 the Press won its third Pulitzer Prize—that is, David John Mays won it for his two-volume biography *Edmund Pendleton, 1721–1803,* published in 1952. Mays was a lawyer of Richmond, Virginia, with no Harvard connections. Pendleton was a Virginia lawyer, judge, governor, and patriot, a rather neglected American Founding Father. Wilson wanted to publish the book but saw no way to pay the costs. The upshot was that Mays owned the book, stood the manufacturing costs of $7,044.09 and part of the advertising costs, received the proceeds, and paid the Press a commission of 25 percent of the list price on all copies sold.[37] Total sales were 1,684, pretty low for a Pulitzer Prize winner.

If *Edmund Pendleton* had been published just three or four years later, it might well have been a Belknap book.

The Belknap Press

"The Belknap Press of Harvard University Press." Those seven words, mysterious to the casual reader, appeared on a Press title page in 1954 and on two hundred others during the Wilson years. This came about because the Croesus who had always eluded Harvard's Press had showed up at last. He was Waldron Phoenix Belknap, Jr., class of 1920, an art historian, art collector, and architect whose fortune included part ownership in some Texas lands. Belknap's invention of

27. Waldron Phoenix Belknap, Jr. (1899-1949), creator of the Belknap Press.

the Belknap Press came to light after he died on December 14, 1949, at the age of fifty. Actually there were two Croesuses, for his mother, Rey Hutchings Belknap, who survived him by ten years, added her fortune to his. The Texas portions of their estates came originally from her father, John Henry Hutchings, a banker of Galveston, Texas, who had died in 1906.

Neither of the Belknaps ever knew that the Texas interests would zoom in value the way they have. A Belknap Press endowment fund, steadily accumulating as a result of their wills, climbed above one million dollars in 1961, two million in 1967, three million in 1978, and four million in 1982, with further increases in store. After the barren decades, the Press had an endowment! In addition to the endowment principal, mother and son channeled into Harvard a stream of oil royalties. And these royalties, combined with the endowment earnings, boosted the investment income of the Belknap Press to about $225,000 a year by the end of Wilson's administration. This of course did not include the sales receipts from Belknap books, then running above $400,000 a year. The investment income and sales grew even larger in the seventies and eighties.[38]

The founding of the Belknap Press was the most important event in the first sixty years of Harvard University Press. Wilson wrote that because of Belknap funds "we have been able to publish effectively books of great cost we could not otherwise have afforded, we have attracted or held authors who would have taken their books elsewhere, and Harvard University Press's share of receipts from sales of Belknap Press books has contributed essentially to the maintenance of Harvard University Press itself."[39]

"What is the Belknap Press?" People ask this, sometimes mistakenly voicing the silent "k." The answer: it is an *imprint*, identifying the books whose costs are paid out of Belknap funds and whose sales receipts are plowed back into Belknap working capital after the parent body has deducted a share for its operating expenses—50 percent until 1976, when it was raised to 60. The Belknap Press has no separate staff, only separate accounts. Waldron Belknap himself supplied the name, specifying that the income from his bequest was to be used for "publishing activities, under the name of the Belknap Press, of the Harvard University Press." (Wilson, taking a small liberty with this language, omitted the word "the" before "Harvard University Press," because by that time the Press was rendering its name simply as "Harvard University Press.")[40]

In the will, Belknap said it was his intention "that the relationship of the Belknap Press to the Harvard University Press shall be as closely analogous as may be to the present relationship of the publishing activities of the Clarendon Press to the Oxford University Press." The Clarendon Press imprint was known for books of long-lasting importance, superior in scholarship and physical production, chosen whether or not they might be profitable. Those principles were adopted for the Belknap Press. At first, when the funds were just a trickle, the subject matter was confined to Belknap's own main interests, American history and civilization, but the benefactor imposed no restrictions and in 1961 the scope was expanded to all fields.[41]

Why did Belknap decide to leave money to the Press? A good question. He must have heard about Wilson and about the general optimism concerning Wilson's advent. But he and Wilson were not acquainted, and neither Wilson nor the Harvard Corporation knew of the bequest in advance.[42]

The Press's fund raising at that time was confined to "the Friends of the Harvard University Press," a program which the Press and its Visiting Committee, led by Frederick Lewis Allen, revived with the University's permission and which raised $4,585 for specific books over a seven-year period. In the spring of 1948 the Press opened this drive with letters to 131 prospective "Friends," signed by various members of the Visiting Committee. An attached leaflet explained that the Press had no endowment and needed help. Belknap was one of 24 people who enrolled at that time; he did so in May 1948 by returning a self-addressed postcard with the signature "W. Phoenix Belknap" (his friends called him Wally).[43] In November he apparently did not reply to a letter seeking his help for three books. The next month, on December 13, he signed the will that changed the Press's history. He died a year later of chronic lung disease.

But there was more to the story. Houghton Library, a Harvard repository for manuscripts and rare books, seems to have played an important part. Belknap, like James Loeb and Paul Sachs, had abandoned New York banking for more congenial pursuits. He had then studied architecture at Harvard, had taken up residence on Beacon Street in Boston, and had done research on colonial painting.[44] Belknap had long been planning to do something for Harvard that would have a real impact. In his research on art he had become aware that many important source materials were not being edited and published because funds were lacking. He discussed with William A. Jackson, head of Houghton Library, the establishment of a fund limited to the publication of manuscripts in Harvard's collections. Jackson and Philip

Hofer, who directed Houghton's Department of Printing and Graphic Arts, influenced him to broaden the scheme.[45] So Belknap elected to strengthen Harvard's up-and-coming press, and in this way he met his twin objectives of striking a blow for Harvard and fostering the publication of scholarly works.

The strengthening, however, was not supposed to take place right away. After making a few bequests, Belknap directed that the residue of his estate be held as a trust fund, the entire income of which would go to his mother. Upon her death, one half of this Belknap Trust was to be transferred to Harvard and its income used for publishing as described earlier. The other half was to be divided into three equal shares and the income paid to individuals whom he named. Two of those shares were to be transferred to Harvard upon the deaths of the named beneficiaries—a condition not yet fulfilled as this is written. This meant that five sixths of the Belknap Trust would ultimately wind up at Harvard for the use of the Belknap Press.

Enter Rey Hutchings Belknap. With the unrelenting encouragement of Wilson and his representatives, she decided to be present at the birth of her son's brainchild. In 1951, a year and a half after his death, she gave $100,000 to begin the endowment. In March 1954 the Belknap Press was publicly announced and its first book appeared: the *Harvard Guide to American History,* which had been in process long before Belknap's death. Mrs. Belknap now proceeded to build her son's monument—and her own. During the next five years she turned over to Harvard the income she was receiving from the Belknap Trust, more than half a million dollars in all. Wilson and the Board of Directors transferred $270,500 of this income to the endowment principal.[46] The rest was applied to the publication of thirty Belknap Press titles before she died on December 28, 1959, at the age of eighty-six.

Mrs. Belknap was not the easiest person to deal with. She wanted to be sure that her son would be suitably honored and the Belknap funds properly used. She needed attention and was apt to feel put upon. The mollification of Mrs. Belknap was a major project during the 1950s for Wilson and others on his behalf, including Howard Mumford Jones and the Press designer Burton Jones.[47]

The difficulties of that period have all but faded from the Press's institutional memory; the historic results of Mrs. Belknap's generosity remain. She not only enabled the Belknap Press to get an early start but also made it her own principal beneficiary in a will which she signed a week before her death. Her residual estate, plus one half of Waldron Belknap's, added almost a million dollars to the Belknap

Press endowment in the early 1960s.[48] Certain holdings, namely some shares in a Texas firm called the Hutchings Joint Stock Association, were assigned only a nominal value in the endowment fund but have brought in about nine tenths of the oil royalties mentioned earlier. The Hutchings Joint Stock Association owns a tract in West Texas which is leased to the Gulf Production Company and which in 1981 contained 448 producing oil wells.[49]

The endowment itself—the capital account—kept growing for several reasons. One was that part of the oil income each year was capitalized in accordance with a clause in Belknap's will. The most dramatic jump in the capital account, $369,000, took place in 1982 when Harvard sold the surface rights to a tract in South Texas while retaining the mineral rights.[50]

The largest projects of the Belknap Press have been the Adams Papers and the John Harvard Library. The Press could not have undertaken them without the Belknap bonanza. On the other hand, many Belknap books were such good publishing ventures that they would have been published Belknap or no.

The *Harvard Guide to American History* was one of these, a volume bearing many of Harvard's most illustrious names in the field of American history. Arthur M. Schlesinger, Sr., had been interested in this project ever since 1934 when the Press had acquired the *Guide to the Study and Reading of American History* from Ginn & Company. After the Second World War he and other professors of American history at Harvard decided to produce a new edition. The all-star cast, as listed in the 1954 book: Oscar Handlin, Arthur Meier Schlesinger, Samuel Eliot Morison, Frederick Merk, Arthur Meier Schlesinger, Jr., and Paul Herman Buck. Much of the responsibility fell upon Handlin, then an associate professor in his thirties, and upon his wife and collaborator, Mary F. Handlin. After publication the group voted that he should get 40 percent of the royalties, the rest being divided into four shares of 15 percent each. (Buck declined any share on the ground that he did not do any of the actual writing.)[51]

The 1954 book had a twenty-year sale of 22,000 in hardcover and another 13,000 in a paperback edition from Atheneum Publishers. Its importance to the history profession was even greater than the figures suggest. Nearly half the book consisted of sixty-six essays on historical research and writing. The rest consisted of reading lists on hundreds of topics, grouped in twenty-five historical periods. In 1974 the Press published yet another edition, edited by Frank Freidel.

In the fifties, under the Belknap imprint, the Press became the publisher of Emily Dickinson. Houghton Library had acquired from the poet's heirs all of their Emily Dickinson papers together with all rights of publication and all of their copyrights covering poems already in print. Chosen as editor was Thomas H. Johnson of the Lawrenceville School, a well-known literary historian.[52] In 1955 appeared *The Poems of Emily Dickinson,* in three volumes, with variant readings. It brought the Press the Carey-Thomas Award for Creative Publishing. This landmark edition presented, for the first time, the entire canon of the poet's work in approximately chronological order, reproducing the manuscripts as faithfully as possible. In the same year came Johnson's *Emily Dickinson: An Interpretive Biography,* followed in 1958 by *The Letters of Emily Dickinson,* in three volumes, edited by Johnson and Theodora Ward.

The Adams Papers

The series of books known as *The Adams Papers* is an American epic in documentary form.[53] The gradually lengthening row of volumes, seemingly destined to lengthen well into the twenty-first century, contains the diaries, letters, and other records of three generations of Adamses—those of John Adams, John Quincy Adams, and the first Charles Francis Adams, leading characters in United States history and incessant writers all. The Adams descendants, who had carefully guarded the immense collection of manuscripts, decided in 1952 to open it in the service of history. Editorial work began in November 1954 at the Massachusetts Historical Society in Boston, which had long been the custodian of the papers and was soon to become their owner. The editor-in-chief was Lyman Henry Butterfield (1909–1982), one of the most accomplished of the American scholar-editors who were raising the art of editing historical documents to new levels.

On September 22, 1961, the first four volumes, entitled *Diary and Autobiography of John Adams,* were published under the imprint of The Belknap Press of Harvard University Press. An exuberant ceremony took place at the Massachusetts Historical Society. President Thomas Boylston Adams, introducing Thomas Wilson, said that without Wilson's initiative "we would not be gathered here today." Here is Wilson's speech in full:

Ladies and gentlemen:
    I have been a publisher for thirty-one years. If I am remembered, I should like to be remembered as the man who realized that *The Adams Papers* must have a uniform, dignified letterpress edition—that they

THE POEMS OF

Emily Dickinson

*Including variant readings critically compared
with all known manuscripts*

Edited by

THOMAS H. JOHNSON

THE BELKNAP PRESS
of HARVARD UNIVERSITY PRESS
Cambridge, Massachusetts
1 9 5 5

28. The three volumes of *The Poems of Emily Dickinson* won the
Carey-Thomas Award for Creative Publishing, named after the early
American printer-publishers Mathew Carey and Isaiah Thomas. On
this title page of volume 1 the poet's name and the Belknap Press lion
appeared in red. The books were designed by Burton Jones. Six years
later the Adams Papers won another Carey-Thomas Award.

must not be dispersed, volume by volume, among many publishers, with consequent changes of emphasis and format, and necessary loss of public impact and historical influence. I am proud to say that my colleagues in the Press and the governing boards to which I am responsible shared my feeling. Today is the great day of my publishing career.[54]

Wilson's part in the enterprise goes back to 1953. The Adams Manuscript Trust, representing the family, had appointed an editorial advisory committee, whose secretary was Walter Muir Whitehill, librarian of the Boston Athenaeum and future Press author. In February 1953, Wilson began talking with Whitehill.[55]

At that time it was believed that several publishers might be involved, because no single publisher or institution could swing the editing and publishing of such a sizable nonprofit undertaking without a large foundation subsidy, which did not appear to be forthcoming.[56] There were two serious problems: how to pay the publication cost and how to pay for the editorial work.[57]

The job of the historical editor, not only for the Adams project but for the many other documentary collections the Press has published, can be illustrated by listing the activities of Butterfield and his *Adams Papers* associates, once the project started. These included: making an inventory and catalogue of the materials on hand, estimated at 300,000 manuscript pages; conducting a worldwide search for the Adamses' letters and other papers that had come to rest outside the family holdings (more than 26,000 outside documents were found in the United States, Holland, Russia, and elsewhere); arranging the whole into logical categories for publication; selecting the documents to be printed; deciphering them and making accurate typewritten copies; identifying and explaining in footnotes those persons, places, and allusions that were more than trivial and would be apt to puzzle modern users; putting the documents in context by means of introductions to the volumes; preparing the manuscript of each volume for the printer; proofreading the galleys and page proofs; and constructing indexes.

Wilson moved fast in January 1954 to solve the first problem, the publishing costs. By then Mrs. Belknap was beginning to supplement the income of the endowment, and the first Belknap Press book was only two months away. Even so, in view of the current uncertainty about the extent and timing of the Belknap endowment, Wilson's actions were daring.

He told Whitehill that the Press was willing to publish the Adams

Diary and Autobiography of John Adams

L. H. BUTTERFIELD, *EDITOR*

LEONARD C. FABER AND WENDELL D. GARRETT

ASSISTANT EDITORS

———— ☆ ————

Volume 1 · *Diary* 1755–1770

THE BELKNAP PRESS

OF HARVARD UNIVERSITY PRESS

CAMBRIDGE, MASSACHUSETTS

1961

29. The books of the Adams Papers were designed by P. J. Conkwright, of Princeton University Press; Rudolph Ruzicka, of Boston; and Burton L. Stratton, of Harvard University Press. The Adams Papers editor-in-chief, Lyman Butterfield, considered Conkwright and Ruzicka the two best living designers. The text type was Ruzicka's Fairfield Medium. On this page the book title was printed in green.

Papers at its own risk and expense.[58] This was even before he had obtained the approval of his two governing boards and the Harvard Corporation.[59] He won the Corporation's informal approval after writing President Pusey a long letter in which, among other arguments, he reported that Yale University Press had unofficially told the Adams advisory committee that "if Harvard should be unable to cooperate in publishing the Adams Papers, Yale would be confident of finding the necessary resources."[60]

As for the problem of editorial costs, Wilson had a hand in that, too. The main mover was no stranger to our story, Roy Larsen, president of Time Inc. Larsen had again become chairman of the Press Visiting Committee upon the death of Frederick Lewis Allen in February 1954. In May, Wilson brought Larsen together with White-hill and Thomas Adams.[61] The upshot was that Time Inc. underwrote the editorial operation for the first ten years in return for advance serialization rights for use in *Life* magazine. The agreement, signed in August 1954, provided $250,000 in ten annual installments, and *Life* published five illustrated articles.[62]

The John Adams *Diary and Autobiography* was warmly acclaimed. It brought the Press its second Carey-Thomas Award. No other university press and few commercial houses had received this honor more than once.

When Wilson left office six years after publication began, the Adams Papers were up to thirteen volumes, grouped into four series advancing on parallel tracks.[63] Thirteen more volumes came out in the period 1968–1982. Press records show that for these twenty-six volumes the Belknap Press, as of June 30, 1982, had incurred total costs of $439,000, not counting overhead expenses, and had received $456,000 in revenues. Overhead expenses were borne by Harvard University Press as a whole, because the Belknap Press has no separate staff or quarters; and, to cover those expenses, transfers of $225,000 were made from the Belknap Press operating fund. Thus the total cost to the Belknap Press was $664,000, as compared to $456,000 in income.[64]

The John Harvard Library

The John Harvard Library, a series reviving influential books of the American past, absorbed even more of the Belknap funds. It was launched in 1960 after a stupendous amount of discussion, argument, correspondence, and planning over a fifteen-year period. The Belknap

30. John F. Kennedy holding the first four volumes of the Adams Papers after receiving them from Thomas J. Wilson at a *Washington Post* book luncheon on October 3, 1961. The President made a speech congratulating everybody connected with the project, including Lyman Butterfield, editor-in-chief, and Thomas B. Adams, president of the Massachusetts Historical Society and descendant of President John Adams (shown in the portrait). Kennedy began: "First of all, I want to say to Mr. Adams that it is a pleasure to live in your family's old house and we hope that you will come by and see us." Later in the speech he remarked, "I have no doubt that Lyman Butterfield and Thomas Adams are breathing heavy sighs of relief—four volumes out and only eighty or a hundred more to go. Obviously the worst is over."

benefactions made it possible. The first editor-in-chief was Howard Mumford Jones, who had thought up the idea in the 1940s. The second and last was Bernard Bailyn. Eighty-one titles have been published, most of them while Wilson was Director. By 1982, when the series was dormant though not exactly dead, the eighty-one titles had cost $1,072,000, not counting overhead, and had returned $1,001,000 through sales. Including overhead—in the form of transfers to the Harvard University Press general account—the Belknap Press's total costs for these titles were considered to be $1,590,600, or more than half a million dollars above income.[65]

The John Harvard Library had major disabilities and a confused history, but it contributed notably to the understanding of the American past. Like the Adams Papers, the Library lifted source materials into the light of day. It did so in the form of handsome new editions of published works combed from three centuries. The idea was that these important writings had become unobtainable or scarce—or, in some cases, were still easily available but needed new scholarly introductions (*Uncle Tom's Cabin* and *The Federalist,* for example). The project had a distinguished editorial board, and the individual books were edited and introduced by first-rate scholars.

Most of the books sold poorly, and there were jokes about a few of the titles, notably *An Essay on Calcareous Manures,* a work by Edmund Ruffin which in 1832 had been a landmark in the history of soil chemistry but which in its 1961 edition never reached 1,000 in sales. On the other hand, the Press has sold about 63,000 copies of *Narrative of the Life of Frederick Douglass, an American Slave, Written by Himself* (10,000 in hardcover and 53,000 in paperback). Among the other good sales were those of Harold Frederic's *The Damnation of Theron Ware,* George Fitzhugh's *Cannibals All!,* Mason Weems's *The Life of George Washington,* and Andrew Carnegie's *The Gospel of Wealth.* But more typical sales were between 1,500 and 2,000, and by 1982 half of the titles had been allowed to go out of print.

Probably nobody thought the John Harvard Library lived up to its noble purpose, and indeed it suffered from disagreement on what the noble purpose was. Was it to rescue fugitive pieces from oblivion, or was it to publish American classics? In other words, some of the old uncertainty of the Scaife years, when "John Harvard Library" was only a name in search of a series, persisted under Wilson and was never resolved. This innate ambiguity was a tragic flaw.

And there was another difficulty, related to the first one but external in nature. During the project's long period of gestation it was outrun by a historic change in the publishing industry. This was the paperback revolution, in particular the coming of "quality paperbacks," a topic for the next chapter. Mark Saxton, the Promotion Manager, who recalled that he was "always more than half opposed to the John Harvard Library," said that "by the time our books were in print, many had been done in paperback by other publishers. The technology had changed. Others got there ahead of us—cheaper and quicker."[66]

Both the schizoid character of the series and its competitive disadvantage can be illustrated by an incident involving James Parton, then publisher of *American Heritage* and an active member of the Press Visiting Committee. In 1962 he planned to offer twenty-two of the John Harvard Library volumes to the subscribers of *American Heritage* but then discovered what he called "an almost insuperable problem from the viewpoint of mail order selling." He told Wilson he had thought the series was composed of out-of-print writings, but

31. Howard Mumford Jones (left), editor-in-chief of the John Harvard Library, showing President Nathan Pusey a copy of *Narrative of the Life of Frederick Douglass*, which became the most popular book in the series.

"instead it turned out that a number of the books are readily available in various editions already at far lower prices." Wilson replied that the Press was working hard in an attempt to define the nature of the Library.[67]

Concerning the low sales, Howard Jones's position was as follows: "The series didn't sell very well. So what? Nobody expected it to. The primary purpose was to get those important books back into permanent form so that libraries could stock their shelves." Nevertheless, Jones felt that the Press had mishandled the series. In retrospect, he said the John Harvard Library "was a failure to capture the field, in paperback, for itself."[68] To reduce the losses, the Press did issue about a dozen of the books in paper covers—an exception to Wilson's policy of not publishing paperbacks—and in general they sold better than the clothbound versions.

Among the most acclaimed works in the John Harvard Library was the book that put the Harvard historian Bernard Bailyn on the road to being one of the Press's leading authors. He had become editor-in-chief of the series in 1962, when Jones had retired. At that time, twenty-four titles were in print and a great many more in process. Bailyn had been working for years on his own John Harvard Library entry, which Jones had asked him to undertake: a collection entitled *Pamphlets of the American Revolution*. His volume 1, covering the period 1750–1765, came out in 1965. Bailyn's introduction occupied 200 of the book's 800 or so pages. He then expanded the introduction into a book, *The Ideological Origins of the American Revolution*, which the Press published under the Belknap Press imprint in 1967. For this, in 1968, Bailyn was awarded the Pulitzer Prize in history and a Bancroft Prize.

Bailyn ran the John Harvard Library along the same general lines as his predecessor. In 1966 the editorial board was disbanded and the control of the series put in the hands of the Charles Warren Center for Studies in American History—an arrangement canceled by the Press in 1969 after Wilson's departure.[69]

Public Relations

Four Pulitzer Prizes and eight Bancroft Prizes were bestowed on Press books published in the Wilson years. (Bancrofts are the most coveted awards in the history profession except the Pulitzers.) Two of the Pulitzer-winning books have been mentioned, Mays's *Edmund Pendleton* and Bailyn's *Ideological Origins*. The other two, like the Mays

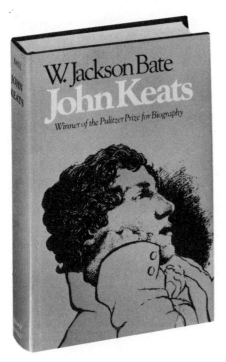

32. *John Keats,* first published in
1963, shown here in the new jacket
used for the fourth printing in
1978. The same design was used for
the paperback edition.

book, were biographies. These were *John Keats,* by Walter Jackson
Bate of Harvard, published in 1963, and the three volumes of Ernest
Samuels's *Henry Adams,* published in 1948, 1958, and 1964. The
Press's reputation for biography was also helped by the first two
volumes of *Justice Oliver Wendell Holmes,* by Mark DeWolfe Howe,
published in 1957 and 1963. Howe died in 1967 without finishing
the biography.

The winning of prizes accomplishes wonders for morale in a publishing house and for relations with authors. One of the steps taken
by the Wilson Press to build itself up in the Harvard community was
the establishment of an annual prize awarded by the Press itself. This
was the Harvard University Press Faculty Prize. Starting in 1956 the
Press awarded $2,000 each year to the Harvard faculty member whose
Press book made "the greatest contribution to knowledge and understanding without limitations as to the breadth or narrowness of
its field." Donald Scott anonymously put up the money.[70] The first
Faculty Prize winner was Harry A. Wolfson for *The Philosophy of
the Church Fathers.* After Scott's death in 1967 his widow, Louise

April 1 9 6 7 : Extra

The Browser

A NEWSLETTER FROM HARVARD UNIVERSITY PRESS

Our first opportunity to observe Thomas J. Wilson closely, without being closely observed ourselves, came when he addressed a gathering at the American Academy of Arts and Sciences. He had just returned from a lengthy mission to the Middle East on behalf of Franklin Book Programs, Inc., of which he was then Chairman, and his subject was the distribution of American books abroad. His ideas were characteristically fresh and arresting. His delivery was faultless, and we instinctively believed everything he said. But what riveted our attention was the gentleman's garb, for he was dressed in an immaculate blue pin-striped suit and desert boots.

We bring up this business of the tan suede boots not because it is Mr. Wilson's habit to go about irregularly shod. Indeed, the boots have made no subsequent appearance, and to this day we have been unable to formulate a satisfactory explanation of their use on that occasion. Perhaps some prankster had hidden all his shoes. Our point, if we have one, is that it takes a man of character to make a good speech before an august body while clad in conspicuous footgear, and we remember the event as our first piece of real evidence that Thomas J. Wilson is a man with a forceful personality. The evidence, we might add, is mounting still.

It is our forlorn duty to report that Mr. Wilson will leave Harvard University Press next January, after twenty years as its Director. He plans to assume new responsibilities in the field of publishing, the details of which have not yet been announced.

Mr. Wilson led the Press during its great period of growth, 1947 to date, when distribution of the books published by us increased six-fold, and when many of our books helped to introduce new ideas into the curriculum. President Pusey, announcing Mr. Wilson's decision, said:

"In his long and influential tenure at Harvard, Mr. Wilson has well served the academic community of the nation and the world. He clearly has seen the University press as one of the primary tools of scholarship. He has set the highest standards of selection,

33. A sample of the prose style of Christopher Reed, author of the Press's newsletter throughout the six years of its existence.

Scott, continued the prize until the Press decided to end it after the 1975 award.

Another kind of boost to the Press's reputation took place in 1963 when a small library was created for the White House in Washington. Of the 1,780 titles chosen, 110 were Harvard University Press books, a showing exceeded only by the 124 from Macmillan.[71]

The Faculty Prize was a deliberate effort to improve the Press's image, and there were others. In 1948 the Press opened a display room in Harvard Square, located first at 22 Dunster Street and finally, after a few moves, in the arcade of Holyoke Center. In 1959 the Press began an annual custom of entertaining the Nieman Fellows at dinner and acquainting those journalists with its purposes and operations. And in 1965 the Press began issuing an approximately monthly newsletter, *The Browser,* which for six years captivated a large audience at Harvard and elsewhere.

The anonymous author of *The Browser* was Christopher D. Reed, who had joined the Press as a traveling book salesman in 1960 and had been put in charge of library services in 1964. (One of his first mailings to libraries, concerning the Loeb Classical Library, cost $83 to print but brought in over $50,000 in orders.)[72] In 1968 he left the Press for the Harvard alumni magazine but continued to write *The Browser* until it fell victim to the Press's financial crisis in 1971.

CHAPTER EIGHT

The Paperback Question, the Double Helix, and Other Stories

A S THE PRESS attracted more and more manuscripts, Wilson became acutely aware that the job of handling them prior to acceptance or rejection—while also recruiting good books for the Press's list—was more than he and Mark Carroll could effectively cope with. In the 1960s, following the lead of other large presses, he began to delegate some of the responsibility for "listbuilding" to editors chosen for that purpose—"specialist editors," as they were called at first. This marked the beginning of the modern, bipartite editorial department, consisting of acquisitions editors and manuscript editors.

Reshaping the Editorial Effort

The most immediate need was to do something about the flood of manuscripts in the social sciences and humanities. As a first step, Wilson created the position of Editor for the Social Sciences. I served the organization in that capacity from July 1, 1960, until I moved to the Harvard Business School in 1973.

My appointment at the Press came by way of the New York Metropolitan Region Study, a project conducted by Harvard's Graduate School of Public Administration. The economist Raymond Vernon was the project's director, and I was the editorial director; both of us moved to Harvard as a result. The undertaking yielded ten books, all published by the Press.

The job of Social Science Editor consisted of responsibility for books mainly in history, economics, and government. The idea was to help the front office determine what to publish and to work with authors before acceptance—and also, to the extent possible, to attract to the Press good books that might otherwise go elsewhere.

As the Press's work expanded, Eleanor Dobson Kewer and Maud Wilcox had to hire more manuscript editors, and by the summer of 1965 there were fourteen full-time people in the editorial operation—nine of them manuscript editors—besides about half a dozen freelance editors who were used fairly often. But this did not solve the problems of congestion. Wilson told the Board of Directors in September 1965 that in addition to "administrative inadequacy," which he said reflected upon him as much as, or more than, it did on Mrs. Kewer, "the most important part of publishing—the choice of the books to be recommended to the Syndics for publication—has become far too much for the Director and his Associates to carry on alone. Vigorous help should come from the Editorial Department, but it cannot be given by that Department as it is now run."[1]

The upshot was that Wilson, with Mark Carroll's active participation, hired David H. Horne as Assistant Director for Editorial Affairs, starting January 1, 1966. During the previous six years he had been Executive Editor at Yale University Press—in effect their chief

34. The Press triumvirate in 1963, year of the fiftieth anniversary. Left to right in the Director's office: Mark Carroll, Associate Director; Warren Smith, Associate Director and Business Manager; and Thomas Wilson, Director.

35. A lineup of editors in 1963. The scene is the Press conference room. Left to right: Joseph Elder, Science Editor; Maud Wilcox, Executive Editor; Eleanor Dobson Kewer, Chief Editor; and Max Hall, Social Science Editor.

36. At the conference table in 1963, left to right: Burton L. Stratton, Production Manager; Grace Briggs, Assistant Business Manager; Loring Lincoln, Sales Manager; and Mark Saxton, Promotion Manager.

editorial officer. Carroll had known Horne at Yale and had suggested him to Wilson. Horne, an energetic man with a strong sense of order, a forceful writer with a flair for humor, was well respected in university press circles. He held a Ph.D. in English from Yale, had taught English at the University of Missouri and Yale, and had gradually formed an association with Yale's Press in the 1950s. He also worked for four Yale departments as editor of the books they developed.[2]

Eleanor Kewer, the Press's longtime Chief Editor, who still had four and a half years before her retirement age, was appointed Chief Editor for Major Special Publishing Projects. Maud Wilcox, who had been Executive Editor for eight years, was appointed Humanities Editor, responsible for books on literature, philosophy, classics, art, music, and so on.

Horne himself took over the assignment of manuscripts to editors and put much emphasis on reducing expenses and making the operation more efficient. But the department continued to expand, and by the end of 1966, when the Press was publishing about 130 titles a year, there were twenty-four full-time editorial employees including fourteen manuscript editors.[3] Horne soon decided he needed a Managing Editor to direct the flow of manuscripts and serve as administrator of the editorial office. To fill that job he hired Dimmes McDowell Bishop, who had been an editor or administrative assistant for five commercial publishers and two university presses. Even so, the Syndics were accepting so many books that manuscripts ready for editing stacked up high in her office.

Starting in 1966 the specialist editors (including Joseph Elder, who had been editing science manuscripts since 1948) received and took action on all incoming manuscripts and proposals in their fields. This was a big change. Mark Carroll delivered to our shelves all the manuscripts awaiting action in the front office. We called it "The Deluge." The specialist editors could say "no" to authors on our own authority but of course could not *accept* in the same way; we could only recommend to the Director that he recommend to the Syndics. And we had to obtain outside readings to back up our judgments.

Acquisitions, or scouting for manuscripts, was always a desideratum and a cause of concern to those who could not find adequate time for it. The crush of reading and acting upon manuscripts—and of dealing with problems that continually arose in connection with books in process—prevented the Press's early specialist editors from giving acquisitions the highest priority. We did not have expense accounts for travel and entertainment. Our solicitation of authors took place mainly among Harvard faculty members and authors already on the Press's list. Wilson did not allow us to approach new authors at other universities that had university presses—and was outraged when an editor from Chicago made calls on professors at Harvard—but he and all of us wanted more from Harvard's finest authors.

In 1967 the Press established a fourth specialist editorship. Ann Orlov, enterprising and aggressive, who had been a manuscript editor for about ten years, became Editor for the Behavioral Sciences— meaning sociology, psychology, and anthropology. She also handled books on religion.

The Paperback Question

Whether to publish paperbacks was the big controversial question of the Wilson era. Wilson firmly answered no, except in a few special

37. David Horne, who transferred from Yale in 1966 to become Assistant Director for Editorial Affairs.

cases. Toward the end, in 1966, he reported that he and Carroll were "less convincedly negative" about starting a paperback line and that the staff was "approaching unanimity" in favor of it. By that time, however, the Press had leased to other publishers the paperback rights to about 250 of its books, and the Harvard Paperbacks did not become a reality until 1971, more than three years after Wilson's departure.[4]

The American paperback revolution was far advanced when Wilson arrived in 1947, but it had scarcely touched academic publishers. The prodigious success of the commercial paperback edition of Susanne Langer's *Philosophy in a New Key* began in 1948. Though Wilson had nothing to do with the leasing of that book to a commercial publisher, the annual sales figures must have impressed him and may have influenced his actions when new paperback opportunities for intellectual books arose.

Those opportunities were created by the advent of "quality paperbacks" in 1953. First came Doubleday Anchor Books, priced at about a dollar. Soon there were Harper Torchbooks, Knopf's Vintage Books, and many others. Paperbacks, hitherto sold at newsstands and cigar stores, appeared in bookstores and became more respectable. Before long, paperbacks dominated the reading lists of college courses and the shelves of college bookstores.

The backlists of university presses contained important works well suited to be given new life and wider circulation through lower-priced editions.[5] Paperbacks could be priced lower than hardcovers not merely because the *covers* were cheaper but because the print runs were larger (and therefore the cost per copy was less), the royalties were smaller, and the hardcover edition had usually absorbed the costs of choosing the book, launching and advertising it, editing the manuscript, and setting the type.[6]

University presses began publishing their own paperback lines in 1955. About twelve presses had them by 1959, reportedly with mixed results at first, and by 1967 about thirty-seven presses were in the field.[7] Harvard's Press traveled a different road because Harvard had many titles that commercial publishers eagerly sought and because of Wilson's conception of the Press's function. He argued that a paperback undertaking would divert the Press's energies from what it existed to do and could do best, that is, publish the maximum number of original books that would add to the sum of knowledge. He also argued that paperback publishing might cause the Press to lose its tax-exempt status, a possible disaster which worried him—even aside from the paperback question—as the Press grew more prosperous. He recognized that authors would receive a higher royalty per copy if the Press itself did the paperbacks, but he obviously believed that the big commercial firms could sell more copies.[8] Moreover, many of the Press's authors were very pleased to be published in such renowned paperback lines as Torchbooks, Anchor, Vintage, and Pocket Books. So his convictions favored leasing the paperback rights, and the more good books he committed to others the harder it would have been for him to change his course even if he had wanted to.

Warren Smith and Grace Briggs, the traditional custodians of reprint rights and permissions at the Press, were not in sympathy with Wilson's paperback strategy. In the fifties, until Wilson put an end to their plans, they turned down requests for paperback rights and built up a file of titles for the Press to reprint eventually in paper. Smith argued that the Press should not make the error of bucking the obvious tide of the future.[9] Wilson, disagreeing about the tide of the future, leased out a number of titles in 1956, including *Eleanor of Aquitaine and the Four Kings*. And in 1959 the acceptance of commercial offers became the Press's official policy.

The hardening of the paperback policy coincided with Mark Carroll's elevation to real power at the Press, and the two events were related. Wilson put the paperback question before the Board of Directors on January 5, 1959, the same day the board approved Carroll's title of Associate Director. The board, unprepared for a paperback decision, asked for further discussion at the next meeting. Wilson assigned Carroll to study the question and write a report that could be taken to the board.

Meanwhile Wilson, in the interim between the board's January meeting and its next meeting in April, negotiated two paperback contracts of special importance. As mentioned earlier, he sold the rights to *The Harvard Brief Dictionary of Music* to Pocket Books without limit of time. Then he solicited bids for Lovejoy's *The Great Chain of Being* (1936). Meridian Books had offered a $2,500 advance, a large offer in the 1950s. Now Random House bid $3,000, Doubleday Anchor bid $3,500, and Harper Torchbooks bid $5,000. Wilson accepted the Torchbook offer.[10]

While this bidding was in progress, Carroll submitted his report. He opposed starting a paperback line. He acknowledged that such publishing could be done successfully on a large scale but quoted various people on the uncertainties and risks of the paperback market at that time. Carroll said that the Press staff had all it could do in publishing more books than any other university press, and that its primary allegiance was to original works of scholarship.[11]

Wilson commended the document to the Board of Directors on

April 8, and they approved it. This action, and especially the support of the elder statesman Donald Scott, gave Wilson a strong weapon in defending his policy to authors, faculty members, and the Visiting Committee during the years that followed.

By the end of 1961, the year in which the paperback rights to *The United States and China* and *The United States and Japan* went to the Viking Press, Wilson and Carroll had leased about fifty of Harvard's books to other publishers. And the movement was just beginning. During the next nine years an average of twenty-nine Harvard books per year came out in paperback under the imprints of other publishers. Among the busiest reprinters were Harper & Row, W. W. Norton, and Vintage Books (by then a part of Random House), but the firm with the most reprints of Harvard books (about one third of the total during the sixties) was Atheneum Publishers, with which the Press made a special arrangement in March 1962.

Atheneum Publishers, of New York, had been founded three years before. Wilson's agreement gave the company a first option—"the right to make the first offer"—on all existing Press books that had not been leased or definitely committed, and on all future Press books. A joint announcement began by saying that Press titles released for softcover publication would "normally" appear under the Atheneum imprint. Atheneum agreed to offer to publish at least ten books a year. The Press could decline any offer if the terms were unsatisfactory. Atheneum agreed to state on the cover and title page of each book that it had originally been published by Harvard University Press— a provision that was one of Wilson's reasons for liking the arrangement.[12]

Both Smith and Carroll had misgivings. Both feared bad feelings on the part of other publishers. Smith opposed the whole arrangement as offering no significant advantages to the Press.[13] But Wilson, with Scott's backing, persuaded the Board of Directors to approve the negotiations.[14] He said the arrangement would provide a large outlet for paperback distribution of Harvard's books, including many that were out of print or not salable to other firms. He shared the concern over possible negative reactions from other publishers and took the precaution of writing to them before the announcement to explain that the Atheneum agreement would not be an exclusive one. Wilson thought the only other disadvantage of the agreement was that it would automatically tend to discourage the Press's own entry into the field, but he discounted this on the ground that the Press was not likely to take that course.[15]

Atheneum put about eighty Harvard titles into its paperback line during the next eight years or so. In the seventies the Press took back some of them—an action that did not fit into Wilson's philosophy— but about sixty were still on the Atheneum list as late as 1980. Many have had a good sale; many have not. The leader by far was *The Republican Roosevelt*, by John M. Blum, with sales of 120,000 during the fifteen years Atheneum had the rights. Under a separate agreement, Atheneum, outbidding Houghton Mifflin, paid $104,000 for the right to publish twenty-six volumes of the Adams Papers in paper covers (80 percent of this money went to the Adams Papers editorial oper- ation). But only eleven volumes appeared, for their sales (except for the first four) were too disappointing to justify publishing the rest.

Although Harvard University Press itself issued paperbound edi- tions of some books in the Muses' Library and the John Harvard Library in the middle sixties, Wilson did not think of these as prelim- inaries to general paperback publishing.[16] Given the Director's com- mitment to his philosophy and to the publishers with whom he had done business, he was considerably shaken in 1966 when confronted with something like a rebellion within the Press.

Dissatisfaction over paperbacks had long existed among the staff. The dissidents gained a new voice when David Horne arrived as head of editorial affairs, fresh from Yale where paperbacks were well es- tablished. Moreover Mark Carroll, feeling that the situation had changed since 1959 and that the Atheneum agreement had been a mistake, no longer rigidly opposed the publication of paperbacks.[17] In the fall of 1966, with Wilson's permission, Horne collected the pro-paperback views of four other department heads and circulated them with his own views. Horne said that other presses had not regretted their paperback programs and most were enthusiastic. He asked whether Harvard was using its valuable backlist to best advantage for itself and its authors, dismissed the claim that university presses lack the necessary sales force as "a myth perpetuated by commercial houses," said no new employees would be needed in the editorial department, and concluded that "the risk would appear minimal and the potential gain great enough to make the venture attractive to a forward-looking management."[18]

Wilson reacted sharply. He scribbled vehement comments in the margins of the five memoranda. At a meeting of department heads on November 23, he forcefully rejected their arguments. Two days later he circulated a memorandum in which he apologized for cutting the meeting short and for seeming to be less sympathetic than in fact he was. He said he now was "on the fence" because he was strongly

influenced by "you, my colleagues." He also said that their memoranda "failed utterly to give me any policy or program I could honestly
and firmly back to our Board and our lawyers," and that the writers
gave no recognition of "the *fact* that every department of the Press
is at present behind in one or more of its commitments." He ordered
Carroll and Horne to come up with a plan that could be taken to the
Board of Directors.[19] But they produced no plan, feeling that Wilson
was not ready to try paperbacks in any case.[20]

It was about this time that Wilson, in his Annual Report for 1965–
66, publicly acknowledged that he was less negative than before.
Almost certainly he now knew that (1) the change was inevitable, and
(2) he would never be the one to carry it out. He had already decided
to leave, and his administration had only one year to go.

The Double Helix

Toward the end of the Wilson administration the Press was drawn
little by little to the frustrating conclusion of one of the strangest
embroilments in its history. This was the case of *The Double Helix*.
The Syndics thrice approved the book, but two men across the Atlantic
Ocean waged war on the manuscript so effectively that the Harvard
Corporation took the unheard-of action of forbidding publication—
after which the book was published commercially and was a best
seller. The episode brought Harvard some undesirable publicity, and
there was wide misunderstanding of what had happened. The principal facts are as follows.

The author was James D. Watson, a Harvard biology professor.
In 1962, when he was thirty-four, he and two British scientists shared
a Nobel Prize for their discovery, nine years earlier, of the spiral
molecular structure of DNA (deoxyribonucleic acid). The British scientists were Francis H. C. Crick and Maurice F. H. Wilkins. In the
mid-sixties Watson wrote a behind-the-scenes account of the race for
DNA, naming his brief manuscript "Honest Jim" and beginning it,
"I have never seen Francis Crick in a modest mood." Sir Lawrence
Bragg of Cambridge University wrote the foreword and never wavered
in his support of the book.

Around January 1966 the Syndic Ernst Mayr, director of the Museum of Comparative Zoology, called the manuscript to the attention
of Thomas Wilson. Wilson found it faulty and vulnerable to lawsuits,
"yet one of the few genuinely exciting manuscripts I have read in 36
years of publishing."[21] He suggested changes, including a change of

title, and signed Watson to a contract. Watson, with much reluctance, eliminated many risky passages. Wilson sought legal advice and was told that he should not publish the book without written consent from Crick, Wilkins, and several others.[22] Wilson felt that these could be obtained, and the Syndics accepted the manuscript in September.

Wilson sent copies of the new version to Crick and Wilkins. They both responded by asking the Press to drop the undertaking. The Press refused.[23] Crick, apparently astonished that Harvard would consider such an informal manuscript, protested to President Nathan Pusey, who until then had not heard of the book. Wilson defended the manuscript, and the president told Crick he did not believe he should intervene. Crick wrote again, more abrasively, and returned again and again to the attack.[24] His arguments were that it was unethical for a scientist in a collaboration to publish an account to which his collaborators objected, also that the manuscript was gossip pretending to be history, was in poor taste, and invaded his privacy. But Wilson's views were reinforced by a number of readers at Harvard and elsewhere who found the story fascinating and revealing of scientific rivalry, thought that reputations would not really be damaged, and discounted the ethical question because this was a personal account rather than a formal research report. The Syndics again supported Wilson on January 9, 1967. Meanwhile Wilson and one of the Press's best editors, Joyce Backman, continued to work with the author to make the manuscript more acceptable.

In February Maurice Wilkins wrote to Pusey, agreeing with Crick on the ethical question and saying the manuscript was unfair to him and inaccurate. Pusey replied that as president he did not interfere with the Press's editorial judgments.[25]

In March Watson completed his "final final" version. Wilson told Pusey that if the two collaborators still objected, he thought he would have to ask the president for "instruction or guidance." The Syndics for the third time approved publication—"unanimously," Wilson reported.[26] But Wilson's tormenters still objected, and Wilson told some of the Syndics he had not changed his opinion about the book but was "discouraged and somewhat weary." He told a lawyer he thought this would "necessitate a final decision by Mr. Pusey himself."[27]

In those early months of 1967 the amount of correspondence on the Watson project was enormous. According to a list in the Press file, dated April 19, the manuscript had been read by thirty-three scientists and fourteen others. This did not include those few who disapproved of it, one of whom was the chemist Linus Pauling, twice a Nobelist, whose failure to solve the DNA riddle was described in Watson's book. He conveyed his unhappiness to Pusey.[28]

Crick and Wilkins had not yet wheeled up their heaviest artillery. They now did so. On May 12, Wilson received a special delivery letter from New York on the ominous letterhead of Paul, Weiss, Rifkind, Wharton & Garrison. That law firm said that in the opinion of its clients the manuscript was defamatory and invaded their right of privacy. Legal proceedings would be brought unless Wilson sent word within the next few days that publication had been abandoned.[29]

On that same day, Oscar Shaw of Harvard's law firm, Ropes & Gray, addressed two letters to President Pusey in response to a request for advice. In the first, he said he had told Wilson there were passages in the manuscript which could be made the basis of suits for invasion of privacy and for defamation and that such suits might succeed. In the second letter he took account of the message just received from New York, saying it materially changed the complexion of the problem and that publication of the manuscript would be unwise, at least in its present form.[30]

Wilson made one more try. He took a few Syndics with him to the president's office to explain their point of view. But there was no real chance of reversing the course of events. Three facts should be kept in mind. First, Wilson was not arguing for the right of the Press to decide the matter; on the contrary, he placed the decision squarely on the President and Fellows, who had not sought this honor but now were forced into a position of saying yes or no.[31] Second, this being true, they had to consider the legal risk overhanging their deliberations. A lawsuit, even if successfully defended, would bring notoriety of a distasteful sort. Third, the Syndics were not completely wholehearted in their stand. Ernst Mayr wrote later that "even among the Syndics, in spite of our vote, there were quite a few who were not altogether happy about this manuscript." The Syndic Konrad Bloch, himself a Nobel laureate, told Wilson and Pusey that because of the continuing opposition, especially that of Wilkins, he had come to the opinion that publication would put the Press and the University in the unhappy position of taking sides in a bitter controversy among top-ranking scientists. He hoped that the book would become available to the public by some other means.[32]

The final verdict was stated in terms of this third consideration. The president took the question before the Corporation on May 22, 1967, and the next day wrote Wilson a letter in which the legal threat was not mentioned. He said the Corporation, after long and careful thought, had concluded that "to publish this work, despite its apparently considerable value, would lead to an outright quarrel in the scientific world in which Harvard as a University has no business to take part. Publication by Harvard would imply to some degree an endorsement of the views of Professor Watson in the face of overwhelming opposition by his former associates, and it seems neither fair to them nor in the long-range interest of the University for Harvard to become involved in this matter."[33]

Wilson, reporting the outcome to the Syndics in June, expressed the hope that the book would be published elsewhere. It was. With Watson's permission, Wilson had already redirected the manuscript to Atheneum Publishers. This firm published *The Double Helix* on February 26, 1968, very successfully. No lawsuits were reported, either in the United States or in England, where the book was issued by Weidenfeld & Nicolson. Clearly, Crick's most passionate desire had not been to block publication per se, but to block publication backed by the prestige of a great university.

Surprisingly, the Corporation's action had escaped public notice. The public notice began on February 13, 1968, just before the book was published and after it had appeared in two installments in the *Atlantic Monthly*. The *Harvard Crimson* spread a story across the top of page one headed "Corporation Vetoed Watson Book." The story created wide ripples. For example, the *New York Times* printed a front-page story under the headline "A Book That Couldn't Go to Harvard," and the *Boston Globe* printed an editorial entitled "Has Harvard lost its guts?"[34] The publicity gave the general impression that the Harvard administration had suddenly stepped in of its own volition to suppress a book. Little or no mention was made of the legal situation.

The belated public attention to the "book that couldn't go to Harvard" had one clear result, if no other: it contributed to the large sales of *The Double Helix*.

It is easy, in the 1980s, to look back on this tragicomic episode and see that Thomas Wilson could have saved many people a great deal of time, effort, and unpleasantness by simply advising Watson at the outset that his manuscript was better suited to a commercial publisher. He did that sometimes for other authors. But how often does a director of a university press get a chance at a book so lively, so revelatory, so bursting with sales potential, on such an important subject, and written by a Nobel-Prize-winning full professor on the local faculty?

End of an Era

The Press's fiftieth anniversary in January 1963, like the twenty-fifth in 1938, was vigorously observed, but with one big difference. Whereas the earlier keynote had been *hope,* the later one was *success.* Events, it seemed, had caught up with President Conant's 1938 toast to "the future of the Harvard University Press—solvent, significant, successful." A dinner was held at the Club of Odd Volumes, where Wilson had happily presided over many gatherings of his governing boards and Visiting Committee, and there was an exhibition at Widener Library. The golden-anniversary theme was carried into June when the Press was host to the Association of American University Presses. At about that same time Wilson returned to Chapel Hill to receive an honorary degree from his alma mater, and in 1965 Harvard made him Doctor of Humane Letters with Donald Scott as his escort and President Pusey citing him as "sympathetic and imaginative disseminator of the achievements of scholarship; sapient leader of a fine university press." When Wilson stepped down, the Press in its fifty-five-year history had published more than 4,000 titles, and more than half of them had come out while he was Director.

Wilson's Press, like Harold Murdock's, saw the introduction of many new series. Four of special distinction were: (1) books from the Center for the Study of the History of Liberty in America, founded by Oscar Handlin; (2) the Library of Congress Series in American Civilization, edited by Ralph H. Gabriel of Yale and including books by Thomas C. Cochran, Frank Luther Mott, Oscar Handlin, and others; (3) publications of the Joint Center for Urban Studies of the Massachusetts Institute of Technology and Harvard University, published jointly by the presses of the two institutions and including books by James Q. Wilson, Raymond Vernon, Stephan A. Thernstrom, Sam B. Warner, Jr., and many others; (4) RAND Corporation Research Studies, examples being *The Urban Transportation Problem,* by John R. Meyer, John F. Kain, and Martin Wohl, and *The Economics of Defense in the Nuclear Age,* by Charles J. Hitch and Roland N. McKean.

Most of the older series continued through the Wilson years. The largest of them, the Loeb Classical Library, inched up to nearly 440 volumes, and its sales grew mightily, especially in the sixties, so that in the fiscal year 1966–67 they were $217,000 as compared with $32,000 in the last year of Roger Scaife's administration. The Charles Eliot Norton Lectures provided thirteen books in Wilson's time. The

38. Thomas J. Wilson in June 1965 on the occasion of his honorary degree from Harvard. His escort (left) was his associate and friend Donald Scott.

ones that sold best—not necessarily the most important—were by Aaron Copland, E. E. Cummings, and Ben Shahn. The Godkin Lectures yielded a number of significant works. One of the most talked-about was *The Uses of the University* (1963), in which Clark Kerr, president of the University of California, analyzed the modern "multiversity." But the Godkin book that made the biggest splash was *Science and Government* (1961), by C. P. Snow. It was a Book-of-the-Month Club selection, the Press's first. When Sales Manager Loring Lincoln retired in 1973 he was asked what Press book was the easiest to place in bookstores during his twenty-eight years in the sales department. "The C. P. Snow," he replied without hesitation. In the book, Snow dealt with the problem of how to make use of scientists in government most effectively and with least risk. The Press sold 19,000 copies in its regular hardcover edition, and the New American Library sold 72,000 in paperback.

Most of the books of Wilson's era were owned by the Press rather than by outside parties, but Books Not Owned (BNO's) continued to be numerous. For example, the Harvard Economic Studies accounted for about fifty titles during his administration and the Harvard Historical Studies and Harvard Historical Monographs for sixty-six between them. The amount of the Press's Books Not Owned commission again was a sore question. In 1953 the Press raised the commission charged to Harvard departments from 25 percent to 30 percent of the list price on books sold and added an additional fee of 5 percent of the manufacturing costs. As in Dumas Malone's time, there was a mixed reaction and considerable outcry. Some compromises were made.[35]

Much could be written about each of the important books of Wilson's second decade, 1957–1967. Many of them have already been mentioned. A few other titles: *Village in the Vaucluse,* by Laurence Wylie; *Boston, A Topographical History,* by Walter Muir Whitehill; *The Strategy of Conflict,* by Thomas C. Schelling; *From Empire to Nation,* by Rupert Emerson; *Industrialism and Industrial Man,* by Clark Kerr, John T. Dunlop, F. L. Harbison, and Charles A. Myers; *Set Theory and Its Logic,* by Willard Van Orman Quine; and the early volumes in a prodigious continuing stream of Ralph Waldo Emerson's journals and notebooks, published under the Belknap Press imprint from the manuscripts in Houghton Library.

Two other books of that period, written by members of the Board of Syndics, hold places of special honor in the Press's history. One had 125 pages, the other 813. They were:

1. *The Process of Education* (1960), by the Harvard psychologist Jerome S. Bruner. Its worldwide sales have exceeded 700,000; only the *Harvard Dictionary of Music* has sold more. *The Process of Education,* a very small volume, was built around the memorable idea that children could be taught the fundamentals of a subject at a much earlier age than was generally believed. In the book's first twenty-four years the Press sold about 86,000 copies in hardcover; Vintage Books sold 353,000 in paperback; and the Press beginning in 1977 sold 30,000 of its own paperback. In addition, the known sales in about twenty foreign languages have exceeded 240,000.

2. *Animal Species and Evolution* (1963), by Ernst Mayr. This large work, a comprehensive summary of the findings and thinking of evolutionary biology, was a landmark in biological writing. It was also the opening event in the Press's rise to distinction in the twin fields of evolution and animal behavior, a rise which owed much to Mayr.

He had joined the Harvard faculty in 1953 and for many years was director of Harvard's Museum of Comparative Zoology. Under his leadership, Harvard University developed fast as a center of studies grounded on evolutionary theory. He was also one of the most helpful Syndics the Press ever had.

Wilson transferred more and more responsibility to Mark Carroll, so that by 1967 Carroll had become a sort of executive vice-president,

39. A sample of books from the first half of the sixties.

supervising just about everything except accounting and shipping. Wilson built Carroll up in his Annual Reports and brought him into the business side of things via the Board of Directors, of which Carroll had become secretary in 1962.[36]

Wilson's place in history rests partly on his activity in the international aspects of book publishing. The Press under his direction was one of the U.S. publishers that led the way toward a truly world market for American scholarship. Foreign sales were and still are important; in 1966 they amounted to about one sixth of the Press's total.[37] The Press joined half a dozen other university presses in the International Book Export Group (IBEG), with home office at Princeton. (In the United Kingdom the Press continued to market its books through Oxford University Press.) In the early sixties Wilson served four years as chairman of the board of Franklin Book Programs, a nonprofit corporation devoted to fostering the translation and publication of American books in less-developed countries and to encouraging local book industries. Wilson's part in Franklin Book Programs included major fund raising (for example, $1 million from the Ford Foundation) and a round-the-world trip to visit thirteen of the Franklin operating offices.

At that time the Harvard rule was that an administrative officer had to retire on the June 30 following his sixty-sixth birthday. When Warren Smith retired as Associate Director and Business Manager on June 30, 1967, he was succeeded as Business Manager—though not as Associate Director—by John A. Nilson, who had been chief accountant since 1964. Both the Production Manager, Burt Stratton, and the Senior Designer, Burt Jones, left before their mandatory retirement age. Stratton was succeeded in 1967 by Christopher C. Kellogg, who had been Assistant Production Manager since 1965. The position of Senior Designer was filled by David Ford, who had joined the Press in 1960. Wilson had strong views about book jackets, insisting, for example, that the author's name be as large as the book title; but he did not have as much interest in the esthetics of book production as Harold Murdock had shown in the 1920s.[38]

Wilson's own retirement was due June 30, 1969. In the mid-sixties he realized that he wanted to continue in publishing beyond that date and would need the money to educate his two children and contribute to the support of another family by a previous marriage. In October 1966 he notified President Pusey that he wanted to take early retirement at either the beginning or middle of 1968 in order to get started in a financially rewarding position. This notification took place a little before the paperback rebellion within the Press and about seven months before the Corporation decided against publication of *The Double Helix*.

Wilson's close friend Marc Friedlaender, who was second in command at the Adams Papers and had previously been at Atheneum Publishers, knew of his intentions and told Atheneum about them. The result was that Alfred Knopf, Jr., and Simon Michael Bessie, the Atheneum partners, made Wilson an offer he could not afford to pass up: he would move to the New York firm as a vice-president and senior editor. In March 1967 he formally requested early retirement as of December 31, telling Pusey that he must begin his new job then or give up the opportunity. He recommended Mark Carroll as his successor. Listing sixteen other possible appointees, he found something wrong with each and argued that Carroll was "the one right choice."[39]

At that time Donald Scott, eighty-seven years old, was at his western home in Santa Barbara, California. Wilson sent him a copy of his letter recommending Carroll. Thereupon Scott sent Pusey his own recommendation of Carroll, saying among other things that Carroll was a man of great strength of character and positive convictions who was soundly versed in the finances of publishing and had a sympathetic understanding of the several fields of scholarship. He warned against recruiting someone from commercial publishing, which he said had been deteriorating in quality.[40] Five days later, on April 4, 1967, Donald Scott died.

The Board of Directors was now left with six members: Chairman L. Gard Wiggins, who had succeeded Edward Reynolds as Harvard's administrative vice-president in 1960; Thomas Wilson; George P. Baker, dean of the Business School; Erwin N. Griswold, dean of the Law School; Merle Fainsod, director of the University Library; and the economist Edward S. Mason, former dean of the Graduate School of Public Administration. A few months later Baker resigned and was succeeded by Bertrand Fox of the Business School; Griswold resigned and was succeeded by Archibald Cox of the Law School; and Oscar Handlin was appointed to fill Scott's vacancy.

One of the last collaborations between Wilson and Scott was their strenuous plea to the authorities not to interfere with the Press's natural growth to 200 titles a year by 1970–71. They must have had reason to fear that some limits would be imposed after Wilson's retirement. Scott sketched out the argument early in 1967. Wilson edited Scott's notes and sent them to the Board of Directors on March 13 with his own long memorandum, entitled "The Press's Need for

More People and More Space."[41] He said the Press would need at least twenty-two more people by 1971, nine of them at once. Then an extraordinary thing happened: the Syndics themselves instructed Wilson to compose a memorandum to the Harvard Corporation "setting forth the unanimous opinion of the Board that the natural growth of the Press should be allowed to continue unimpeded." Wilson did so, and all the Syndics signed the document: W. J. Bate, Konrad E. Bloch, Crane Brinton, Frank M. Cross, Jr., John P. Dawson, Bertrand Fox, George M. A. Hanfmann, Manfred L. Karnofsky, Simon S. Kuznets, Juan Marichal, Ernst Mayr, John W. M. Whiting, and Wilson as chairman. Direct appeals from the Syndics to the Corporation were nothing novel, but all the others had come in times of adversity. Wilson was officially notified that the memorandum had received careful attention from the Corporation and that the reaction was entirely favorable, but that no action was taken because none was required.[42]

President Pusey did not appoint a committee to search for a new Director. He spent a good deal of his own time in the summer of 1967 satisfying himself that Carroll was indeed the right choice. He talked with the directors Wiggins, Baker, Griswold, Fainsod, and Mason, and they all went along with Wilson in favoring Carroll. He also corresponded with sixty or more people, including heads of other university presses, and he told the Corporation members on September 13 that he did not recall a single letter adverse to Carroll. On September 18 the Corporation approved the appointment.[43] "The joy that shot through this Press when news of his election came to us is indescribable," Wilson said in his Annual Report for 1966–67, which was his last. Carroll, he said, "will carry the Press to new heights."

Wilson left behind a publishing organization with annual sales of $3,000,000, a high reputation for scholarly merit, solid support from the University, a comfortable cash balance, an endowment, income from oil wells, about 2,500 titles in print, and ambitious plans for continued growth. It also had large overhead expenses. It did *not* have some things it might need in the future, including adequate computer facilities for a computer age and a paperback program for a paperback age. And there was another significant fact, almost unrecognized at that prosperous moment. Among the hundreds of thousands of books in the Press's warehouse, many were never going to be sold.

In New York, Wilson had all too short a time to work enthusiastically at his new career. His death of a heart attack on June 27, 1969, at the age of sixty-six, came three days before the date on which he would have had to retire from Harvard.

CHAPTER NINE

Crisis and Reorganization

1968–1972

> Publishing the highest quality of scholarly books is indeed costly, and in a
> time like this it leads to deficits. But if a scholarly press's success is to be
> judged primarily in bookkeeper's terms, it will soon become something other
> than a scholarly press.
>
> —L. H. Butterfield to President Bok, February 1972

> I fully share your feeling that the Press cannot be regarded simply as a
> business; it is a very important part of scholarship at Harvard. At the same
> time, the losses at the Press had become very heavy indeed—and at a time
> when University finances were sufficiently tight that such losses could only
> jeopardize other educational programs.
>
> —President Bok to L. H. Butterfield

MARK CARROLL was Director of the Press for four years and
forty-nine days—from January 1, 1968, to February 18, 1972.
The number and quality of the publications remained high. Beginning
in his first full fiscal year, however, the Press incurred annual losses
of $43,000, $220,900, $548,200, and $349,900. The deficits were
due in part to worsening external conditions, which plagued all university presses in that period. They were also due to inheritances from
the Wilson administration, including policies, people, and unsold books
that had to be written off as losses. They were increased by interest
payments on the Press's high-climbing loan for working capital and
by costly difficulties in processing book orders through a University-
owned computer.

It is also clear from the historical evidence that Carroll, bent on
continuing along the lines laid down by Thomas Wilson, was slow
in recognizing the speed, magnitude, and persistence of the Press's
financial slide. Wilsonian expansionism went out of date but the publishing program had a momentum of its own—manuscripts accepted,
contracts signed, projects in full swing—a momentum not easy to
reverse, especially if one kept hoping that renewed prosperity was just

around the corner. Thus, as sales income leveled off, the staff continued to grow and expenses of all sorts continued to rise. Even the separate account of the Belknap Press ran deficits because of the heavy costs of long-term Belknap projects, notwithstanding the income from the Belknap endowment and from the Texas oil properties. Carroll finally made strenuous efforts at retrenchment. They were not as early or as effective as they might have been if he and his helpers could have made better forecasts of the future from year to year and from month to month.

Because of the financial setbacks, this chapter is a story not only of publishing achievements but also of trouble upon trouble leading to Carroll's dismissal in the worst time of shock and confusion since the Press's wartime crisis of 1942. Unlike the crises of 1919 and 1942, the crisis of the early 1970s broke into the open and became a topic of buzzing interest at Harvard and in the publishing world.

Books

Mark Sullivan Carroll, the sixth Director of the Press and the first to rise through the ranks to the top position, was born in Boston on April 25, 1924. He graduated from Boston Latin School in 1943 and spent the next four years in the army. He graduated from Harvard in 1950. In college he was correspondent for the *Boston Post,* and after graduation he became news editor of a Boston radio station. In 1951, after taking the Radcliffe Publishing Procedures Course, he began five years as promotion manager of Yale University Press. But Harvard University Press was his goal, and starting in 1956, as assistant to Wilson and then as Associate Director, he performed with such zest for work, such quickness, such readiness to take responsibility, and such capacity for making friends (both at Harvard and elsewhere) that he achieved the Directorship when he was only forty-three.

Under Carroll the Press put its publishing imprint on about 580 new titles and new editions. The average annual number published was 140, ten more than the average of Wilson's last four years. The fiscal year 1970–71, which was the year of the Press's greatest deficit, $548,200, was likewise the all-time record year in number of titles published: 163.[1] The most prolific earlier year had been 1967–68, when 144 titles had been published.

According to my calculations, the total number of books published by the Press during its first six decades—1913 through 1972—was

40. Mark Carroll,
sixth Director of the Press.

about 4,800. (If we add the output from the next decade, 1973–1982, which is not covered by this history, the grand total slightly exceeds 6,000.)

Not only in quantity but also in quality the Carroll Press shone brightest just before it passed into history. Several books of unusual importance appeared in the calendar year 1971. One of the most highly praised books ever published by the Press came out only three months before Carroll's departure. This was *A Theory of Justice,* by John Rawls.

Rawls, a professor of philosophy at Harvard, had been working on *A Theory of Justice* for many years, and his articles on the subject had drawn attention. The Humanities Editor, Maud Wilcox, followed his progress, read a draft of the book, and counteracted the author's first leaning toward Princeton (his alma mater). In the book, Rawls developed the concept of justice as *fairness.* He argued that utilitarian philosophy, which had become widely accepted as the main tradition of moral philosophy, cannot form an adequate foundation for our political rights or our intuitive notions of what is just. His alternative was the older tradition of social contract, which he explained, defended, and rehabilitated. The book won several prizes and has sold well over a hundred thousand copies.[2]

Another product of 1971 was *The Insect Societies,* by the Harvard zoologist Edward O. Wilson. This book further advanced the Press's position in evolution and animal behavior. It was the first of E. O. Wilson's books for the Press, the one that was featured in the *New York Times Book Review* with a long line of ants marching between the columns. Wilson agreed to publish with the Press partly because of Ernst Mayr's influence and partly because of his own admiration for a Press book of 1967, *The Dance Language and Orientation of Bees,* by Karl von Frisch—a book designed by David Ford, who also designed *The Insect Societies.* Wilson's early dealings with the Press were with Murray Chastain, who had just been hired as Biomedical Editor with the financial help of the Commonwealth Fund, and whose advent brought the number of specialist editors to five. Wilson in *The Insect Societies* covered the natural history and life cycle of social wasps, social bees, ants, and termites in 560 pages and 258 illustrations. His last chapter, "The Prospect for a Unified Sociobiology," presaged his books to come.

In 1970, when Wilson was finishing *The Insect Societies,* he succeeded Ernst Mayr on the Board of Syndics. That same year the Press enlarged the audience for Mayr's 1963 opus, *Animal Species and*

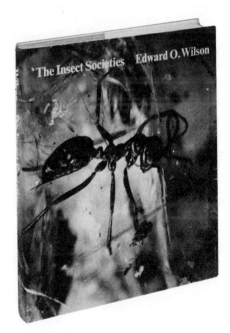

41. E. O. Wilson's first book for the Press, an event of the banner year 1971.

Evolution, by publishing an abridged edition in less technical language under the title *Populations, Species, and Evolution.* For this, Mayr asked for a manuscript editor without biological expertise and insisted that she query any passage that was not clear to her. The editor, Nancy Clemente, complied. Still another zoological product of the Carroll years was an American edition of an important European work, *Studies in Animal and Human Behavior,* by Konrad Lorenz, an old friend of Mayr's.

In 1971 the Press brought out *Notable American Women, 1607–1950: A Biographical Dictionary,* in three volumes, edited by Edward T. James and Janet W. James under the auspices of Radcliffe College. It contains biographies of 1,359 women. Nothing like it had been done before. The elder Arthur M. Schlesinger thought up the project. The editorial work, at Radcliffe's expense, began in 1958. Thomas Wilson made an offer in 1959 and signed a contract under which the Belknap Press eventually stood the heavy publication costs and paid royalties to Radcliffe.

The year 1971, too, was the time when the Press entered the paperback field, ten or fifteen years behind most other major university presses. Carroll decided in 1970 that the time had come. He told the Board of Directors that a number of Press authors and staff members had urged a formal paperback program and that he thought this would "provide needed income with a minimum of investment."[3] The board gave its approval in January 1971 and Carroll established the Harvard Paperbacks. The Press began retrieving paperback rights from commercial publishers.

A Paperback Committee headed by Christopher Burns, one of Carroll's assistants, managed to issue the first ten Harvard Paperbacks in May of that same year. No extra people were hired and no extra office space had to be found, notwithstanding the earlier contentions of Wilson and Carroll. The first ten books were not mentioned in the spring catalogue, because it had gone to press earlier. Eleven more paperbacks were ready in the fall, and all twenty-one were advertised together. The sales staff was happy over its sudden new entree into the nation's bookstores. The Harvard Paperbacks were successful from the start, and Carroll said in his Annual Report for 1970–71 (his last) that they had brought a "much-needed flexibility" to the Press's entire publishing program.

The Press was fortunate in having the ideal book for Number 1 in the series. John K. Fairbank finished the third edition of *The United States and China,* the most popular volume in the American Foreign

Policy Library, in time for publication in the spring of 1971, and the Press decided to issue it simultaneously in hardcover and paperback. Thus it became available for course adoption right away, and about 40,000 copies of the paperback version were sold in the first year and a half alone. Number 10, too, was a new book: *Marihuana Reconsidered,* by Lester Grinspoon, a psychiatrist at the Harvard Medical School. All the others that first year were drawn from the Press's backlist, including Bernard Bailyn's *Ideological Origins of the American Revolution,* Chester Barnard's *Functions of the Executive,* Arthur Lovejoy's *Great Chain of Being,* Susanne Langer's *Philosophy in a New Key,* and Amy Kelly's *Eleanor of Aquitaine and the Four Kings—* books that seemed destined to sell forever.

During the Carroll period, the Press published a number of other outstanding books, among them *Economic Growth of Nations,* by the Harvard economist Simon Kuznets; *The Entropy Law and the Economic Process,* by the Vanderbilt economist Nicholas Georgescu-

42. The first ten Harvard Paperbacks, a marketable crop in the 1971 harvest.

Roegen; *The Exceptional Executive,* by Harry Levinson of the Harvard Business School; *Guide to the Study of United States Imprints,* by G. Thomas Tanselle of the University of Wisconsin (an example of the many Belknap Press projects that were expensive to manufacture but were received with joy by their specialized audiences); and *Congress v. the Supreme Court,* by Raoul Berger, a retired New York lawyer who became a research fellow at the Harvard Law School and produced, in the 1970s, three more books with the timely titles *Impeachment, Executive Privilege,* and *Government by Judiciary.* Legal history was a lively subject in the Carroll years, and a new series called Studies in Legal History was founded in 1971. Another new series, Harvard Studies in Urban History, began about the same time.

Inside Kittredge Hall

Any Press Director needs competent lieutenants whom the Director trusts and is willing to listen to—and who can work together. Carroll badly needed such support, especially on the business side but also in other areas. He did not always get it. The Press during the Wilson and Carroll administrations was "relatively unstructured" and subject to "incomplete touching of bases," as Carroll said later.[4] In the fall of 1971 he hired an Operations Manager—Brian P. Murphy—to correct shortcomings of financial management and to control costs. This was a successful stroke for the Press, but it came too late to save Carroll's own position.

When Carroll was promoted to Director in 1968, he made David Horne the Associate Director, and Horne continued in that job throughout the Carroll administration. Carroll looked to Horne to improve and run the editorial department, itself a large order, and to be secretary of the Syndics. Carroll did not give Horne the broad authority over Press operations that he himself had obtained from Wilson in the middle sixties. For reasons unknown or at least too complex to be untangled here, relations between Carroll and Horne cooled, as both men confirmed in interviews later. As for the editorial operation, Horne was never satisfied with the results of his efforts to make it more efficient. He tried to institute more planning—the setting of goals and the reporting of progress—but could not enforce the reforms. Horne felt that this failure of planning was true of the whole Press.[5]

The department head to whom Carroll was closest during the major part of his administration was his Promotion Manager, Costello Bishop. Harvard's Press Directors always come into office determined to build a fire under the promotion effort. This had been true of Roger Scaife and Thomas Wilson, and it was true of Mark Carroll (also, later, of Arthur J. Rosenthal). One of Carroll's first acts was to reorganize the promotion department. Mark Saxton departed after fifteen years as Promotion Manager and was replaced by a man from New York who lasted only a few months. Carroll then gave the job to Bishop, a former New York salesman of advertising space who had been working for a textbook-development firm in Cambridge and whose wife, Dimmes, was the Press's Managing Editor.

Bishop took over in November 1968. He gathered an eager young staff with high morale. He also increased the number of Harvard books adopted by book clubs and chose a Boston advertising agency, Quinn & Johnson, to replace the New York firm Franklin Spier. In 1970 Carroll created for him the title Assistant Director and gave him control over both the promotion and sales departments. In the spring of 1971, when the financial troubles were fast becoming worse, the Director placed Bishop in high company by making him secretary to the Board of Directors. Long afterward in an interview, Carroll commented that Bishop's methods had not improved sales income relative to promotion expenditures.

Christopher Burns, already mentioned in connection with paperbacks, was another newcomer who had Carroll's confidence for a time. Carroll hired him in February 1970 as Assistant to the Director, a title Burns had held earlier at Yale University Press.

"Assistant *to* the Director," of course, is a lesser rank than "Assistant Director." Carroll on taking office had appointed two assistants *to* him. One was his former secretary, Lois Wotherspoon, who managed his appointments and correspondence, was given vague responsibility for "the operational activities of the Press," and handled the sale of translation and reprint rights. The other was Nanine K. Hutchinson, who exerted somewhat more power than her title suggested. Nanine Hutchinson had worked about ten years in the promotion department, where she had inaugurated the Press's busy program of exhibiting its books at scholarly meetings and had risen to the post of Assistant Promotion Manager. Among her new duties under Carroll, she collected information from the Press departments so that she could make recommendations (which Carroll usually accepted) on how many copies to print, how many to bind, what price to charge, what discount to give booksellers, and when to reprint a book or let it go out of print.[6]

Christopher Burns was an assistant of another kind. He studied the Press's operations and made various proposals for improving accounting, customer relations, and order processing. Some of his ideas were put into effect but encountered implacable resistance. His most lasting contribution was setting up the paperback program. Burns left the Press in August 1971, having served a year and a half.

At the beginning of 1971 the Press had more than 140 employees, an increase of about 30 during Carroll's first three years. Most of the staff, working hard to produce the Press's huge list that year, little suspected what was going on between Carroll and the Board of Directors. Some would remember that period as a time of pride in accomplishment and the Press as "a great place to work,"[7] and it would be incorrect to picture the Carroll administration as a period of unrelieved gloom and discord. The gloom descended mainly in 1972. Internal discord, however, existed earlier.

In March 1970 four of Harry Levinson's doctoral students at the Business School presented the results of a five-month study of the Press.[8] They had conducted about fifty interviews and had persuaded ninety-three Press employees to fill out a questionnaire. They found one major unifying theme—devotion to scholarly books of high quality—but said the staff disagreed widely on "what the Press is." The basic problem, according to the report, was the "underlying uneasiness and confusion over where the Press is and where it is going." The level of communication among departments was found to be low, and thus there was "little sense of shared responsibility for a common task." Also: "A good deal of hostility is reverberating unnecessarily within the Press." The investigators recommended that the Press define its goals and then set policies for moving toward the goals. The report had a mixed reception at the Press.[9]

Carroll himself became so concerned about internal communication that he issued a spirited memorandum to "all staff" on January 19, 1971. He was appalled, he said, at the number of times he had been called upon to deal with persons or groups who could not reach decisions among themselves. "We are associated with one of the world's leading publishing houses, regarded as a powerful educational instrument, but the sniping, snapping, and assorted flak that catches me in its cross-fire are clearly indicative that this fact is frequently overlooked in attempts at self-justification that lowers our standard in our eyes and in those of our publics."

Budgets and Deficits

Carroll was caught in flak from another direction, too. The Press's Board of Directors gradually lost confidence in his ability to assess what was happening to the Press's finances and to remedy the situation.

Earlier, when Thomas Wilson was in control with Donald Scott at his side and the Press's prosperity was taken for granted, the Board of Directors did not have a great deal of governing to do. The board did not even see the annual budget. But when a younger man succeeded Wilson, the board felt a renewed sense of its responsibility.

Besides, there were three vigorous new members, Fox, Cox, and Handlin, each with a deep interest in the Press. Professor Bertrand Fox, director of research at the Business School, was fresh from a term on the Press's Board of Syndics. Archibald Cox, law professor and future Watergate prosecutor, had been chairman of the Press's Visiting Committee in the early 1960s while he was Solicitor General of the United States, and his book *The Warren Court* was soon to be published by the Press. Oscar Handlin had served two terms as a Syndic and had eight Press books to his credit, besides many other Press books that he had edited or supervised in the Department of History and at the Center for the Study of the History of Liberty in America. Fox, Cox, and Handlin joined Chairman L. Gard Wiggins, Edward S. Mason, Merle Fainsod, and Carroll.

A central factor in the board's worry about Press management was the large gap between the Press's budget predictions and the actual results. The annual losses were serious enough; but even more damaging to Carroll's position were the annual surprises. True, there was no cause for alarm in the first year or so. The fiscal year 1967–68 brought record sales of $3,149,000 and a solid profit of $40,000, a bit higher than Carroll had expected. Even so, the directors sought more information about monthly trends, asked for target figures by which to measure performance, and in October 1968, with Fox taking the lead, insisted that annual budgets be brought before the board for approval.[10] For the next three years the task of preparing budgets of even approximate reliability under changing conditions was simply too much for Carroll and the Press's accounting staff. As a result, the Press lost its financial credibility.

For 1968–69, Carroll expected another surplus. But sales suddenly declined in the winter and spring, so that the twelve-month total was only $3,210,000, not much above that of the year before; and thus the Press, with its payroll and other costs increasing, suffered a deficit of $43,000, its first since the early 1950s.

For 1969–70, the budget had to be submitted in the spring of 1969, three months before the start of that fiscal year, long before the book list for the year was completely known. This was the first budget reported in the minutes of the Board of Directors. It projected a large increase in sales and a surplus of $10,000.[11] But sales income seesawed during the fiscal year and finally fell off so badly that the twelve-month total was only $3,047,000. This drop in annual dollar sales was something almost unprecedented in Carroll's fourteen years at the Press. By March 2, 1970, when the fiscal year had four months to run, the Press was projecting a $20,000 loss. On May 18, when the year was only six weeks from completion, Carroll submitted a revised budget in which the loss was put at $51,500.[12] The actual loss was $220,900.

For 1970–71, the first budget again projected a $10,000 surplus. As if to justify this expectation, the sales figures, compared with the preceding year, rose considerably during the first five months. Then, however, a surprising number of books were returned by bookstores, thus whittling the sales total. At the same time the Press's expenses continued to increase very fast, and in May 1971, two months from the end of the fiscal year, the Press was predicting a loss of $148,500.[13] The actual loss was eventually determined to be $548,200.

In March 1971, before anyone dreamed that the 1970–71 loss would exceed half a million dollars, and even before the Press had made its $148,500 estimate, Carroll had to submit his budget for the *next* year, 1971–72. This time, instead of predicting a surplus, he budgeted for a loss of $135,000. It was a realistic thing to do. It was also inflammatory. By then, the Board of Directors had had enough of big losses, and so had the Harvard administration, from whose pocket the lost dollars were being extracted. Nathan Pusey, about to leave the presidency, was said to be "absolutely horrified" by the deficits.[14] The Harvard Corporation rejected the budget. Gard Wiggins, nearing the end of his vice-presidency, told Carroll at a special meeting of the Board of Directors on May 7 that it would be impossible to get a deficit budget approved. He asked Carroll to cancel his travel plans until an acceptable break-even budget could be prepared. Carroll, feeling that he had been placed in an impossible dilemma, simply changed some predictions in order to make the budget balance. He told the Board of Directors, in effect, "Well, you wanted a break-even budget." This was not received with joy, either. As calculated more than a year later, the actual loss for 1971–72 was $349,900. [15]

The unrealism of a break-even budget at that stage is suggested by the fact that losses continued for two years after Carroll's departure. The amounts were $110,500 in 1972–73 and $79,300 in 1973–74.

The four deficits through 1971–72 came to a total of $1,162,200. The negative profit-and-loss balance on the University's books was somewhat less—$959,000—because there had been a substantial *plus* balance before the losses began.[16] With the two additional deficits after the Carroll administration, the cumulative profit-and-loss balance was a minus $1,148,800. It took the Press seven years to repay this sum to the University.

The astonishing size of the deficits in the Carroll years puzzled a lot of people, not only in the Harvard administration but also within the Press. Obviously, income grew only sluggishly while payroll and other operating expenses grew fast; there was no mystery about that. But some of the financial factors entering into the income and expense figures were less obvious.

First, the sluggish income. Sales receipts in Wilson's last four years had increased 57 percent—by well over a million dollars. In the next four they increased only 16 percent, from $3,149,000 to $3,663,000. This rise was more than accounted for by higher pricing of books.[17] In the national economic uncertainty the level of sales moved up and down. Collecting from customers became more of a problem. Book returns by booksellers were unexpectedly high. Student unrest and the "politicizing" of campuses may have interfered with book buying, but that would be hard to document. Carroll several times made it clear to the Board of Directors that other presses were having economic troubles too. And they were. It was commonly said in academic publishing that the general sales lag was due in part to the cuts in federal aid to universities and libraries that took place beginning in 1969.[18]

And there was another kind of income that fell away during those years—subsidies from foundations. In particular, the Ford Foundation grants of $290,000, which had enabled the Wilson Press to publish many books with weak sales prospects and still show annual profits, were entirely lacking. Belknap funds continued to come in, and without them the Press's output would have been smaller and less distinguished; but Belknap funds were running behind the costs of the Belknap projects to which they were obligated. (In the years immediately following Carroll's administration, the Mellon Foundation made important grants to university presses, including $250,000 to Harvard University Press.)

Three of the less obvious factors in the deficits were: (1) the requirement that old unsalable inventory be written off as a dead loss, (2) interest on debt, and (3) the computer nightmare.

The inventory write-offs have often been misunderstood.

Publishing is a manufacturing industry. Manufacturers commonly borrow from banks to finance the production of their goods. The Press's banker is the University. The Press draws from the Harvard treasurer what it needs to finance its operations, and the withdrawals, minus the deposits of Press income, constitute a revolving debt which is secured mainly by the value of the inventory. Manufactured goods that are not sold have to be considered a loss. The Press's long-established method of recording such losses was to write off the total cost of unsold Press-owned books during the sixth year after publication. To provide enough funds to cover expected write-offs, the Press made monthly transfers into an inventory reserve account. Such transfers were expenses, and, like other expenses, were entered into the calculations of profit or loss at the end of each fiscal year.

Concerning the half-million-dollar deficit of 1970–71, word got around at the Press that most of it was due to write-offs. Indeed, a Harvard student newspaper quoted a Press executive to that effect in 1972.[19] The write-off was sometimes said to have been more than $300,000. This was a mistake, which may have occurred through a misinterpretation of a statement in an auditors' report for 1970–71. Press records (and the auditors' report itself) show that the write-off amount actually charged to expenses was $96,000.[20] This was the highest that had been paid up to that time; but the write-off expense in the Carroll period was not vastly larger than it had been under Wilson. The heaviest write-offs came later, as a result of increased output in the Carroll period; in fact, the heaviest expense the Press has ever had for this purpose, $295,000 in a single year, came in 1976–77, six years after the record output of 1970–71.[21]

A weightier factor in the deficits was the payment of interest. Just as the federal budget includes a large sum for interest on the national debt, the Press's expenditures include interest on all but $500,000 of its revolving debt to the University for working capital, and this interest took a violent leap in the Carroll years. In the year of the $548,200 deficit, the Press paid $144,500 interest on the debt. During the four years in which the total deficit was $1,162,000, the interest was $471,600. During the previous four-year period it had been only $133,800. The reason, of course, was that the debt itself expanded rapidly as the Press drew heavily upon the University for expense money and restored less from income than anybody expected. The debt, which in the sixties had fluctuated just above and below $1 million, was increasing in Wilson's last year or so; and under Carroll it kept rising until it passed $3 million in 1970–71 and hit $3,436,000 in June 1972. (In June 1982 it was $2,107,000.)

The computer troubles are not so easy to put into dollar terms, but they caused much expense and at the same time interfered with sales.

The expanding Press under Wilson, needing more efficiency in handling the enormous amount of paperwork, gradually made more use of the Harvard Computing Center, an agency which, like the Press, came under the jurisdiction of Vice-President Wiggins. The Press under Carroll wanted to acquire a computer of its own, but Wiggins said no. The Computing Center was in even worse financial trouble than the Press was about to be in, and it badly needed the Press's business. So the Press, flooded with book orders and having nowhere else to go, took a plunge and agreed to transfer all its invoicing functions and inventory record-keeping to the Computing Center.[22]

To estimate the final net cost of this arrangement—its advantages and disadvantages as compared with alternative systems—is too complicated for this narrative. At least the actual payments to the Computing Center are precisely known. The Center's records show that from February 1968 through June 1972, the Press paid the Center $266,000. Of this, $86,000 was for systems analysis and programming, and $180,000 for computer usage and data handling. In the single year 1969–70, when the Press's deficit was $220,900, its payments to the Center came to $104,000.

The computer problem also had indirect costs. When the system was put into operation in the summer of 1969, it contained so many bugs that for many months the shipment of books from the Press's warehouse was extremely ragged. There was an appalling backlog of orders, and complaints from customers swamped the sales department. Morale at the Press suffered. The business staff, instead of being reduced by the addition of an electronic system, had to be greatly increased so as to put book orders into suitable form, first for the warehouse and then for the Computing Center.

Attempts were made to improve relations between the Press and the Computing Center, but the two organizations deeply distrusted each other, and anyhow the facts of life were against them. The art of applying computer technology to business was then at an early stage. Furthermore, at any stage—even in the 1980s—difficulties have not been unusual. The troubles at Harvard University Press were a classic case. The Press had no experience in building data-processing systems. The Computing Center had little experience with business procedures, much less with publishing procedures.[23]

Christopher Burns, Carroll's assistant, recommended a commercial firm, Technical Impex Corporation, of Lawrence, Massachusetts, which had both a computer and a warehouse, and which already served some publishing clients. Burns and Carroll engaged that firm to handle the paperback series that they started in the spring of 1971.

The meeting of the Board of Directors on May 7, at which Carroll was instructed to prepare a break-even budget, was the signal for the start, or at least a sharp intensification, of an economy wave that shook the Press from top to bottom.

Three days after the meeting, Carroll announced to the Syndics that the Press, along with many other presses, was in difficulties and that the financial situation necessitated a change of policy—namely, that fewer manuscripts would be presented to the board without "expectation of sales or financial support sufficient to allow the Press to break even."[24] This new policy created unfamiliar duties for the specialist editors. When recommending a manuscript they had to attach a budget sheet, showing in one column the anticipated income (that is, the number of copies expected to be sold, multiplied by the retail price as reduced by discounts) and in the other column the manufacturing cost as estimated by the production department, plus costs of overhead, royalties, and advertising. The idea was to make the income and the costs come out even—on paper at least.

The whole Press was asked to suggest ways to save money, and a list of twenty-seven suggestions was circulated.[25] The annual dinner and free books for the Nieman Fellows were discontinued. Telephone extensions were reduced in number; long-distance calls were discouraged. The Press's delegation to the annual meeting of the Association of American University Presses was almost eliminated. *The Browser* was abolished, to the dismay of many who felt that this widely read instrument of sales and public relations was killed at the very time the Press needed it most.

The important step of hiring an Operations Manager was already in the works, for the Board of Directors had agreed that Carroll should look for "an appropriate person to supervise and control the entire range of business activity from receipt of order to shipment of books, together with ancillary activities."[26] Now Carroll also went ahead with a plan for the University's auditors to analyze Press operations.[27]

New Faces

Derek Curtis Bok succeeded Nathan Pusey as president of Harvard on July 1, 1971, moving up from the deanship of the Law School. Before he took office he learned about the large Press deficits from the outgoing Gard Wiggins. During the crowded time of transition, neither Bok nor Carroll approached the other to discuss the causes of the deficits or anything else about the Press. The president left the matter to the Board of Directors and especially to his new administrative vice-president, Stephen S. J. Hall.

Stephen Hall automatically became chairman of the Board of Directors, succeeding Wiggins. He was one of two newcomers to the board in 1971, the other being George Hall, treasurer of Little, Brown, who was appointed at Carroll's suggestion and who became the first non-Harvard member.

The idea of putting the Press under the administrative vice-president did not originate with Bok; the arrangement had begun in the Conant administration. But by 1971 the university press movement in America was almost a century old and there was a solid tradition of resistance to anything that seemed to downgrade the presses' educational mission. A few years before, a handbook published for the Association of American University Presses had contained this statement: "Long experience has shown that lodging the press anywhere else in the university than in the president's lap spells trouble. No other officer combines the breadth of vision of the university's function with the authority to commit the large sums that a press requires. The most common tempting alternative—to place the press, which superficially resembles a business operation, in the hands of the university's business officers—has proven the most destructive."[28]

Stephen Hall joined Harvard after a rapid rise in the Sheraton Corporation and the International Telephone & Telegraph Corporation. At Harvard, like his predecessors Edward Reynolds and Gard Wiggins, he supervised nonteaching agencies, namely Food Services, Buildings & Grounds, Insurance & Real Estate, the Faculty Club, Purchasing, the Police, Personnel, Planning, the Printing Office—and the Press. For this group Hall established stricter and more centralized management controls than had existed before. Each agency was required to prepare a five-year Management Plan, including a budget for the first year with forecasts by months, and then to submit every month a two-page progress report. The heads of the agencies were held accountable for performance, and they met with Hall each week to discuss matters. Carroll soon stopped going, after which the Press was represented by David Horne and later by Brian Murphy.

Hall maintained that the system worked well with one exception, namely that Carroll did not want to be a member of the team and did not cooperate.[29] "Of all those agencies," Hall told me, "the Press was the only one I didn't know anything about. I had never published a book. The Press didn't fit into that group. Mark knew that. I knew that. It was an awkward relationship. But it was up to us to work it out." Hall said Carroll never submitted management-planning reports in a form he could use. To Hall, it seemed that Carroll "took it upon himself to be the standard bearer of academic freedom and freedom of the Press with this new administration." Hall disclaimed any desire to tell Carroll how to run the book publishing operation, but said he did tell Carroll that the Press's freedom could be preserved only if its management was perceived by the University's decision makers as knowing what it was doing. If the *goal* was to lose half a million, that was one thing, "but don't tell us you're going to make money and then surprise us with that kind of deficit. We have to look at the whole operation and find out why it's losing and correct the holes." The Board of Directors, Hall said, could not get Carroll to give them the data to do that. "Mark had some real problems. He was caught in the middle on using the Computing Center. We knew that and offered to help." On the deficit problems, "all he had to do was come in and say, 'You know, Steve, if we could form a little committee'— we'd have stood up and cheered." Hall summarized thus: "In any company that Mark would ever work for, he wouldn't have lasted three weeks with that attitude. But the board wanted very much to see Mark succeed, and so it went on for six months."

From Carroll's point of view, Hall's methods and demands were inappropriate and unworkable in scholarly publishing. He believed that the publisher's role was to preserve and develop culture and that the energies and talents involved could not be completely converted to repetitive procedures. The operations were not susceptible to ordinary cost accounting because the results of a given investment could not be predicted with certainty and because "the intellectual dimension cannot be translated into a line item for financial statements."[30] He felt that Hall's general approach was to divide manuscripts into winners and losers and that this approach, along with the requirement of monthly budgets, created an impossible situation. It was true that he did not want to be a part of Hall's team, for he not only lacked respect for Hall's management ideas but also thought the Press should be answerable directly to the president. It was also true that he saw himself as a standard bearer, not only defending the autonomy of the Press but standing up for academic publishers in general.

Then there was the personal factor. Some observers in the University have always believed that both Hall and Carroll acted stubbornly and self-righteously and that the contest between these two unbending individuals was the most telling factor in the whole affair. At any rate, Hall and Carroll antagonized each other from the start.

At the Board of Directors meeting of October 1, 1971, Chairman Hall reported that President Bok wanted a realistic budget, without surprises. Other board members expressed the same desire. This also was the meeting at which Carroll, with Hall's concurrence, recommended the hiring of Brian Murphy as Operations Manager. The board agreed.

Murphy was a New Yorker, at that time with Harper & Row as assistant vice-president for operations. Carroll found him through an executive employment agency. Murphy had twenty-five years of experience at three publishing houses. From 1946 to 1964 he was at Harcourt, Brace & Company, where he became operations manager, and from 1964 to 1967 he was at McGraw-Hill, where one of his titles was general manager of systems. After four years at Harper & Row, he joined the Press in October 1971, and the Board of Directors almost immediately began looking to him for facts, forecasts, and recommendations. (Later, in the administration of Arthur J. Rosenthal, Murphy became Associate Director for Operations.)

By the autumn of 1971 Carroll was finding a more receptive attitude toward his desire to break away from the Harvard Computing Center. The commercial firm Technical Impex was already handling the paperback program. Now the auditors who were studying Press operations recommended consideration of Technical Impex for all of the Press's books and estimated a saving of more than $200,000 a year. Murphy looked the firm over and favored the shift. The idea was for the Press to make use not only of the firm's computer but also of its warehouse in Lawrence. In other words, Technical Impex would take over most of the books, the shipping, invoicing, and record keeping, and the Press could abolish its shipping department and dispose of its own warehouse, which Murphy thought was very inefficient. Vice-President Hall approved the action and so did the rest of the Board of Directors.[31]

Thus, Murphy's first big task was to supervise the transfer of the

43. Brian Murphy, who was hired by Mark Carroll as Operations Manager in October 1971. The picture was taken in 1985 when he was Associate Director for Operations. Behind him is the Loeb Classical Library.

Press's order processing and more than a million books to a site some twenty-five miles north. The operation began in December 1971. It met with various delays (the shipping department was being asked to ship itself out of existence) and was still going on after Carroll departed. The University bought the Press's warehouse for $317,000, which was put into a reserve fund for use in building a new warehouse later. The arrangement between the Press and Technical Impex lasted until 1976 and was an improvement, but never entirely satisfactory.

The financial stress of Carroll's last few months stimulated some other novel events.

In January 1972 the Press held a cut-rate sale of books in Memorial Hall. This drew eager crowds and brought in more than $50,000.

That same month the Board of Syndics, which had not had to give a thought to financial affairs since the birth of the Board of Directors twenty-five years earlier, officially lent a hand in the retrenchment effort. A possible role for the Syndics had been discussed at a rather gloomy joint meeting of the Directors and Syndics the previous November—attended also by some members of the Press staff, who were shocked by the statements made by Stephen Hall and others concerning the Press's condition. In January, at the request of the Directors, the Syndics when accepting manuscripts began rating them according to scholarly worth, that is, pronouncing them either "exceptional" or "acceptable." The Press obligated itself to publish the "exceptional" ones but not the merely "acceptable" ones if management believed that it would lose money on them.[32] (As it happened, the Press published all the books in both categories.)

The Explosion

While all this was going on in the winter of 1971–72, Carroll's personal standing with the Harvard authorities was not improving.

Stephen Hall told the Board of Directors that Carroll had to be replaced. The faculty men on the board told Hall to go slow; they wanted to make their own investigations. In January, Bok and Carroll met face to face. It was their first real talk. Neither man considered it satisfying. Apparently the president continued to be puzzled about the large deficits and was even more puzzled that he could get little explanation or comment from the Press Director. Meanwhile the members of the Board of Directors were informally questioning Syndics and others, though not letting on that Carroll's job was in peril. Finally the directors gathered in a private dining room at the Business School, without Stephen Hall, and unanimously decided that the Press needed a change of management. Hall and Bok were notified. Bok agreed that the action was necessary. He thought he himself should give the news to Carroll with no one else present. An appointment was set up for Friday, February 18.

In retrospect it appears that three considerations were uppermost in Harvard's decision to replace Mark Carroll: (1) the large and continuing deficits, (2) Carroll's failure to see them coming, and (3) a belief that Carroll was somehow immobilized or that at least he was not a team player and was not adequately cooperating with the University administration to turn the Press around.

The public announcement of the action was badly handled. Both sides seemed uncertain over who was to release the news, and when, and how. A week passed before anything got into print, at which time there was much excitement and confusion. The University never clearly explained its side of the affair in a public statement. The role of the Board of Directors was not publicly mentioned. The public knew only that Carroll had been suddenly fired, and many people in and around Harvard assumed that the firing was "brutal" and that the cause of scholarly publishing had fallen victim to an attempt to run the Press like a hotel chain.

Ironically, the impression of brutality was enhanced by a desire *not* to be brutal. Obviously, Bok did not intend the action to look like a firing. Just as obviously, he did not wish to engage in public criticism of Carroll, then or later. When Bok asked Carroll to resign, Carroll wanted no part of the fiction, but somehow this was not immediately grasped by the president. Carroll asked to be allowed to write the announcement, and Bok agreed. Carroll then went to Philadelphia for a week on a previously scheduled vacation, not telling anyone at the Press what had happened. During the week he telephoned to the president's office a short statement in which he said he had been terminated. Bok apparently was surprised by the wording but found nothing essentially inaccurate in it. On February 24, Stephen Hall visited the Press and read Carroll's statement aloud at a hurriedly called meeting. The next day, Carroll had the statement circulated to the whole staff under date of February 25, with only minor changes.

The statement said: "A week ago today, in his office, President Bok informed me that he no longer wished me to be Director of the Press and that my duties would be terminated effective immediately. Until a successor can be selected, he has appointed David Horne Acting Director, with the intention also that Brian Murphy shall be in charge of all business affairs."

The University's own announcement in the *Harvard University Gazette* on February 25 mentioned neither a firing nor a resignation. It said simply that Horne had become Acting Director, replacing Carroll, and that Murphy would continue to supervise business affairs. Stephen Hall was quoted thus: "The Press, like most University presses in the country, is going through hard times. The basic direction of the Press will continue to be, as it has always been, to pursue its objective of publishing scholarly books. But we must minimize our losses in order to keep up standards."

The daily papers printed incomplete and muddled stories under headlines like "Harvard Drops Mark Carroll, Director of University Press" and "Bok Dismisses University Press Head." The president began receiving letters of surprise, disappointment, and anger. Carroll himself received at least ninety letters, most of them expressing outrage.[33] A group of Syndics, miffed because they had not been consulted about the dismissal or notified in advance of the announcement, visited Bok at his home, where he was recovering from an ankle injury. The dismissal was a hot topic in the Harvard community; some people even speculated that the Press was about to go under. In the absence of information about the circumstances, there was a tendency to make Stephen Hall a symbol of Carroll's misfortunes and to assume that the Press was being taken over by money men.

Lyman Butterfield, editor-in-chief of the Adams Papers, wrote in "astonishment and dismay" that the action would certainly be injurious to Harvard and maybe catastrophic for the Press, and that the scholarly community throughout the nation would consider it high-handed and unjust. Walter Muir Whitehill told Bok that "the abruptness of Mark Carroll's unexplained dismissal seems more in the spirit of a Peruvian military dictatorship than of Harvard University." Howard Mumford Jones, former editor-in-chief of the John Harvard Library, who had been a close associate of Press Directors Malone, Wilson, and Carroll, told the president: "In my thirty-six years of experience here I have never seen so coarse, brutal, and unwarranted an action." Jones, in a letter to the Press, asked for cancellation of the contract for a book he was writing; but David Horne and Maud Wilcox argued eloquently against this, and eventually the press did publish the book—*Revolution and Romanticism.*[34]

The Press staff did not believe the rumors that the institution was going under, and they continued to work hard at publishing books; nevertheless there was much confusion and resentment among them, and in fact morale was so bad that Bok found it desirable to meet with about fifteen leading staff members, without Stephen Hall in attendance. They questioned him rather sharply. Bok said that his administration did not regard the Press as purely a business venture, that the Press over the years had played a leading role in the teaching and research functions of the University, that he was determined to support the Press, and that he thought the administrative difficulties were in the process of being resolved.[35] Presumably he spoke in the same vein to the Syndics. He issued no public statements.

The Association of American University Presses saw the Harvard upheaval as an omen of peril for all. William B. Harvey, director of the University of Florida Press and president of the Association, wrote Bok that the dismissal appeared to be an unseemly action that would reflect no credit on Harvard or upon scholarly publishing. Herbert S. Bailey, Jr., director of Princeton University Press, who was about to succeed Harvey as president of the Association, told Bok he was "stunned" at the news. Bailey said he was aware that Harvard University Press had suffered severe financial losses the year before, "as did nearly all university presses including Princeton," but it seemed to him that the Press had taken the necessary steps to turn itself around and was on the way to recovery.[36]

Within the Association there was a debate on what to do about the Carroll firing. Some press directors urged the officers of the Association to visit Derek Bok and insist upon a full explanation. Others thought this would do no good or would be inappropriate. Carroll ended the controversy with a letter to Harvey, in which he said he did not believe that an investigation of Harvard by the Association would be beneficial to Harvard, to himself, the Association, or its member presses. He did not see that any findings could be used with authority either at Harvard or elsewhere. He suggested instead a broad effort to review and strengthen the place of university presses in their institutions and in the publishing firmament. Harvey congratulated Carroll for statesmanship.[37]

Thereupon the Association passed two resolutions at its annual meeting in June 1972, a meeting whose main theme was the financial crisis of the university presses. One resolution said that whereas it was the judgment of the Association that Carroll's "directed resignation" had "the appearance of abruptness and an erroneous interpretation and exercise of the authority under which a scholarly press ought to function," the Association wished to express its esteem and affection for him. The other resolution, in line with Carroll's suggestion, instructed one of the standing committees to study the administrative relations of member presses to their university officers and to recommend guidelines of university responsibility "that are imperative to reduce and remove the threats increasingly posed to scholarly publishing."[38] The committee's work resulted in a pamphlet adopted by the Association a year later, entitled "Reciprocal Responsibilities of a University and Its Press." This document was considered so important by the university presses that it has been reprinted (as amended) each year in the Association's Directory.

In language very like that used at Harvard by Dumas Malone and Ralph Barton Perry in the thirties and forties, the Association said, "A university press exists to publish works of scholarship, and its purposes are therefore essentially academic, closely related to the educational aims of the parent institution. It should not be confused with auxiliary enterprises such as athletic programs, dormitory management, and food services." Because a press is "an academic function of the university to which it belongs," it should receive support of all kinds—"intellectual support, financial support, and support in the form of services and plant"—and, like libraries, "should be protected as far as possible from short-term budgetary fluctuations." If a press reports to an individual administrative officer, that officer should have both academic and fiscal authority.

A press, too, has responsibilities, and the statement spelled them out. One of the duties of the press director is "to manage all publishing operations with such efficiency that the cost of press operations remains within budget." The management of a university press "may be more difficult than that of a commercial publishing enterprise." The officers of a press should have publishing experience that will enable them to cope with their special problems. To handle them successfully, a press must be organized "as if it were a business."[39]

Meanwhile Harvard continued Carroll's salary until July 1972, when he was appointed chief of professional publications at the National Park Service in Washington. In 1978 he became the founding president of a new organization, the Society for Scholarly Publishing, which includes commercial as well as academic publishers.

The Interregnum of 1972

President Bok appointed a committee to search for the next leader of the Press. It was only the second search committee for a Press Director in Harvard's history; the first had found Thomas Wilson. Bok appointed five men—two from the Board of Directors, two from the Board of Syndics, and one from the Press's Visiting Committee. This gave him an opportunity to show his regard for the importance of the Syndics, who had been left out of the deliberations on Mark Carroll.

One of the Syndics on the search committee became its chairman. This was James Q. Wilson, professor of government and Press author.

During the interregnum, Wilson also acted as chairman of the Board of Syndics for purposes other than that of presiding over the monthly meetings to consider manuscripts. He acted as liaison between the Syndics and the search committee, and in the Harvard community he was an effective force in allaying people's worries and fears about the Press.

While the search committee was at work, the Press had two Acting Directors in succession, David Horne and Oscar Handlin.

Horne moved up from Associate Director on February 24, 1972, the day Stephen Hall notified the Press that Carroll was gone. Horne announced his own resignation a month later in order to accept an offer as director of the University Press of New England, a consortium

44. Oscar Handlin, historian and author, active in the service of the Press.

of New England universities, based at Dartmouth College.[40] He left Harvard on May 15, having been at the Press about six and a half years. During his brief term as Acting Director, he and Brian Murphy were in effect comanagers of the Press, Murphy having the financial control and full responsibility for business operations.

The historian Oscar Handlin now entered yet another phase of his Harvard University Press involvement, which had started with the publication of *Boston's Immigrants* thirty-one years before. There was no Associate Director to take over from Horne; the search committee was just getting organized; the Press was still shivering from the blows it had taken and could use all the solidity and prestige that it could get. Someone suggested, "Why not choose a big-name professor?" President Bok turned to Handlin.

Handlin served as part-time Acting Director from mid-May to early October of 1972. Maud Wilcox, a constant stalwart of the Press during all the troubles, was named Acting Executive Editor, with full responsibility under Handlin for the editorial operation. Thus, after fifteen years in the editorial department, she replaced David Horne in the top position. She also took over his role as secretary to the Board of Syndics. And she continued to perform the function of Humanities Editor.

In the summer of 1972 the Press was almost sixty years old and moving into a new and unknown stage. The passing of the Old Regime was neatly symbolized on June 30. On that date Grace A. Briggs, who had handled copyrights and permissions for as long as anyone could remember, and who had been Assistant Business Manager among other things, retired after thirty-five years of service. On that same date Joseph Elder, the Science Editor, retired after twenty-four years in that job. Warren Smith and Eleanor Dobson Kewer had already left, Smith in 1967 after forty-three years and Mrs. Kewer in 1970 after thirty-four years. The Sales Manager, Loring Lincoln, was due for retirement in 1973 after twenty-eight years. Thus, five people together gave more than a century and a half of service, joining the Press when it was small and immature and helping to preserve its standards during the good and bad times of its middle decades.

The New Regime soon began taking shape. The search committee came up with a Director who delighted President Bok—a successful New York publisher who had made a specialty of publishing books by scientists and scholars, and who had sold his company and was ready for a new venture. This was Arthur J. Rosenthal, fifty-three years old, the founder of Basic Books.

Rosenthal's name was suggested by Simon Michael Bessie of Atheneum Publishers, who was the new chairman of the Visiting Committee and a member of the search committee. Rosenthal's appointment was announced at the end of August 1972, and he took office on October 1.

So the Carroll administration was over, and the Rosenthal administration was beginning. But the showdown with Carroll and the uproar that he caused by refusing to go quietly were not soon forgotten. Besides the general pain and the personal disaster for Carroll and the damage to Harvard's reputation, the affair had some effects of a different sort.

The effect on the community of university presses has already been described. The Association of American University Presses, in its statement on reciprocal responsibilities, put into words the dual nature of a university press. That is, a university press is "an academic function" which must be organized and run "as if it were a business."

At Harvard, too, there was a heightened awareness of Harvard University Press and the importance of reconciling its dual nature. In the past, more than once, the educational mission and the need for sound business management had seemed to come into conflict, es-

45. Arthur J. Rosenthal (left), who became Director in 1972, and President Derek Bok, who appointed him. They are pictured in May 1981 at a party celebrating Rosenthal's winning of the Curtis Benjamin Award for innovation and creativity in publishing, given by the Association of American Publishers.

pecially when external conditions had gone wrong. A firmer agreement on the nature of a university press might have made some of the troubles avoidable.

During the centuries since the first printing press arrived in North America, the publishing of books by Harvard has taken several forms, and the maturing of the central publishing department, even after 1913, has been a slow and erratic process. President Eliot founded the Printing Office and Publication Office, and would have founded a more fully organized university press if the financial means had been available. President Lowell wanted a university press, but only with misgivings did he agree to start one, because he feared that it would not be self-supporting—and it wasn't. President Conant tried to abolish the Press because he did not think the University should be "in business." But he failed, and the University in the second half of his administration strengthened the Press instead, recognizing for the first time the need for making ample funds available for working capital. President Pusey had no financial worries about the Press until the very end of his tenure. President Bok inherited a crisis during which Harvard gained some additional experience with academic publishing. He told the new Director in 1972 that he wanted the best scholarly press and also a very professional press and saw no reason why the two purposes should interfere with each other.

One result of the 1972 uproar, though a delayed one, was that the Harvard administration became persuaded that the Press ought not to be grouped with service agencies such as Buildings & Grounds, Police, and Printing Office under the supervision of the vice-president for administration. No change was made at that time, but it is clear now that the reason for the delay was that the administration thought the change would be unfair to Vice-President Stephen Hall. It would have been perceived as a rebuke to him, a personal rebuke that the administration had no wish to make. So the change took place in 1976, when Hall left Harvard. The Press was put directly under the president. Professor Handlin replaced Hall as chairman of the Board of Directors, and the board welcomed a new member—Derek Bok.

Notes

1. Antecedents and Founding

1. The story of that first printing press has been written many times, in various versions. See esp. Samuel Eliot Morison, *The Founding of Harvard College* (Harvard University Press, 1935), 255–256, 342–348, 379–380; and George Parker Winship, *The Cambridge Press, 1638–1692* (Philadelphia: University of Pennsylvania Press, 1945), 1–20.

2. Glover's first name appears about six ways on documents, including Joseph, Jose, and Jesse. A transcript of his will in Middlesex County courthouse, Cambridge, Mass., folio 6, 1653–1655, begins "I Josse Glover." Day was sometimes spelled Daye.

3. Winship speculated that Glover might have brought along a trained printer who also died on the voyage (*Cambridge Press*, 9, 14–15). The case for Matthew Day as North America's first printer was put forward with much assurance by John Clyde Oswald, *Printing in the Americas* (New York: Gregg Publishing, 1937), 1, 40–52.

4. Dunster was unable to get from the Massachusetts authorities a clear definition of his legal responsibilities under Glover's will, and in 1656, after a great deal of litigation, a court decided that the printing press and certain other properties were parts of the estate and that Dunster's stepson John Glover must be compensated for them. Besides Glover's will, pertinent handwritten documents include: Henry Dunster's petition to Massachusetts General Court (Oct. 10, 1652) in Harvard University Archives, Henry Dunster Papers, folder dated 1652–1655; Middlesex County Records, vol. 1, entries in 1656 for April 1, May 9, June 19, and esp. June 24 (pp. 77–78, 82, 83, 87–90); also an undated document in folio 12 headed "Mr. Dunster's Demands," evidently related to court sessions of May 9 and June 19. Some useful passages in secondary sources: Winship, *Cambridge Press*, 43–44, 45, 126–129, 130–132, 139–145; S. E. Morison, *Harvard College in the Seventeenth Century*, vol. 1 (Harvard University Press, 1936), 315–317, 345; Isaiah Thomas, *The History of Printing in America*, ed. Marcus A. McCorison (New York: Weathervane Books, 1970; orig. pub. 1810), 43–49.

5. William C. Kiessel, "The Green Family a Dynasty of Printers," *New England Historical and Genealogical Register* (April 1950), esp. 81–82.

6. Winship, *Cambridge Press*, 127, 131.

7. On the origins of publishing in America see Lawrence C. Wroth, "The Booktrade Organization in the Colonial Period," in Hellmut Lehmann-Haupt, Ruth Shepard Granniss, and Lawrence C. Wroth, *The Book in America* (New York: R. R. Bowker, 1939), 43–44.

8. Apparently the only printing in Cambridge between 1692 and 1800 took place from May 1775 to April 1776, when Samuel Hall produced a patriotic newspaper in Harvard Yard, the *New-England Chronicle,* Cambridge's first newspaper. See C. S. Brigham, *History and Bibliography of American Newspapers, 1690–1820,* vol. 1 (Worcester, Mass.: American Antiquarian Society, 1947), 353, 394–396; S. E. Morison, *Three Centuries of Harvard* (Harvard University Press, 1936), 148–151; Thomas, *History of Printing,* 176–178, 274–275.

9. On the library catalogue see Harvard Corporation Records, Oct. 3, 1722, and Dec. 25, 1723; Charles Evans, *American Bibliography,* vol. 1 (New York: Peter Smith, 1941; orig. pub. 1912), 319. The Corporation Records of 1734 and 1735 are full of the Monis project.

10. Madeleine B. Stern devotes a chapter to Hilliard as a bookseller in her *Imprints on History: Book Publishers and American Frontiers* (Bloomington: Indiana University Press, 1956), 24–44. John Tebbel, in *A History of Book Publishing in the United States,* vol. 1 (R. R. Bowker, 1972), 415–416, 442–443, 446, brings out Hilliard's influence but gets the dates confused and is completely wrong about the founding of the University Press.

11. C. F. Swift, ed., *Genealogical Notes of Barnstable Families,* a reprint of the Amos Otis Papers (Barnstable, Mass., 1888), 69–70.

12. Harvard University, "Quinquennial Catalogue, 1636–1930." Births and deaths of the various Hilliards are in Swift, *Genealogical Notes,* and Thomas W. Baldwin, comp., *Vital Records of Cambridge, Massachusetts, to the Year 1850,* 2 vols. (Boston, 1914, 1915).

13. Sketch of Pearson by Claude M. Fuess in *Dictionary of American Biography;* also Morison, *Three Centuries of Harvard,* 159, 188–190.

14. On the establishment of the University Press see not only Corporation Records of April and October 1802 but also Pearson's notes in Corporation Papers, folder dated 1800–1803. On procurement of equipment see Joseph Willard to Ebenezer Storer, May 20, 1802, in College Papers, 1st series, IV, 41; also Overseers' Records, IV, 367–368, 391–392. The "Corporation Records" in the University Archives are the minutes of Corporation meetings; they should not be confused with "Corporation Papers" and "College Papers."

15. Corporation Records, Oct. 25, 1802; also *A Check List of Massachusetts Imprints, 1802,* prepared by the American Imprints Inventory Project (Works Projects Administration) in Massachusetts (Boston, 1942), esp. 19–20, 69, 111, 117.

16. William Hilliard to Corporation, April 16, 1813, College Papers, 1st series, VII, 49.

17. Sources on Eliab Metcalf: Joseph T. Buckingham in *Boston Evening Transcript,* Oct. 1, 1859; Frederick Lewis Weis, "Michael Metcalf of Dedham, Mas-

sachusetts, and Some of His Descendants" (1940), typewritten manuscript at American Antiquarian Society, 233–234.

18. For example, the title page of Jacob Bigelow's *American Medical Botany,* the first American book with printed color plates, issued in three volumes beginning in 1817, named Cummings & Hilliard as publisher and the University Press as printer. Richard J. Wolfe, in his *Jacob Bigelow's American Medical Botany, 1817–1821* (Boston: Bird & Bull Press and Boston Medical Library, 1979), 90, concludes that Bigelow himself should be considered the real publisher.

19. Hilliard to Corporation, April 16, 1813, College Papers, 1st series, VII, 49.

20. Corporation Records, Oct. 18, 1827, summarizing the actions of a committee, consisting of Nathaniel Bowditch, Francis Calley Gray, and Ebenezer Francis, which had been empowered to put an end to the University Press contract or modify it as they saw fit.

21. Corporation to Harvard's Board of Overseers, Corporation Records, Jan. 17, 1828; Overseers' Records, VII, 405–417, esp. 412. Another statement on Harvard's financial upheaval, including the sale of the Press, is that of Treasurer Ebenezer Francis, Dec. 20, 1827, in College Papers, 2nd series, II, 169–172.

22. Max Hall, "Cambridge as Printer and Publisher: Fame, Oblivion, and Fame Again," *Proceedings of the Cambridge Historical Society* 44 (1985), esp. table entitled "Publishers and Printers of Harvard's Earliest Annual Catalogues in Book Form, 1819 to 1883."

23. Marshall T. Bigelow, "The University Press at Cambridge," *Harvard Register* (June 1881), 348–349.

24. *Stephen Daye and His Successors, 1639–1921,* a company history published by the University Press in 1921. More on the University Press is told in Hall, "Cambridge as Printer and Publisher."

25. Stern, *Imprints on History,* 342, 352, 356, and esp. 386. The earliest university press on her list was Cornell University Press, dated 1869, but elsewhere she explained that it was discontinued in 1884 and reestablished in 1930.

26. Richard Macksey, "Shadows of Scholars, 1878–1978," in "One Hundred Years of Scholarly Publishing" (pamphlet, Johns Hopkins University Press, 1978). Macksey, after saying the press customarily marks its beginning in 1878 (pp. 1, 4), adds on page 4: "It is probably more accurate, however, to speak of the evolution of this Press rather than of its founding, since at Johns Hopkins it acquired only gradually the features of what would today be considered a 'university press.' " Its first publication was a periodical; its first book came out in 1882; it began calling itself The Johns Hopkins Press in 1890 and The Johns Hopkins University Press in 1972.

27. Peter Sutcliffe, *The Oxford University Press: An Informal History* (Oxford: Clarendon Press, 1978), xiii, xiv, xviii.

28. M. H. Black, *Cambridge University Press, 1584–1984* (Cambridge: Cambridge University Press, 1984), foreword and appendix.

29. See report of Sept. 28, 1857, by a faculty committee headed by Professor Francis Bowen, College Papers, 2nd series, XXIV, 219–223. (The report is erroneously dated in the College Papers; its true date appears in Faculty Records,

XV, 174.) See also Faculty Records, 1869–1872, p. 297; and 1872–1874, pp. 88–91.

30. The first head of this printing office was William H. Wheeler; he was succeeded around 1878 by Gustave Weinschenk. On Wheeler see Cambridge City Directories, 1875–1880; and Frank T. Hull et al., "The Printing Art," *Cambridge Tribune*, May 9, 1914. On cost of printing office: University Archives, Treasurer's Statement, 1872–73, pp. 35, 37. On job printing for Harvard: Printing Office Account Book, May 1878–Sept. 1879, University Archives UAV 713.202. On Weinschenk: City Directories, 1878 et seq. The approximate date of the move to University Hall was established by Weinschenk's office address in City Directories of 1889 and 1890.

31. Macksey, "Shadows of Scholars," 5.

32. Corporation Records, Sept. 30, Nov. 30, Dec. 16, 1885; and May 24, 1886.

33. Arthur E. Sutherland, *The Law at Harvard* (The Belknap Press of Harvard University Press, 1967), 197–198.

34. Title pages of the Harvard Oriental Series after the first volume say "Published by Harvard University," but apparently this meant only that the books could be ordered from the Publication Office and were edited and financed from Harvard. As late as 1912 the Harvard Publication Office continued to list the series as "published by Ginn & Company." The formal transfer to Harvard University Press seems to have taken place around 1915.

35. "A.P." [Arthur Perrin], obituary of Williams in *Harvard College, Class of 1877: 40th Anniversary Report* (1917), 311–314.

36. Ibid., 312.

37. W. Warren Smith, memo to me, Oct. 17, 1979. Gustave Weinschenk had left Harvard for Ginn & Co. in 1892—see Thomas Bonaventure Lawler, *Seventy Years of Textbook Publishing: A History of Ginn & Company* (Boston: Ginn, 1938), 89; and Weinschenk's address in Cambridge City Directories, 1892 and 1893—and had been succeeded as head of the Printing Office by his son, Frederick William Weinschenk, who was succeeded by Wilson.

38. Adam K. Wilson, "Harvard College Printing Office," July 1900, in University Archives, "Chest of 1900."

39. James Loeb in *Harvard College, Class of 1888: Secretary's Report No. V* (February 1905), 61. For biographical sketches of Loeb see obituary by Fred Bates Lund in *Harvard College, Class of 1888: 50th Anniversary Report* (1938), 206–211; and entry by Ashton Rollins Sanborn in *Dictionary of American Biography*.

40. C. E. Norton to D. B. Updike, Nov. 20, 1903 (Providence Public Library, Providence, R.I.); Norton to Charles W. Eliot, March 2, 1906 (University Archives, Eliot Papers, box 235).

41. D. B. Updike to C. W. Eliot, March 9 and April 14, 1906; Warren & Smith (Warren's architectural firm) to Updike, April 10, 1906 (Eliot Papers, box 254, Updike folder).

42. The list is in Updike to Eliot, April 14, 1906.

43. Norton to Eliot, March 6, 1906 (box 235).

44. For good descriptions of the spirit of the time, see Ray Nash, *Printing as an Art: A History of the Society of Printers, 1905–1955* (published for the Society by Harvard University Press, 1955), passim, esp. 23–24, 26–33, 37–47, 64.

45. Updike to A. Lawrence Lowell, March 31, 1910; James Loeb to Lowell, Aug. 30, 1910 (University Archives, Lowell Papers, 1909–1914, folder 1348).

46. Mrs. Donald Scott, interview Dec. 12, 1973. On C. C. Lane's early career, see Lane to Dean Byron S. Hurlbut, March 21, 1908 (Eliot Papers, box 224, Lane folder); and Lane's piece in *Harvard College, Class of 1904: Second Report, June, 1910*, p. 177.

47. C. C. Lane in *Harvard College, Class of 1904: 25th Anniversary Report* (1929), 439.

48. *Harvard College, Class of 1904: Fiftieth Anniversary Report* (1954), 271.

49. Publication Office Annual Report, 1911–12 (pp. 229–231 of President's Annual Report); also "The Publications of Harvard University, 1912," a copy of which, annotated by Lane, is in Donald Scott Papers, Harvard Business School Archives. On printing apparatus see correspondence in University Archives, Eliot Papers, box 224, Lane folder; crumbling ledger entitled "H.U. Press—Type and Supplies Purchased 1909–1926" (University Archives, UAV 711.288), 9, 10, 59; Lane to A. L. Lowell, May 3, 1912 (University Archives, Lowell Papers, 1909–1914, folder 1348); and Corporation Records, June 19, 1912.

50. Once, after the Medical School had complained about the cost of printing its catalogue, Lane told President Lowell that if the Medical School could get the bulk of its printing done outside for "less than the prices that we charge," and maintain its quality, "I think it would be a very good argument for the abolition of the printing office and the discharge of the Publication Agent" (Lane to Lowell, Nov. 14, 1910, folder 1348).

51. C. C. Lane to J. D. Greene, April 24, 1909 (Eliot Papers, box 224, Lane folder). To this letter Lane attached a list of nineteen periodicals and series and described their methods of publication. On the importance of the meeting of editors (April 8, 1909) see Harvard University Press, first Annual Report, 1912–13 (pp. 239–241 of President's Annual Report).

52. The costs of the Harvard Historical Studies were paid from the Henry Warren Torrey Fund, established by William M. Prichard. Until 1912 the publisher, who took a commission of 10 percent of the retail price of each book, was Longmans, Green, & Co., of New York. The costs of the Harvard Economic Studies were paid from the David A. Wells Fund and the William H. Baldwin, Jr., 1885 Fund. The publisher until 1912 was Houghton, Mifflin & Co.

53. C. C. Lane to Donald Scott, April 24, 1912, four-page attachment (Donald Scott's files).

54. Ibid.; also Lane to A. L. Lowell, April 8, 1911 (Lowell Papers, 1909–1914, folder 1348).

55. W. Warren Smith, interview Oct. 24, 1973; Smith's memo to me Oct. 17, 1979. On the 1912 takeover see "The Publications of Harvard University, 1912" (Donald Scott Papers); and Publication Office Annual Report, 1911–12.

56. The contract, dated June 14, 1912, is on file at the Press. The Press's name appeared on the cover of the monthly magazine from 1913 to November 1919.

57. Publication Office Annual Reports, 1910–11, 1911–12.

58. The detailed story of the printing and publishing courses appears in Max Hall, "A West Point for Printers," *Harvard Business School Bulletin* (January–February 1979), 12–16, reprinted in *Graphic Arts Monthly* (January 1980), 126–131. The basic first-year course, in which Updike lectured more than anyone else, was held each year except for a year and a half during the World War. The second-year course, which Rogers taught in 1911 and Dwiggins in 1915–16 and 1916–17, was given only four times in all. The other course, called "The History of the Printed Book," was taught by Harvard's Department of Fine Arts and did not involve C. C. Lane, but the Business School instigated it, advertised it as part of the instruction in printing, and paid the professor's salary for the first two or three years.

59. Minutes of the meeting are in folder labeled "Courses—Printing #1," Business School Archives. A copy of the proposal dated March 29, 1912, is in University Archives, UAV 711.232, second folder, unlabeled. Its author was Walter S. Timmis.

60. C. C. Lane, "A Summary of some of the steps in the development of the Harvard University Press," in longhand, bound into vol. 1 of the Minutes of the Press's Board of Syndics.

61. Donald Scott to E. F. Gay, April 22, 1912; Gay to Scott, April 24; C. C. Lane to Scott, April 24. These letters are in Donald Scott Papers, Harvard Business School Archives; so are those cited in the following notes unless otherwise stated. (Scott's own letters in those records are carbon copies; the originals of his letters to Gay are in Gay's files at the Business School.) Sales of Taussig textbook are from Joseph Dorfman, *The Economic Mind in American Civilization*, vol. 4 (New York: Viking, 1959), 211.

62. E. F. Gay to Donald Scott, June 27, 1912; Scott to Gay, July 19.

63. Herbert Heaton, *A Scholar in Action: Edwin F. Gay* (Harvard University Press, 1952), 85.

64. Lane, in "A Summary," listed those who attended. Besides Lowell, Gay, Lane, and Scott, they were professors Kittredge and W. H. Schofield, D. B. Updike, Ellery Sedgwick, J. D. Phillips, and A. W. Shaw.

65. A. L. Lowell to E. H. Wells, Oct. 11, 1912 (University Archives, Lowell Papers, 1909–1914, folder 1462).

66. Donald Scott to Ellery Sedgwick, Oct. 7, 1912.

67. Lowell to Wells, Oct. 11.

68. The committee had no agreed-upon title. Scott and Lane used various wordings. Scott later called it "the committee appointed by Mr. Lowell which founded the Harvard University Press"; see his autobiographical sketch in *Harvard College, Class of 1900: Fiftieth Anniversary Report* (1950), 557.

69. Obituary of Robert Bacon by "H.J." [Henry Jackson], *Harvard College, Class of 1880: Report IX* (1920), 15–18. Other biographies: James Brown Scott, *Robert Bacon: Life and Letters* (Garden City, N.Y.: Doubleday, Page, 1923), and sketch by Montgomery Schuyler in *Dictionary of American Biography*.

70. Lane, "A Summary."

71. Lowell to Scott, Dec. 21, 1912.

72. E. F. Gay to Scott, Dec. 23, 1912. The postscript is on the original letter in Donald Scott Papers, though not on the carbon copy in Dean Gay's own files at the Business School.

73. Among five definitions of "syndic" in the Oxford English Dictionary, the pertinent one is as follows: "One deputed to represent, and transact the affairs of, a corporation, e.g., a university; *spec.* [specifically] in the University of Cambridge, applied to members of special committees of the senate, appointed by grace for specific duties."

74. Letter dated Jan. 20, 1912 (he meant 1913) in University Archives, Lowell Papers, 1909–1914, folder 1462.

2. First Steps under C. C. Lane

1. Throughout this book, in reporting the number of titles published by the Press, I depend on my own estimates, based mainly on the lists appended to the Press Annual Reports, with adjustments for known duplications and mistakes. Such estimating is hardly an exact science. For example, when is a pamphlet to be counted as a "book"? I have tried to judge each case on its merits, not purely on the number of pages. Is a two-volume work one book or two? I have counted it as one if both volumes came out together with exactly the same title. Thus, here and in later chapters, I draw no distinction between the number of "titles" and the number of "books," except that if volumes appeared at different times I counted them separately even if the title was identical. A revised edition is considered a new book; a mere reprinting is not. An "import"—a work originating in another country and given an American edition by the Press—is counted as a new Press book. As for books merely distributed for other organizations, I have not included them in the total numbers of Press books published, even though the distinction between "published" and "distributed" has often been disregarded in the statistics of the Press itself.

2. Items listed in "The Publications of Harvard University, 1912," a copy of which is in Donald Scott Papers, Harvard Business School Archives, plus four books published through the Publication Office in the latter part of 1912.

3. "The Harvard University Press," a printed statement dated June 19, 1913 (Donald Scott Papers).

4. *Harvard Graduates' Magazine* (June 1913), 630–631, 665.

5. The longest-lived of the new series was the Harvard Studies in Romance Languages, volume 1 of which, in 1915, was *The Poems of Giacomo Da Lentino*, ed. E. F. Langley. Others included the Harvard Studies in Education and the Harvard Bulletins in Education (both 1914) and the Harvard Theological Studies (1916).

6. A. L. Lowell to G. L. Kittredge, Jan. 21, 1913, carbon copy in University Archives, Lowell Papers, 1909–1914, folder 1462.

7. Syndics minutes, Oct. 9, 1913.

8. C. C. Lane to A. L. Lowell, Aug. 27, 1919 (Lowell Papers, 1917–1919, folder 58).

9. Information on royalties and other contractual matters is from the Press's

contract files. Kittredge's royalty on *Chaucer* was 15 percent of receipts—higher than usual. In 1918 the Press was given the rights to Kittredge's *The Old Farmer and His Almanac,* which had been published in 1904 by Horace E. Ware.

10. C. C. Lane to Donald Scott, April 16, 1913 (Donald Scott Papers); F. W. Hunnewell to Anson Phelps Stokes, of Yale, Jan. 23, 1914 (University Archives, Lowell Papers, 1909–1914, folder 1406); Syndics minutes, April 1 and May 20, 1914.

11. Putnam, Putnam & Bell to President and Fellows, May 22, 1914 (Lowell Papers, 1909–1914, folder 1462).

12. A. L. Lowell to William L. Putnam, July 31, 1914 (Lowell Papers, 1914–1917, folder 180).

13. E. F. Gay to A. L. Lowell, June 17, 1912 (Lowell Papers, 1909–1914, folder 1348); also Press Annual Report, 1914–15. The expert was C. B. Thompson.

14. D. B. Updike to E. F. Gay, May 24, 1913, in Harvard Business School Archives, Merrymount folder, along with carbons of Gay to Updike, May 29 and July 29, 1913. Also see Donald Scott to Gay, Sept. 26, 1913, and Gay to Scott, Sept. 29, 1913 (Business School Archives, General Files, Donald Scott folder).

15. James Brown Scott, *Robert Bacon: Life and Letters* (Garden City, N.Y.: Doubleday, Page, 1923), 177, 185.

16. Donald Scott to C. C. Lane, June 23, 1913; Scott to Judah H. Sears, July 25, 1913 (carbons in Donald Scott Papers).

17. The architectural plans are mentioned in twelve letters in Donald Scott Papers, Sept. 23–Nov. 5, 1913.

18. Donald Scott to A. L. Lowell, Oct. 23 and Nov. 5, 1913 (University Archives, Lowell Papers, 1909–1914, folder 1462); Lowell to Scott, Oct. 28, 1913 (Donald Scott Papers).

19. "The Needs of the Harvard University Press," printed in June 1914, is in University Archives, HUF 710.10. Several drafts are in Donald Scott Papers. There was much correspondence about what Scott called the "campaign against Loeb"—for example, Scott to C. C. Lane, Feb. 9, 1914 (Donald Scott Papers).

20. J. H. Sears to Donald Scott, May 18, 1914 (Donald Scott Papers).

21. Donald Scott to E. F. Gay, Aug. 13, 1914, and March 17, 1915 (Business School Archives, General Files, Scott folder).

22. Copies of Gay's report, an undated document of eight pages, are in Lowell Papers, 1909–1914, folder 1462, and in Donald Scott Papers—in each case amid correspondence dated in May 1914.

23. A. L. Lowell to C. F. Adams, May 29, 1914 (Lowell Papers, 1909–1914, folder 1462).

24. On Randall Hall's history see William Bentinck-Smith, *Building a Great Library: The Coolidge Years at Harvard* (Harvard University Library, 1976), 71–73, 99–100. On the Press and Randall Hall, see *Harvard Alumni Bulletin,* Nov. 16, 1916, pp. 138–140; Press Annual Report for 1915–16; interview with W. Warren Smith, Oct. 24, 1973.

25. See Lane's autobiographical items in *Harvard College, Class of 1904:*

Decennial Report, June, 1914, and *Fourth Report, 1920.* Also A. L. Lowell to Joseph Warren, July 15, 1918 (Lowell Papers, 1917–1919, folder 1654).

26. A large amount of the printed matter is in the University Archives and in Donald Scott Papers for 1914. In the University Archives see especially the folders in UAV 711.202, UAV 711.205; the folders labeled "Posters," "Literary Notes," and "Advertising" in UAV 711.232; and the copy of *Literary Notes* of Oct. 21, 1914, in Lowell Papers, 1914–1917, folder 180.

27. Syndics minutes, March 19, 1913. The head of Oxford University Press was the agent in Great Britain, as he had been for the Publication Office. K. W. Hiersemann, Leipzig, was the Press's agent in Continental Europe.

28. On the University Press Association see Press Annual Report for 1914–15; *Harvard Alumni Bulletin,* Dec. 8, 1915, p. 190, and Nov. 16, 1916, pp. 139–140; Syndics minutes, May 10 and Oct. 30, 1916; W. W. Smith to me, Nov. 10, 1980; John B. Putnam, "Highbrow Tobacco: The Origins of AAUP," *Scholarly Publishing* (July 1974), 301–302.

29. This $61,000 may not be comparable with the earlier one, because the treasurer's figure for 1913–14 had been $43,540. All during the Lane administration there were discrepancies in the sales figures between the Press's Annual Reports and the Treasurer's Statements, due no doubt to different methods of calculation.

30. J. B. Scott, *Robert Bacon* (note 15 above), esp. 210–214, 219n, 269, 272.

31. Ibid., passim; also Henry Jackson, obituary of Bacon in *Harvard College, Class of 1880: Report IX, 1920,* pp. 18–19; Montgomery Schuyler's essay on Bacon in *Dictionary of American Biography.*

32. Entry for Gay in *Who's Who in America, 1928–1929;* Herbert Heaton, *A Scholar in Action: Edwin F. Gay* (Harvard University Press, 1952), 139–140, 147–148, 156–183.

33. C. C. Lane in *Harvard College, Class of 1904: Fourth Report, 1920;* and on selection of Dwiggins, C. C. Lane, "Early Years in Hingham," in *Postscripts on Dwiggins,* vol. 2, ed. Paul A. Bennett (New York: Typophiles, 1960), 158; also Syndics minutes, May 31, 1918. Dwiggins's duration of office and salary are shown in his work journals in the Boston Public Library.

34. Dorothy Abbe, "William Addison Dwiggins" (pamphlet, Boston Public Library, 1974), esp. 5–6, 8–9, 16–17, 22.

35. Rudolph Ruzicka, interview June 11, 1977.

36. This account of the wartime troubles is from "Report of the Committee to Visit the Harvard University Press," May 14, 1923, in *Reports of the Visiting Committees, Harvard College, 1919–1924* (in University Archives), 239. One of the committee members was C. C. Lane. The name of his assistant was not given.

37. Walter Stone, a member of the Business School faculty and staff, told Donald K. David in a letter dated March 8, 1920, that in 1918 he was "transferred to the Press for the period of the war" (Harvard Business School Archives, folder labeled "Courses—Printing #1").

38. Roger Pierce, Secretary to the Corporation, to C. F. Adams, May 15, 1918 (University Archives, Lowell Papers, 1917–1919, folder 58). Letters cited in next few notes are in the same folder.

39. C. C. Lane to Robert Bacon, May 6, 1919, carbon.

40. C. C. Lane to A. L. Lowell, June 30, 1919.

41. From a typed manuscript in folder 58, preserved with carbon of letter from F. W. Hunnewell to C. C. Lane, July 8, 1919.

42. C. C. Lane to F. W. Hunnewell, July 10, 1919.

43. Amount from Harvard Treasurer's Statement for 1918–19, p. 150.

44. "Demoralizing" and "chaotic": A. L. Lowell to F. W. Hunnewell, July 23, 1919, and to G. L. Kittredge, July 30, 1919; G. L. Kittredge in the Press's Annual Report for 1933–34. The copy of Lowell's telegram in folder 58 is undated; Lane replied by telegram July 29, 1919.

45. C. C. Lane to A. L. Lowell, Nov. 8, 1919, Lowell Papers, 1919–1922, folder 51.

46. *New York Times,* Dec. 28, 1967.

47. Lowell Papers, 1917–1919, folder 58.

48. President's Annual Report, 1918–19, dated Dec. 18, 1919.

49. C. C. Lane to A. L. Lowell, Dec. 29, 1919, Lowell Papers, 1919–1922, folder 51.

50. C. C. Lane to A. L. Lowell, Aug. 11 and Aug. 19, 1919 (Lowell Papers, 1917–1919, folder 58); Lane to Lowell, Oct. 8, 1919 (Lowell Papers, 1919–1922, folder 51).

3. The Murdock Years

1. Quotation is from the Press's Annual Report for 1933–34, signed by G. L. Kittredge as "Acting Chairman of the Syndics." My source on Murdock's troubleshooting and reorganization of firms, also his friendship with Lowell, is David W. Bailey (interview Dec. 8, 1973). On the work of the three-man committee see University Archives, Lowell Papers, 1919–1922, folder 39, and Lowell's Annual Report for 1921–22, p. 28.

2. Murdock's precarious health and his short hours in the office ("ten to noon") are discussed by David T. Pottinger in "Harold Murdock," *Proceedings of the Massachusetts Historical Society* 68 (1944–1947, pub. 1952), 455–457. Warren Smith (interview Oct. 24, 1973) said Murdock typically came to the Press in a chauffeur-driven Ford, rode to Boston by subway at noon, had lunch at the Union Club, visited Goodspeed's Book Shop for transactions and conversation about rare books, and spent the rest of the afternoon in the library of the Massachusetts Historical Society.

3. On estimating number of titles see Chapter 2, note 1.

4. Calculated on basis of Harvard Treasurer's Statement, 1918–19; Press Annual Report, 1919–20; and Press sales records for 1933–34. Here and elsewhere I have not attempted to render time series in "real dollars"; that is, I have not adjusted the figures to allow for inflation and deflation.

5. Memorandum from the Syndics to President J. B. Conant, appended to Syndics minutes of April 26, 1934.

6. Biographical facts from *Who's Who in America* and obituary in *New York Times,* April 6, 1934.

7. Syndics minutes, Jan. 8, 1920.

8. From July 1, 1913, through June 30, 1919, according to the Treasurer's Statements, the receipts of the Printing Office were $512,479, its expenditures $490,969.

9. Report dated May 14, 1923, in *Reports of the Visiting Committees, Harvard College, 1919–1924,* pp. 239–241.

10. George Grady to Harold Murdock, Nov. 12, 1930, Appendix II, p. 2 (University Archives, Conant Papers, box 41, folder dated 1934–35). Outside printing, which did not endear the Press to the commercial printers of the town, continued to be done in later eras for nonprofit organizations, though presumably without aggressive sales efforts.

11. David T. Pottinger, "Organization of the Harvard University Press," a memorandum to President J. B. Conant, Sept. 10, 1934 (University Archives, Conant Papers, chronological files on the Press), 1–2, 5; also Pottinger, "Harold Murdock," 456.

12. Press Annual Reports, 1919–20 and 1920–21, and ledger entitled "H.U. Press—Type and Supplies Purchased 1909–1926," in University Archives (UAV 711.288), 60, 62. Also in the Archives is a blueprint document entitled "Inventory of Harvard College Printing Office Equipment, January 1, 1920" (UAV 711.232), itemizing $73,733 worth of equipment.

13. F. W. Hunnewell, Secretary to the Corporation, to R. W. Beach of the Cosmos Press, Sept. 16, 1931 (University Archives, Lowell Papers, 1930–1933, folder 80). Beach had suggested that the work of the Printing Office be turned over to his firm.

14. Harold Murdock to A. L. Lowell, April 5, 1926; Lowell to Murdock, April 6 and April 26, 1926 (Lowell Papers, 1925–1928, folder 67).

15. See also the interesting correspondence in folder 67 between Lowell and the lawyer C. P. Curtis, Jr.

16. Pottinger, "Organization," 1–2.

17. Ibid., 2.

18. *Reports of the Visiting Committees, Harvard College, 1919–1924,* pp. 239–241.

19. *Harvard Alumni Bulletin,* Feb. 21, 1924, p. 568.

20. Stanley Morison, in Morison and Rudolph Ruzicka, *Recollections of Daniel Berkeley Updike* (Boston: Club of Odd Volumes, 1943), 2. See also the judgment by Lawrence C. Wroth in H. W. Kent et al., *Daniel Berkeley Updike and the Merrymount Press* (New York: American Institute of Graphic Arts, 1940), 33.

21. On "Printer's Bible" see Max Farrand, Foreword to *The Work of the Merrymount Press and Its Founder,* catalogue of an exhibition (San Marino, Cal.: Huntington Library, 1942), 8; and Mark Antony DeWolfe Howe in *Updike: American Printer and His Merrymount Press,* by many authors (New York: American Institute of Graphic Arts, 1947), 95.

22. The planned publication is mentioned in "Forthcoming Publications," November 1913 (Donald Scott Papers, Harvard Business School Archives), and in at least fifteen letters between Edwin F. Gay and D. B. Updike, beginning Nov.

27, 1911, and ending Nov. 27, 1916, in Business School Archives, folder labeled "Merrymount (Printing Course)." Updike received a royalty of 15 percent of sales receipts, which Murdock later voluntarily raised to 15 percent of the list price (Press contract files). New printings of the first edition were made in 1923 and 1927. A second edition was published in 1937 and reprinted in 1951. A third edition came out in 1962 under the imprint of The Belknap Press of Harvard University Press and was reprinted in 1966. The Press allowed the work to go out of print in 1975. Dover Publications later published a paperback edition.

23. "Harvard University Catalogue, 1974–1975," pp. 949–950.

24. Ibid., 956–957.

25. Press's semiannual "Announcements" for Spring 1934, Autumn 1934, Spring 1935, and Autumn 1937; Syndics minutes of Oct. 19, 1933, May 25, 1938, and Dec. 7, 1938; the Press's "Out-of-Print Catalogue, 1913–1976" under names of Copeland, Eliot, Grandgent, Perry, and Robinson; Frederick C. Packard, Jr., interview March 15, 1981; Stratis Haviaras, introduction to *The Poet's Voice: Poets Reading Aloud and Commenting upon Their Works* (cassettes, Harvard University Press, 1978).

26. *New York Times*, April 6, 1934; *Inland Printer*, May 1934. The *Boston Herald*, April 6, 1934, changed the statement to say that the books were *rated* as unsurpassed. The *New England Printer*, April 1934, changed it to "were in the front rank in this country in printing and design"—a safer statement.

27. George Parker Winship, "Good Printing at Harvard," a letter in *Harvard Alumni Bulletin* (May 29, 1924), 981–982; *Publishers' Weekly* (May 17, 1924), 1587–1589; also a list provided to Harvard University Press around 1963 by American Institute of Graphic Arts and amended in two letters to me from Edward M. Gottschall of the institute, March 19 and April 8, 1974. Besides *Doctor Johnson,* the Harvard books in the 1924 group were: *Modern Color,* by Carl Gordon Cutler and Stephen C. Pepper; *Wordsworth in a New Light,* by Emile Legouis; *Prophets of Yesterday and Their Message for Today,* by John Kelman; and *A Handful of Pleasant Delights,* edited by Hyder E. Rollins.

28. Herbert H. Johnson of the Rochester Institute of Technology, who gave me helpful advice on Rogers's Harvard University Press Books, pointed to two of them that had not appeared in the Fifty Books exhibits but that he (Johnson) considered "great" in design—"without peer." They are *The Wedgwood Medallion of Samuel Johnson,* by C. B. Tinker (1926), and *A New Portrait of James Boswell,* by C. B. Tinker and F. A. Pottle (1927). Melvin Loos was associated with the printer William E. Rudge. One of the Harvard books in the 1926 Fifty Books was a book *about* Bruce Rogers—also *designed* by Rogers. This was *Bruce Rogers: Designer of Books,* by Frederic Warde.

29. See discussion in Joseph Blumenthal, "Bruce Rogers," *Gazette of the Grolier Club* (October 1970), 5–6, 15, esp. 8.

30. Press Annual Report for 1919–20.

31. David T. Pottinger, "B.R. at the Harvard University Press," in Paul A. Bennett, ed., *BR Marks & Remarks* (New York: Typophiles, 1946), 91–95, 100–101; also Rogers's own recollections, ibid., 65, 67.

32. W. W. Smith, interview Oct. 24, 1973; Bruce Rogers to Dumas Malone, Jan. 5, 1938 (the Press's General File 1938, "R" folder).

33. Biographical facts in Pottinger's own words are in *Harvard College, Class of 1906,* anniversary reports of 1926, 1931, 1936, 1941, 1946, 1951, 1956 (the longest of which is the *25th Anniversary Report,* published in 1931).

34. Grace A. Briggs, interview Dec. 5, 1973. On the Cambridge experience in general, see David T. Pottinger, "I, Too, in Arcadia," *Proceedings of the Cambridge Historical Society* 35 (1953–1954, pub. 1955), 113–114.

35. D. T. Pottinger to C. C. Lane, May 17, 1931, carbon copy found in 1974 among Pottinger's papers by his daughter, Ann Pottinger Saab.

36. This paragraph is based on W. W. Smith, interview Oct. 24, 1973.

37. A copy of Ryder's pamphlet, apparently published in 1922, is in the Harvard University Archives. The Press tried to explain to Ryder that Professor Charles Lanman had the responsibility for pricing the Oriental books. Ryder said this was inconsistent with the Press's claim to be the publisher.

38. The sequence of events is mainly from G. A. Reisner's preface, dated Nov. 15, 1930. Statistics are from Press records.

39. C. C. Lane to D. T. Pottinger, June 6, 1930, letter among Pottinger's papers in possession of Ann Pottinger Saab. For Lakeman's career see his own accounts in the Anniversary Reports of the class of 1904, in the University Archives, especially those dated 1934, 1939, and 1954. On Grady see brief obituary in *New York Times,* Jan. 23, 1956, p. 25.

40. George Grady to Harold Murdock (note 10 above), 2, 3, esp. 8, 10. Warren Smith remembered Adam K. Wilson as "a masterly manager of staff and plant" who "kept peace in the organization and got very fine printing done year after year" (memoranda to me Oct. 17, 1979, and May 6, 1981).

41. D. T. Pottinger to C. C. Lane, May 17, 1931, carbon in possession of Ann Pottinger Saab.

42. Pottinger to Lane, March 28, 1931.

43. Pottinger to Lane, May 17, 1931.

44. Date of Wilson's retirement: University Archives, Personnel Records. The new foreman was Walter Stanislaus Gregson, an English-born printer who had been in the organization since 1902.

45. On Gregson's and Arnold's duties, Pottinger to Conant (note 11 above). For Arnold's career see his own accounts in the Anniversary Reports of the Harvard class of 1924, in University Archives.

46. A. L. Lowell to Harold Murdock, March 7, 1928 (University Archives, Lowell Papers, 1925–1928, folder 67). See also Press Annual Reports for 1926–27 and 1927–28.

47. Murdock to Lowell, Sept. 21, 1928; Lowell to Murdock, Sept. 22, 1928; Press Annual Report, 1929–30.

48. For history of the house see David T. Pottinger, "Thirty-Eight Quincy Street," *Proceedings of the Cambridge Historical Society* 23 (1934–1935, pub. 1937). In 1950, when the house was about to be demolished to make way for the Allston Burr Lecture Hall, Denys P. Myers, class of 1940, in a letter to the *Harvard Alumni Bulletin* (Nov. 25, 1950, p. 199), pleaded in vain for its preservation and called it "the most charming example of romanticism in mid-nineteenth-century American domestic architecture still extant in Cambridge." On the move in general see Murdock to Lowell, April 27, 1932; Lowell to

Murdock, April 28, 1932 (Lowell Papers, 1930–1933, folder 80); Press Annual Report, 1931–32.

49. Day's account in Anniversary Reports of Harvard class of 1912.

50. *Harvard College: Class of 1912: Twentieth Anniversary Report* (1932), 71–72.

51. Eleanor Harman, "A Reconsideration of Manuscript Editing," *Scholarly Publishing* (January 1976), esp. 147, 148.

52. Ibid.

53. W. W. Smith, interview Oct. 24, 1973.

54. For Syndics' resolution on Murdock, see Syndics minutes, April 12, 1934, and *Harvard University Gazette,* April 21, 1934.

55. G. L. Kittredge wrote in his Press Annual Report for 1933–34, "The Financial Vice-President has supervised and determined such matters as were beyond the powers and functions of the Syndics," and in his Press Annual Report for 1934–35, "All questions of finance have been referred to the Financial Vice-President of the University, who has shown keen interest in the Press and spared no pains in furthering its activities." On the creation of the position see J. B. Conant's Annual Report, 1933–34.

56. J. B. Conant to Cass Canfield, March 12, 1934. This and the other documents on the search for a Director, unless otherwise stated, are in University Archives, Conant Papers, Harvard University Press folders, beginning with 1933–34. Conant's own letters are carbon copies.

57. The memorandum and Kittredge's short letter of transmittal are appended to the handwritten Syndic minutes of April 26, 1934, preserved at the Press. The minutes of April 12 and 19 also deal with the document. The final draft was made by Professor Blake and Professor William S. Ferguson.

58. Conant to A. W. Page, Dec. 7, 1934; Page to Conant, Dec. 13, 1934; Conant to Page, Dec. 20, 1934; memo by Jerome Greene about the Corporation's approval in January 1935; and, for the *"de novo"* statement, Conant to W. W. Norton, Feb. 4, 1935.

59. Conant to A. W. Page, June 18, 1935, in Conant Papers along with the communications from MacLeish.

60. On Ginn transfers, see Syndics minutes of March 1, 1934 (fourteen titles listed); Feb. 7, 1935; April 11, 1935.

61. David Horne, "The Loeb Classical Library: Background and Problems," April 19, 1972, a lengthy report. This and James Loeb's will, dated July 18, 1931, are in Press files.

62. Press Annual Report, 1933–34.

63. David Horne report, esp. Exhibits V and VI.

64. M. A. DeWolfe Howe to J. B. Conant, Aug. 6, 1935, in Conant Papers along with other letters about Malone.

65. Press Annual Report, 1934–35.

66. Correspondence of 1935 in David T. Pottinger's papers in possession of Ann Pottinger Saab. No copy of Grady's report is available but its gist can be inferred from the correspondence cited, from Warren Smith's recollections, and from what happened in early 1936.

67. J. B. Conant to Dumas Malone, Oct. 16 and Nov. 12, 1935; Corporation Records of Nov. 18.

68. *Harvard Alumni Bulletin* (Dec. 6, 1935), 339.

69. D. T. Pottinger to Dumas Malone, Nov. 25, 1935, carbon in Pottinger's papers. Pottinger described himself as "temporarily in charge of the Press; advertising, designing, contracts, general correspondence." The duties of Warren Smith: selling, inventory records, adjustments. Herbert Jacques: in charge of Printing Office, general oversight of bookkeeping and accounting. Helen L. French: secretary to Pottinger and in charge of Syndics' records. Eleanor Peterson: stenographer, assistant in advertising records. Charles M. Thompson: book review files. Mildreth Camia: order desk, telephone operator. Clara M. Durkee: head bookkeeper. Mary Dee: cashier. Dorothy Dee and Margaret Dee: bookkeepers. Fred Batstone: shipper. Donald Maxwell: assistant to shipper. Ruth H. Sawyer: general stenographer.

4. Malone and a Wider Audience

1. Malone's "Brief Account of the Enterprise" in *Dictionary of American Biography,* vol. 20 (reprinted in vol. 1 of twelve-volume edition).

2. Press Annual Report, 1937–38, p. 439 (the reason for the high page numbers in these reports is that they are printed as a part of the President's Annual Report). Malone said in that report that the Press, with eighty-four new offerings, still ranked among the three largest university presses. On policy of selectivity see also Press Annual Reports of 1936–37 (pp. 393–394) and 1938–39 (p. 483). On author-subsidized monographs see Syndics minutes of Nov. 4, 1936, and Jan. 6, 1937.

3. Press Annual Reports: on imports, 1939–40 (p. 455) and 1941–42 (p. 487); on shrinkage of funds and slowing of series, 1937–38 (p. 441), 1938–39 (pp. 483, 484), and 1939–40 (p. 456). For example, the Harvard Studies and Notes in Philology and Literature went under in 1938 and the Harvard Studies in English in 1939—each after about twenty volumes—because funds ran out (James B. Munn to Dumas Malone, June 21, 1938, in the Press's General File 1938, folder labeled "M–O").

4. Press Annual Reports, 1938–39 (p. 482), 1939–40 (p. 456), and 1940–41 (pp. 460, 461). The sales receipts, by fiscal years, are from Press records.

5. Malone interview, Nov. 28, 1973; "Report of the Committee to Visit the Harvard University Press," Feb. 27, 1939, in *Reports of the Visiting Committees, Harvard College, 1937–1942,* p. 155.

6. Press Annual Report, 1937–38 (p. 438); *Harvard Alumni Bulletin* (Jan. 28, 1938), p. 479. The banquet was at the Fogg Art Museum on Jan. 7, 1938.

7. Dumas Malone, "The Scholar and the Public," *Proceedings of the American Philosophical Society* 80, no. 1 (1938), 28, 29, 31, 32.

8. Ibid., 29–30 and esp. 35.

9. Malone interview Nov. 28, 1973.

10. The firings took place Jan. 7, 1936. Later, J. T. Day expressed his bitterness in three letters to Dumas Malone, Jan. 7 and Jan. 11, 1938, and one undated

(Press's General File 1938, folder labeled "D"). Personnel Records in the University Archives show that foreman Walter Gregson survived the cut and continued in the shop, though not in charge, until he retired in 1948 at age seventy-one. His total service in the organization was forty-six years.

11. Press Annual Reports: 1936–37 (pp. 391–392) and 1937–38 (pp. 440–441). David Pottinger, like some other good designers of his time, had always preferred the Monotype. According to Warren Smith, Pottinger resisted the Linotype and also offset printing. On Lakeman see his autobiographical sketch in *Harvard College, Class of 1904: Fiftieth Anniversary Report* (1954).

12. On Rugg see *Harvard College, Class of 1921: Twenty-fifth Anniversary Report* (1946).

13. Dumas Malone, interview Nov. 28, 1973.

14. James B. Conant, *My Several Lives: Memoirs of a Social Inventor* (New York: Harper & Row, 1970), 112–115. Until Conant's administration the University had no retirement age. In *My Several Lives* Conant did not mention Kittredge's Press connection, but Malone recalled that Conant told him, concerning the Syndics, that Kittredge had "dominated the thing too long." Kittredge died in 1941 at age eighty-one.

15. Corporation Records, June 1 and Oct. 5, 1936; May 16, 1938; June 19, 1940; Dec. 7, 1942. Edward S. Mason moved to Washington for defense work in 1941, and Edward H. Chamberlin served as his substitute on the Syndics until 1943, when he too went to Washington.

16. Edward S. Mason forty years later spoke feelingly of the "animosity" between McNair and Malone. In an interview Feb. 14, 1981, he said that McNair scorned Malone as not knowing anything about business and that Malone considered McNair a "philistine of the worst kind."

17. Syndics minutes, Nov. 4 and Dec. 2, 1936; Dumas Malone, "Memorandum," Nov. 19, 1936 (Conant Papers); and see esp. Press Annual Reports, 1935–36 (p. 379) and 1936–37 (p. 392).

18. Press Annual Report, 1936–37 (p. 392).

19. Malone, "Memorandum"; also Press Annual Report, 1935–36 (p. 379).

20. Dorothy Greenwald to me, June 29, 1981.

21. Sales figures for this and other books are from Press records and were supplied by Joan O'Donnell and others.

22. Press Lovejoy file, Melvin Arnold to Thomas J. Wilson, March 30, 1959.

23. Royalty information is always from Press contract files, in this case from letters in 1935 which served as a contract.

24. Press Annual Report, 1936–37 (pp. 392, 396); 1937–38 (p. 443).

25. S. E. Morison to Dumas Malone, June 4, 1937 (University Archives, Press correspondence, UAV.711.5, folder "M").

26. Bernard Bailyn, "Morison: An Appreciation," *Proceedings of the Massachusetts Historical Society* 89 (1977), 118.

27. Chester I. Barnard to Harvard University Press, Sept. 12, 1956; also William B. Wolf, *Conversations with Chester I. Barnard* (Ithaca, N.Y.: New York State School of Industrial and Labor Relations, Cornell University, 1973), 14. The 1937 and 1938 correspondence is in the Press's Barnard file.

28. Malone to Barnard, April 12, 1938.

29. Malone to Barnard, Aug. 17, 1938; Eleanor Dobson to Barnard, Nov. 17, 1938.

30. Chester I. Barnard, *The Functions of the Executive* (Harvard University Press, 1938). See esp. (in 1968 edition) pp. xxviii, xxix, xxx, 73, 82, 216, 217. For an analysis of the book and its influence, see Kenneth R. Andrews's introduction to the 1968 edition.

31. F. J. Roethlisberger, *The Elusive Phenomena: An Autobiographical Account of My Work in the Field of Organizational Behavior at the Harvard Business School* (Division of Research, Harvard Business School, 1977; distributed by Harvard University Press), 46, 48–51.

32. See Alfred D. Chandler, Jr., "Comparative Business History," in D. C. Coleman and Peter Mathias, eds., *Enterprise and History* (Cambridge University Press, 1984).

33. The "racial" groups Elin Anderson wrote about were Irish, Yankees, French Canadians, Jews, Italians, and Germans. She had entitled the manuscript "Relationships of Nationality Groups in Burlington, Vermont." The title *We Americans* was suggested by the Press's outside reader, the sociologist Robert S. Lynd of Columbia University, except that he put quotation marks around the word "Americans." Lynd received $25 for criticizing the manuscript—possibly the first reader's fee ever paid by the Press. Almost all outside readers were Harvard professors, who at that time received no fee. On Loubat award see Press Annual Report, 1937–38, p. 440, and *New York Times,* May 9, 1938, p. 2.

34. Press Annual Report, 1938–39 (p. 483); *Harvard Alumni Bulletin* (May 12, 1939), 907.

35. Howard Mumford Jones, foreword to Frank Luther Mott, *A History of American Magazines,* vol. 5 (The Belknap Press of Harvard University Press, 1968), ix.

36. Frank Luther Mott, "Unfinished Story; or, The Man in the Carrel," which is chapter 11 in his *Time Enough: Essays in Autobiography* (Chapel Hill: University of North Carolina Press, 1962), 169–180. That chapter, which tells the story of the magazine project, is reprinted in *A History of American Magazines,* vol. 5, pp. 341–350.

37. Mott, "Unfinished Story," 174 (as reprinted, 345).

38. Arthur M. Schlesinger, *In Retrospect: The History of a Historian* (New York: Harcourt, Brace & World, 1963), 113–114.

39. When Dumas Malone wrote to Frankfurter, June 29, 1938, proposing a 10 percent royalty, Frankfurter replied on July 20, 1938, "Of course your terms are O.K. by me, to use a phrase sanctified by the King James version" (Press contract files).

40. To Malone's overture Raymond replied that he did not know what he would do with the book, for he was trying to make it a "readable account" and it fell "between two stools," being neither "popular" nor a textbook. Said Malone: "Just the sort of thing that we are specially interested in."

41. Malone learned about the Cohen project from Professor Perry Miller. In the Press's Cohen file these letters are especially interesting: Perry Miller to Dumas

Malone, Jan. 12, 1940; Malone to I. B. Cohen, Jan. 16, 1940; Carl Van Doren to Malone, Oct. 7, 1940. Cohen received no royalties, because the first 1,500 copies were exempt.

42. Edward S. Mason, "The Harvard Department of Economics from the Beginning to World War II," *Quarterly Journal of Economics* (August 1982), 424. Through a misunderstanding the Press later lost Leontief as an author (Press's Leontief file, correspondence between him and T. J. Wilson in 1949 and 1950).

43. She was Theodora Kimball, a librarian, coauthor (with J. S. Pray) of *City Planning*.

44. William Ernest Hocking to Dumas Malone, Aug. 6, Aug. 16, and Sept. 10, 1941 (Press files).

45. Susanne K. Langer, preface to the first edition, dated Cambridge, 1941. The italics are hers.

46. W. W. Smith, memo to Press Director Roger L. Scaife, Jan. 25, 1944 (University Archives, Conant Papers).

47. On the Giedion book the Press does not control the rights to editions in foreign languages. The translation sales figures are unavailable but presumably large.

48. Dumas Malone to Sigfried Giedion, March 3, 1939; see also Syndics minutes, March 15 and Nov. 8, 1939.

49. *Space, Time and Architecture,* 1st ed., v.

50. "Harvard University Press, Spring Announcements 1941."

51. W. W. Smith letters to me, June 23, 1981, and March 15, 1982.

52. "Study of Publishing Overhead," which Dumas Malone sent to Financial Vice-President J. W. Lowes on March 17, 1937, and which is preserved in the Conant Papers.

53. Press Annual Report, 1940–41, pp. 461–462.

54. Minutes of Board of Trustees of Loeb Classical Library Foundation, June 9, 1941. Harvard collected war risk insurance for the bombing losses.

55. Trustees minutes, Nov. 25, 1946.

56. Press Annual Report, 1941–42, p. 487; Glen W. Baxter, interview Dec. 11, 1981.

57. For example, David W. Bailey to Roy E. Larsen, Nov. 20, 1942 (copy in Fogg Art Museum Archives, Paul J. Sachs Archive, folder labeled "Harvard University Press: Roy E. Larsen").

58. W. W. Smith, interview Nov. 24, 1973.

59. J. B. Conant to R. L. Scaife, March 6, 1944 (Press out-of-print files, Conant folder labeled "Our Fighting Faith").

5. Wartime Shock

Epigraph: Paul Buck, in "The Adams Papers: A Ceremony Held at the Massachusetts Historical Society on September 22, 1961" (Boston: Massachusetts Historical Society, 1962), 8–13. By then Buck was director of the Harvard University Library and Carl H. Pforzheimer University Professor; he was also a member of the Press's Board of Directors. The speeches by Buck and others appear also in the *Proceedings of the Massachusetts Historical Society* 73 (1961).

1. Press Annual Report, 1937–38, p. 438.

2. J. B. Conant to Dumas Malone, Jan. 8, 1938 (University Archives, Conant Papers, chronological files on Harvard University Press).

3. "Study of Publishing Overhead," sent by Dumas Malone to Vice-President J. W. Lowes on March 17, 1937 (Conant Papers), esp. p. 5.

4. J. W. Lowes to Dumas Malone, April 20, 1937 (Conant Papers); Dumas Malone, "A Report on the Financial Reorganization of the Harvard University Press: With Special Reference to the Separation of Publishing from Printing," Oct. 28, 1941 (Conant Papers), 1; Syndics minutes, Oct. 13, 1942.

5. Press Annual Report, 1936–37. Malone's next four Annual Reports were increasingly urgent on the need for such income.

6. Press Visiting Committee files: Dumas Malone to Jerome D. Greene, Secretary to the Corporation, May 29, 1940; Malone to Roy E. Larsen, Nov. 21, 1940.

7. Press Annual Report, 1939–40, p. 457; Press Visiting Committee files, esp. Malone to H. C. Lodge, Feb. 23, 1940, with enclosure, and Malone to Maurice Smith, Dec. 2, 1941.

8. James B. Conant, *My Several Lives: Memoirs of a Social Inventor* (New York: Harper & Row, 1970), 111, 158, 168–171.

9. Ibid., 211–212, 222, 234–235, 242–244, 272, 274–275, 299.

10. Ibid., 363.

11. J. W. Lowes to Dumas Malone, Nov. 10, 1938; Malone to William Rugg, Nov. 14, 1938 (Press General File 1938, folder labeled "L").

12. Evidence concerning the Harvard Sociological Studies is in Dumas Malone to John D. Black (chairman of the Committee on Research in the Social Sciences), Jan. 17, 1939 (Conant Papers); Black to Jerome D. Greene, June 9, 1939 (Conant Papers). About this matter and also the Harvard Studies in International Law, see Syndics minutes, Feb. 8, 1939; Malone to J. W. Lowes, March 15, 1939 (Conant Papers).

13. Syndics minutes, April 26, 1939, to which is attached a printed circular from Jerome Greene to the permanent officers of the University, April 15, 1939, transmitting the text of the Corporation action of March 27.

14. Syndics minutes, Nov. 8 and Dec. 6, 1939.

15. Conant to Malone, May 12, 1941 (Conant Papers).

16. Harvard news release Sept. 26, 1941.

17. Dumas Malone, interview Nov. 28, 1973, and letter to me April 2, 1982.

18. Malone to W. H. Claflin, June 16, 1941 (Conant Papers).

19. Conant to Malone, June 20, 1941 (Conant Papers); Syndics minutes, Oct. 1, 1941.

20. Malone to G. H. Chase, Aug. 12, 1941 (Conant Papers); Malone, "A Report" (note 4 above), 2–3, 8.

21. Lybrand, Ross Bros. & Montgomery to W. H. Claflin, Aug. 1, 1941 (copy in Fogg Art Museum Archives, Paul J. Sachs Archive, folder labeled "Harvard University Press: Financial Repts.").

22. When the separation of publishing and printing took place, the printer

J. Albert Meyer and the accountant William C. Rugg were not retained. Grace Briggs recalled that people at the Press considered them the scapegoats of the type-metal affair. Malone, who again had to be the "lord high executioner," told me: "I always felt an injury had been done to Bill Rugg."

23. James W. McFarlane, interview Feb. 22, 1974.

24. Press Annual Report, 1941–42, pp. 488–489. On divided salaries see also Malone, "A Report" (note 4 above), 3–4; on accounting changes, Syndics minutes, March 4 and April 8, 1942.

25. Malone, "A Report," 12, 14.

26. Syndics minutes, Feb. 18, 1942.

27. Chafee to Sachs, Aug. 20, 1942 (Fogg Art Museum Archives, Paul J. Sachs Archive, folder labeled "Harvard University Press: Committee of Press").

28. Memo, Treasurer to Bursar, Nov. 25, 1941 (Conant Papers).

29. The new commission is explained in Dumas Malone to Edward W. Forbes, March 2, 1942, in Press contract files, Giedion envelope; also W. Warren Smith interview Oct. 24, 1973. Of the 25 percent, 15 percent of the list price was charged on copies sold, as before. The additional 10 percent was charged before sales took place, that is, when the books were printed—except that after the first 500 copies printed, the charge was not made on unbound books, only those bound. Later this complicated arrangement was changed to a flat 25 percent of the list price on all copies sold. Malone's contract negotiations are mentioned in Syndics minutes, March 4 and May 6, 1942. A long, forceful letter of protest from Frederick Merk, chairman of the Department of History, dated May 3, 1943, is in Fogg Art Museum Archives, Paul J. Sachs Archive, folder labeled "Harvard University Press: Board of Syndics."

30. About five years later, near the start of Thomas J. Wilson's administration, it was stated in the minutes of the Press Board of Directors (Oct. 22, 1947) that the Press was losing about $5,000 a year on department books because the handling charge was only 25 percent.

31. Syndics minutes, Feb. 18, March 4, April 8, and May 6, 1942; Corporation Records, June 29, 1942.

32. Press Annual Report, 1941–42, pp. 489–490.

33. R. L. Scaife, memorandum, May 21, 1942 (carbon in Press file labeled "Reports on the Press"). "Atlantic" is a reference to the Atlantic Monthly Press and its Atlantic–Little, Brown books.

34. R. L. Scaife to J. B. Conant, July 9, 1942 (Conant Papers).

35. Syndics minutes, July 13, 1942.

36. David W. Bailey to Roy E. Larsen, Nov. 20, 1942 (copy in Fogg Art Museum Archives, Paul J. Sachs Archive, folder labeled "Harvard University Press: Roy E. Larsen"); also Bailey's notes in preparation for his appearance before the Syndics on Nov. 17, 1942 (shown to me by Bailey, May 17, 1982).

37. Dumas Malone to J. B. Conant, July 17, 1943 (Conant Papers).

38. The Syndic Edward Mason recalled (interview Feb. 14, 1981) that even before 1942 Pottinger had been venting his dissatisfaction with Malone. Mason formed the impression that Pottinger, in talking about the Director, was "affable but with all kinds of innuendoes."

39. The Syndics' undated statement, drafted by Ralph Barton Perry, Thomas Barbour, Baird Hastings, and Sachs, is in the Sachs Archive at the Fogg Museum (folder labeled "Harvard University Press: Committee of Press") along with the letter to Claflin. Actually there are two versions of the statement in the folder, but they differ only in the first sentence of the second paragraph.

40. [Paul J. Sachs], "Memorandum," July 29, 1942 (Sachs Archive, folder labeled "Harvard University Press: Committee of Press"). The Syndics at dinner July 28 were McNair, Perry, Hastings, Munn, and Sachs.

41. See note 45 below. Malone's publications during the late thirties and early forties are mentioned in Steven H. Hochman and Katherine M. Sargeant, "Dumas Malone: A Select Bibliography" (pamphlet, Charlottesville, Va., 1981), 7, 10.

42. Eleanor Dobson Kewer, interview Nov. 14, 1973; Malone interview Nov. 28, 1973.

43. Pottinger's letters to Claflin are in Conant Papers; the one to Sachs is in Sachs Archive, folder labeled "Harvard University Press: Board of Syndics."

44. W. W. Smith, letter to me June 23, 1981. Pottinger did not name the important University officer. Mr. and Mrs. Horace Arnold (interview March 19, 1981) said they always believed that Pottinger resigned in protest over Arnold's impending discharge.

45. Notes by Zechariah Chafee on Pottinger's testimony Oct. 3, 1942 (Sachs Archive, folder labeled "Harvard University Press: Board of Syndics").

46. P. J. Sachs to J. B. Conant, Oct. 6, 1942 (Conant Papers). See also Chafee to Sachs, Oct. 5, 1942 (Sachs Archive, folder labeled "Harvard University Press: Committee of Press").

47. Syndics minutes, Sept. 7, 1943.

48. R. L. Scaife to W. H. Claflin, Sept. 11, 1942 (Conant Papers).

49. Corporation Records, Oct. 19 and Nov. 23, 1942; also Sachs to Conant, Oct. 8 and Nov. 6, 1942 (Conant Papers).

50. Quotations are from a memorandum by Sachs in preparation for a meeting with Malone on Nov. 9, 1942 (Sachs Archive, folder labeled "Harvard University Press: Board of Syndics").

51. [Paul J. Sachs], "Memorandum of Meeting at Faculty Club November 17, 1942" (Sachs Archive, folder labeled "Harvard University Press: Board of Syndics").

52. D. W. Bailey to R. E. Larsen, Nov. 20, 1942 (copy in Sachs Archive, folder labeled "Harvard University Press: Roy E. Larsen").

53. Ibid. On Arnold's role, my source is D. W. Bailey, interview May 17, 1982. The meeting took place Nov. 17, 1942; see note 51 above.

54. D. W. Bailey, interview May 17, 1982.

55. Conant Papers: P. J. Sachs to J. B. Conant, Nov. 6, 1942; A. Calvert Smith to Conant, Nov. 7, 1942; Dumas Malone to Conant, Nov. 25, 1942.

56. W. W. Smith, interviews Oct. 24, 1973, and Nov. 13, 1981, and letter May 6, 1981.

57. J. W. McFarlane to P. J. Sachs, Dec. 9, 1942; memo by McFarlane entitled "Conversation with Dumas Malone, Friday, December 11, 1942" (Sachs Archive, folder labeled "Harvard University Press: Board of Syndics").

58. [Paul J. Sachs], "Memorandum for Meeting of Syndics at Shady Hill, December 9, 1942" (Sachs Archive, Syndics folder). The same folder contains a longer version, entitled "Memorandum Presented by PJS at the Meeting of the Ad Hoc Committee at Shady Hill, December 9, 1942," and at the top is a handwritten note saying this was "used in a 2 hr. talk" in the Naumburg Room of the Fogg Museum on December 28. The audience was not specified.

59. Mimeographed Syndics minutes, March 3 and March 17, 1943 (Sachs Archive, Syndics folder). These minutes preserved by Sachs contain matter omitted from the regular Syndics minutes preserved at the Press, which, beginning in the fall of 1942, were devoted almost entirely to manuscripts submitted.

60. Mimeographed minutes, April 5, 1943 (Sachs Archive, Syndics folder). The regular April 5 minutes preserved at the Press are very brief and about manuscripts only.

61. Dumas Malone to W. W. Smith, May 6, 1943 (copy in Sachs Archive, folder labeled "Harvard University Press: Dumas Malone").

62. Dumas Malone, interview Nov. 28, 1973; "Dumas Malone," *Publishers Weekly* (July 3, 1981), 10.

63. Dumas Malone to J. B. Conant, May 6, 1943 (Conant Papers).

64. J. B. Conant to P. J. Sachs, May 22, 1943 (Sachs Archive, folder labeled "Harvard University Press: President Conant—Calvert Smith").

65. Sachs to Conant, June 3, 1943 (Conant Papers).

66. J. B. Conant, interview Nov. 9, 1973.

67. Corporation Records, July 19 and Aug. 2, 1943; University News Office, release no. 1943–153, for papers of September 16. Malone's resignation letter is in Conant Papers.

6. Scaife and Survival

1. R. L. Scaife, memorandum, "Random Comments on the Harvard University Press after a Year Spent at Quincy St.," January 1945 (Press file labeled "Reports on the Press").

2. W. Bentinck-Smith, interview Sept. 20, 1982; Donald Scott to Mark Carroll, April 17, 1962 (Press file labeled "Fremd, Edward, History of HUP"). Fremd began a brief history of the Press that was never published.

3. On shortages: Press Annual Reports, 1943–44 (p. 370) and 1945–46 (p. 447).

4. Annual output is from Press Annual Reports; net sales are from Press records.

5. N. P. Breed, "A General Descriptive Summary of the Harvard University Press," September 1946 (Press files), 48; R. L. Scaife to K. D. Metcalf, Jan. 9, 1946 (Press file labeled "Reports on the Press"). The Harvard Treasurer's Statements show the annual profits.

6. A. Calvert Smith to J. B. Conant, undated, telling of Syndics action of July 27, 1943; Dean Paul H. Buck to Conant, Sept. 9, 1943 (University Archives, Conant Papers, chronological files on Harvard University Press). Also Paul J. Sachs to P. H. Buck, Sept. 8, 1943 (carbon in Fogg Art Museum Archives, Paul

J. Sachs Archive, folder labeled "Harvard University Press: General"). The Corporation on Sept. 20, 1943, appointed Scaife as of Sept. 1.

7. Syndics minutes, Nov. 2, 1943.

8. Copies of the Syndics' document of Nov. 18, 1943—entitled "A Tentative Statement of the Purposes of the Harvard University Press and an Outline of Appropriate Fields of Activity"—are in Press file labeled "Reports on the Press" and in the Conant Papers.

9. R. L. Scaife to J. B. Conant, Nov. 29, 1943 (Conant Papers).

10. J. B. Conant to Henry James, Dec. 6, 1943 (carbon in Conant Papers). The Corporation approved Scaife's three-year salaried appointment Dec. 20. He resigned his Little, Brown vice-presidency, retaining his membership on the board.

11. Henry James to J. B. Conant, Dec. 2, 1943 (Conant Papers).

12. Conant to James, Dec. 6.

13. A copy is in Conant Papers.

14. Letter to me from Robert Shenton (Secretary to the Corporation) Feb. 18, 1983. The text of the report by James and Clark is unavailable. It was first presented to the Corporation on Feb. 21, 1944.

15. J. B. Conant, "To Members of the University Faculties and Their Associates," May 11, 1944 (Conant Papers).

16. Syndics minutes, Nov. 27, 1944; R. L. Scaife to J. B. Conant, Nov. 30, 1944 (Conant Papers).

17. Eleanor Dobson Kewer, interview Nov. 14, 1973; Dumas Malone to Willi Apel, April 17, 1940, and Malone to W. C. Rugg, May 10, 1940 (Press's Apel files); Syndics minutes, esp. Feb. 2, 1940; March 1, 1943; and March 17, 1943.

18. Kewer interview; R. L. Scaife to T. J. Wilson, "Personnel," March 17, 1947 (Press file labeled "For Mr. Wilson When He Becomes Director").

19. Breed, "Descriptive Summary" (note 5 above), p. 38 and esp. Exhibit 7.

20. Press contract files: contract between the Press and Apel, April 26, 1950, giving him 10 percent of list on first 7,500, then 12½ percent on the next 7,500, and 15 percent thereafter; letter from Apel and R. T. Daniel to T. J. Wilson, April 7, 1958, agreeing that Apel's beginning royalty would be 9 percent and Daniel's 1 percent; contract between the Press and Pocket Books, Jan. 22, 1959, providing a royalty of 4 percent of list on first 150,000 copies of the paperback and 6 percent thereafter (the Press kept half of this revenue, according to its contract with Apel). Pocket Books paid $3,000 as a minimum guarantee on royalties and $1,468 more as one-half the Press's costs of composition, artwork, and engraving.

21. T. J. Wilson to Freeman Lewis of Pocket Books, Feb. 26, 1959, granting paperback rights without limit of time "as we had agreed in our original negotiations." The Jan. 22 contract had specified a five-year term.

22. In 1978 the Press published another music dictionary, called *Harvard Concise Dictionary of Music,* compiled by Don Michael Randel.

23. James Bryant Conant, *My Several Lives: Memoirs of a Social Inventor* (New York: Harper & Row, 1970), 363–365, 369–370. On Lamont Library, K. D. Metcalf, interview June 8, 1982.

24. On Scaife's displeasure, William Bentinck-Smith, interview Nov. 13, 1973.

On Scaife's expectations, Scaife to J. B. Conant, Nov. 1, 1946 (Conant Papers). On the various printings and the finances, Breed, "Descriptive Summary," 14–15.

25. R. E. Larsen to R. L. Scaife, Sept. 8, 1943 (Press contract files); Syndics minutes, passim, including Jan. 10, 1940; Oct. 13, 1942; Nov. 3 and 24, 1942; Jan. 6, 1943; esp. Sept. 7, 1943. Ray had undertaken the project at the request of Thackeray's literary executor, Hester Thackeray Fuller.

26. R. L. Scaife to Horace Arnold (by then assistant director of the Printing Office), July 19, 1945; Scaife to N. P. Breed, Sept. 17, 1946 (Ray folder at the Press).

27. H. M. Jones, interview Oct. 13, 1973; Syndics minutes, May 15, 1944. Jones was a guest at this meeting, one week before the Corporation appointed him a Syndic.

28. Syndics minutes, June 12, 1944; R. L. Scaife to J. B. Conant, same date, and Conant to Sumner Welles, June 26, 1944 (Conant Papers).

29. Harvard University Press catalogue, Spring 1945, back cover.

30. A similar proposal from McCord is reported in the Syndics minutes of April 21, 1937, though the name John Harvard Library does not appear in those minutes.

31. L. P. Belden, interview Jan. 19, 1982. The matter appears also in Syndics minutes, March 29, May 23, June 4, and Sept. 23, 1946, also April 11, 1947; draft memo from R. L. Scaife to the Syndics, ca. April 8, 1946, given to me by William Bentinck-Smith; Scaife to Syndics, July 3, 1946, with attachments (University Archives, Keyes D. Metcalf papers, UAIII.50.8.11.3).

32. H. M. Jones, interview Oct. 13, 1973; R. L. Scaife to Mrs. Arthur H. Sulzberger, April 2, 1946, enclosing Jones's proposal and seeking funds for it (carbon given to me by William Bentinck-Smith). Though Jones evidently did not know it, the Syndics minutes of Dec. 5, 1929, had contained this passage: "Voted: That the Director be requested to consult Professor Kenneth B. Murdock and Professor C. N. Greenough regarding a plan for republishing in a series important older American books now out of print."

33. David McCord, interview Dec. 4, 1973; Syndics minutes, Oct. 5, 1938. The contract is dated Jan. 10, 1939.

34. Dictionary of invention was discussed in a memo by R. L. Scaife, May 15, 1944, in which he attributed the idea to Buck (Conant Papers); Syndics minutes April 10, May 15, June 12, and Nov. 27, 1944, also Feb. 24 and May 13, 1945. On Melville, Syndics minutes, Feb. 24, 1945. On Harvard Classics, Syndics minutes, Oct. 29, 1946.

35. Scaife in Press Annual Report, 1944–45. See also Syndics minutes, Feb. 2 and March 17, 1943; April 10 and June 12, 1944; March 28 and May 13, 1945; and esp. Nov. 5, 1945; also Harvard Corporation, Informal Record, June 27, 1945.

36. *In and Out of the Ivory Tower: The Autobiography of William L. Langer* (New York: Neale Watson Academic Publications, 1977), 205–206. On termination of project, see minutes of Press Board of Directors, Aug. 8, Sept. 16, and Dec. 16, 1947; T. J. Wilson to J. B. Conant, Sept. 29, 1947 (Conant Papers).

37. On marketing revolution: Frank Luther Mott, *Golden Multitudes* (New York: Macmillan, 1947), 268, 271–272. For Penguin offer: Eunice E. Frost to R. L. Scaife, Sept. 13, 1945 (Press's Susanne Langer file).

38. W. W. Smith to me, March 15, 1982.

39. On Catherine Scott and Francesca Morgan, University Archives, Personnel Records. See also *Publishers' Weekly* (July 1, 1944), pp. 26–28.

40. W. Bentinck-Smith, interview Nov. 13, 1973. He gave me four issues of *Book News.* Norman A. Hall, business manager of the *Bulletin,* worked half-time at the Press on direct-mail advertising for several years.

41. L. B. Lincoln, interview Nov. 18, 1973.

42. J. B. Conant, Annual Report, 1945–46, pp. 14–15.

43. R. L. Scaife to J. B. Conant, March 20, 1946 (Conant Papers). Before this, Scaife had considered himself directly under Conant rather than under Treasurer William Claflin. On Oct. 23, 1945, and Jan. 9, 1946, Scaife had said in letters to Keyes Metcalf that the Press was under the control of Conant and that the Printing Office was under Claflin (carbons in Press file labeled "Reports on the Press").

44. Breed, "Descriptive Summary" (note 5 above), 55, 50, 51. R. L. Scaife discussed Reynolds and Breed in a memorandum, "Future Harvard University Press Policies," Jan. 13, 1947 (Press file labeled "For Mr. Wilson When He Becomes Director").

45. F. L. Allen to J. B. Conant, Oct. 8, 1946 (Conant Papers).

46. Memorandum, "To the Members of the Visiting Committee of the Harvard University Press," March 30, 1946, signed by Maurice Smith, chairman of the fund-raising subcommittee, and Roy Larsen. This document spelled out the Guarantee Plan. Mimeographed copies were given to me by William Bentinck-Smith.

47. J. B. Conant to F. L. Allen, Dec. 17, 1946; Allen to Conant, Dec. 30, 1946 (Conant Papers).

48. Scaife, "Random Comments" (note 1 above). On Scaife's being "much upset," Edward Reynolds to F. L. Allen, May 5, 1947 (copy in Press file labeled "For Mr. Wilson When He Becomes Director").

49. At the suggestion of Jordan, who as a professor at the University of Chicago had served as a general editor of the University of Chicago Press, Scaife set up a Publishing Committee consisting of thirty-one Harvard professors. See Syndics minutes, Dec. 13, 1943; R. L. Scaife to J. B. Conant, March 21, 1944 (Conant Papers); R. L. Scaife to T. J. Wilson, memo entitled "Meetings," March 25, 1947 (Press file labeled "For Mr. Wilson When He Becomes Director").

50. As an example of Scaife's suggestions, he proposed a new position which would "resemble that of a Dean" and which would have charge of the Press, the Printing Office, the Publication Office, and a few other things, adding that the group might conceivably include, later, the *Harvard Alumni Bulletin* (R. L. Scaife to J. B. Conant, Nov. 30, 1944, Conant Papers).

51. K. D. Metcalf, interview Nov. 15, 1973.

52. R. L. Scaife to K. D. Metcalf, Nov. 28, 1945 (carbon in Press file labeled "Reports on the Press").

53. The committee's report and Metcalf's letter are in Conant Papers. The names on the report are Cass Canfield, Donald K. David, E. Pendleton Herring, Roy E. Larsen, Frederick G. Melcher, Donald Scott, and Keyes D. Metcalf.

54. T. J. Wilson to J. B. Conant, Jan. 28, 1947 (Conant Papers).

55. Minutes of Press Board of Directors, Sept. 23 and Dec. 2, 1955, and Corporation Records, Dec. 12, 1955. Background correspondence is in Donald Scott Papers, Harvard Business School Archives.

56. W. Bentinck-Smith, interview Nov. 13, 1973.

57. T. J. Wilson as quoted in John T. Winterich, "Harvard's Press Marks Half Century of Publishing," *Publishers' Weekly*, April 22, 1963.

58. J. B. Conant, interview Nov. 9, 1973.

59. J. B. Conant to T. J. Wilson, Oct. 25, 1951 (carbon in Conant Papers, initialed "JBC" in pencil).

7. Wilson and the Rise of the Press

1. This is the form in which Wilson's dictum was usually quoted—for example in John T. Winterich, "Harvard's Press Marks Half Century of Publishing," *Publishers' Weekly* (April 22, 1963), 16. Chester Kerr, in *A Report on American University Presses* (New York: Association of American University Presses, 1949), 13, said Wilson made the remark in 1947. Twenty years later, in a similar statement to the President of Harvard, Wilson changed "bankruptcy" to "within its financial capacities" (letter to Nathan M. Pusey, July 14, 1967, University Archives, Pusey Papers, chronological files on the Press).

2. Quotation is attributed to Wilson in Board of Directors minutes, Feb. 25, 1948. All figures are from Press records, except that the statistics on titles published are my own estimates based on a study of the Press's Annual Reports. The 2,300 total does not include books only distributed for Harvard departments (not brought before the Syndics). For example, the figure 144 for 1966–67 does not include 21 books only distributed. (The Press sometimes included such books in announcing its output.) The "published" figures include imports, that is, books of foreign publishers imported by Harvard and issued in American editions. Imports were numerous in some years—33 in 1953–54, when the total published was 117.

3. T. J. Wilson to Board of Directors, March 13, 1967 (Donald Scott Papers, Harvard Business School Archives, folder labeled "H.U. Press—Miscel."); memorandum from Board of Syndics to President and Fellows of Harvard College, May 23, 1967, written by Wilson (Syndics minutes, vol. 4, pp. 154–156).

4. On public relations see Thomas J. Wilson, "A Publisher Speaks Out," *Harvard Alumni Bulletin* (Sept. 24, 1949), 19. Quotation is from Press Annual Report, 1965–66, pp. 5–6, one of Wilson's most eloquent statements.

5. Mainly from *Who's Who in America*, 1956–1957. Biographical details are in many places—e.g., University news release of April 11, 1947, and *New York Times*, June 28, 1969 (the day after Wilson's death), 31. Wilson's book was published by Henry Holt & Co.

6. John King Fairbank, *Chinabound: A Fifty-Year Memoir* (New York: Harper & Row, 1982), 358.

7. N. M. Pusey to Howard Mumford Jones, Oct. 30, 1967 (carbon in Pusey Papers).

8. Press monthly balance sheets; Board of Directors minutes, May 8, 1958; Edward Reynolds to N. M. Pusey, May 14, 1958, and Corporation vote of May 19, 1958 (Pusey Papers).

9. U.S. Department of Commerce, Bureau of the Census, *Historical Statistics of the United States: Colonial Times to 1970,* pt. 1 (Washington, D.C.: Government Printing Office, 1975), 382–387.

10. Board of Directors minutes, Sept. 28, 1964. See also Press Annual Report, 1963–64, p. 10. On the Ford grants in general see Gene R. Hawes, *To Advance Knowledge: A Handbook on American University Press Publishing* (New York: American University Press Services, 1967), 13–16.

11. *Harvard Alumni Bulletin* (Dec. 10, 1955), 252. On need for new quarters in the 1940s: Press Annual Reports for 1944–45, 1945–46, and 1946–47. On Jewett House: Board of Directors minutes, Aug. 8, 1947; Syndics minutes, Sept. 19, 1947, Nov. 18, 1947, and Jan. 16, 1948. On 1955 urgency: Board of Directors minutes, May 6, 1955, and Press Annual Report, 1954–55.

12. Board of Directors minutes, Sept. 23, 1955, Nov. 4, 1955, Jan. 6, 1956, and Jan. 26, 1956; Press Annual Report, 1955–56. On the building itself see *Harvard University Handbook* (Harvard University, 1936), 239; *Education, Bricks and Mortar* (Harvard University, 1949), 66.

13. Who first suggested the name Kittredge Hall is not clear, but apparently these men took part in the naming: Edward Reynolds, Thomas Wilson, David W. Bailey (Secretary to the Corporation), President Nathan Pusey, and Pusey's assistant, William Bentinck-Smith. An interesting letter from Bailey to Reynolds, April 20, 1956, is in the Pusey Papers. The Corporation approved the name June 4, 1956. See also University news release, July 2, 1956.

14. On space shortage: Press Annual Reports for 1957–58, 1958–59, and 1959–60. On its easing: Annual Reports for 1960–61, 1961–62, 1962–63, 1963–64. On its return: Annual Report for 1965–66; Board of Directors minutes, Oct. 28, 1966; and the documents of 1967 cited in note 3 above.

15. University news release, Jan. 4, 1948; *Publishers' Weekly,* May 17, 1952.

16. Mark Saxton, interview Nov. 5, 1973.

17. On science publishing, see Michael A. Aronson, "Building the Science List of a University Press," *Scholarly Publishing,* October 1973. On science books at the Press: J. D. Elder to me Oct. 10, 1973; Syndics minutes, March 1, April 12, and esp. June 14, 1951. On Commonwealth Fund: the same minutes plus those of June 7, 1951, and Press Annual Report, 1951–52. On Harvard Books in Astronomy: Syndics minutes, Nov. 8 and Dec. 8, 1951; Board of Directors minutes, Dec. 20, 1951; and esp. William I. Bennett, memorandum for the files, Nov. 15, 1973. Blakiston published eight titles in the Harvard Books on Astronomy. By 1982 the Press had added four more and still had four of the Blakiston titles in print (in later editions)—namely, *Earth, Moon, and Planets,* by Fred L. Whipple; *Galaxies,* by Harlow Shapley; *The Milky Way,* by Bart J.

Bok and Priscilla F. Bok; and *Atoms, Stars, and Nebulae,* by Lawrence Aller (originally Aller and Leo Goldberg). The first book published by the Press in the series, in 1952, was *Stars in the Making,* by Cecelia Payne-Gaposchkin; it sold 12,700 in hardcover and 78,000 in a Pocket Books paperback.

18. Burton J. Jones, interview Dec. 6, 1973.

19. Maud Wilcox, interview June 10, 1981; Eleanor Dobson Kewer, interview Nov. 21, 1973.

20. T. J. Wilson to Board of Directors, Sept. 14, 1965 (Donald Scott Papers, file labeled "Harvard University Press, Correspondence—Wilson, 1964–").

21. Board of Directors minutes, April 28, July 28, and Oct. 27, 1950. Wilson was named president-elect of the Association of American University Presses in 1950 and was president 1951–1953.

22. T. J. Wilson to N. M. Pusey, March 31, 1954 (Pusey Papers). The Corporation acted on April 5.

23. Press Annual Report, 1966–67, p. 3. Wilson's letter to Donald Scott, Sept. 5, 1958 (Donald Scott Papers, file labeled "HUP, Current Action"), contains very high praise of Smith in the first decade.

24. Board of Directors minutes, Jan. 5, 1959; Corporation Records, Jan. 19, 1959.

25. Quotation is from Press Annual Report, 1958–59, p. 3. Specific responsibilities in T. J. Wilson, "Important Memorandum to the Press Staff," undated but probably January 1959 (Donald Scott Papers, file labeled "HUP Personnel").

26. Here are the five, with the dates of the reviews: Fairbank, *The United States and China* (July 11); Ruth Fischer, *Stalin and German Communism* (Sept. 5); Seymour E. Harris, *The European Recovery Program* (Nov. 7); *The Keats Circle,* ed. Hyder E. Rollins, and *The Letters of Edgar Allan Poe,* ed. John Ward Ostrom (both Dec. 19).

27. For the background and substance of the book see Fairbank, *Chinabound* (note 6 above), 326–327.

28. Press Annual Report, 1949–50.

29. In the voluminous Press files on the Kelly book these items are of special interest: T. J. Wilson to Amy Kelly, Sept. 29, 1948; Syndics minutes, Jan. 10, 1949; contract in Press files, dated Jan. 24, 1949; Kelly to Wilson, June 9, Nov. 16, and Dec. 5, 1949, and June 30, 1950. Also see *Harvard Alumni Bulletin* (Nov. 11, 1950), 156.

30. Winterich, "Harvard's Press" (note 1 above), 18. To be precise, Wilson told Winterich, according to the article, that the Press around 1950 had given up "the practice of requiring or accepting cash subsidies from authors of scholarly but unsalable books." Amy Kelly's book did not belong in the "unsalable" category; but the Press staff, at least in my time (1960–1973), was given to understand unmistakably that *all* cash subsidies from authors were taboo.

31. Syndics minutes, Sept. 7 and Oct. 11, 1943; R. L. Scaife to T. J. Wilson, memos of March 17 and 25, 1947 (Press file labeled "For Mr. Wilson When He Becomes Director"); Board of Directors minutes, Oct. 22, 1947, March 30, 1964, and Feb. 3 and March 31, 1969. Apparently no limit was ever imposed for non-Harvard readers, but almost always the same maximum has applied.

32. Syndics minutes, March 28, 1950; Nov. 4 and Dec. 15, 1953; July 8, 1954.

33. Syndics minutes, Jan. 16, 1950, and esp. March 28, 1950.

34. An example of an acceptable textbook is *A New Introduction to Greek,* by A. H. Chase and Henry Phillips, Jr., published by the Press in 1946 and still in print in the 1980s.

35. Fairbank, *Chinabound,* 357–360. Another series prepared at the Center, the Harvard East Asian Monographs, which the Press only distributes rather than publishes, has exceeded 100 titles.

36. Syndics minutes, Jan. 16, 1948. Funds for the editing were provided by the Theodore Roosevelt Memorial Association.

37. All this is from two enormous Mays folders at the Press.

38. Statistics are from (1) the University's annual Financial Report to the Overseers (which before 1948–49 was called Treasurer's Statement), and (2) the Press's annual statistical reports headed "Belknap Press Fund" (Press accounting files). For example, in Financial Report for 1966–67 the Belknap figures are on p. 303 and other pertinent Harvard University Press data on pp. 15, 17, 19, 376.

39. Press Annual Reports, 1963–64 (p. 10) and 1965–66 (pp. 7–8).

40. Transcript of Belknap's will is in Office of the Recording Secretary, Harvard. The "official" name of the Press (in Harvard Corporation documents) is "The Harvard University Press," and the Press itself used the "the" until the late forties.

41. On Belknap Press guidelines, Board of Directors minutes, March 4, 1952. The board that day approved a memorandum by T. J. Wilson on the Clarendon Press and other aspects, dated Feb. 27, 1952 (an undated copy is in Donald Scott Papers), and also adopted a resolution by Scott establishing the Belknap Press. The Harvard Corporation approved this April 7, 1952. On the question of subject matter, Press Annual Report, 1960–61, p. 2.

42. T. J. Wilson, Press Annual Report, 1963–64, p. 9; Mrs. T. J. Wilson (Phoebe Rous Wilson), interview March 15, 1974.

43. Grace A. Briggs, interview Dec. 5, 1973, and correspondence in her "Friends" files, esp. Frederick Lewis Allen to Waldron P. Belknap, Jr., March 31, 1948, and Belknap's card postmarked May 27. For contributions totaling $4,585 see Harvard Financial Reports, 1947–48 through 1953–54 ("gifts for current use"). Many other subsidies for specific books were received during that period, but apparently not through the Friends.

44. For a biographical account see Alice Winchester, "Waldron Phoenix Belknap, Jr., 1899–1949," in "Waldron Phoenix Belknap, Jr." (pamphlet, The Belknap Press of Harvard University Press, 1956), 5–13.

45. William A. Jackson, "The Belknap Press," ibid., p. 15; T. J. Wilson, "Publisher's Foreword" in *Records of a Bibliographer: Selected Papers of William A. Jackson* (Harvard University Press, 1967); Philip Hofer, interview March 16, 1982.

46. Board of Directors minutes, Sept. 27, 1957. The gifts from Mrs. Belknap (who is not identified) and the annual capitalizations of income appear in the Harvard Financial Reports.

47. Howard M. Jones, interview Nov. 16, 1973; Burton J. Jones, interview Dec. 6, 1973; T. J. Wilson to D. W. Bailey, William Bentinck-Smith, Edward Reynolds, and James Reynolds, Nov. 19, 1959 (Pusey Papers). Much of the trouble came in connection with a posthumous book by Waldron P. Belknap, Jr., *American Colonial Painting: Materials for a History,* prepared for publication by Charles Coleman Sellers (The Belknap Press of Harvard University Press, 1960).

48. Transcript of Rey Belknap's will is in Office of the Recording Secretary, Harvard. The additions to capital are shown in Harvard Financial Reports.

49. Robert L. Wareham (a senior trust officer at the Old Colony Trust Division, First National Bank, Boston), interview July 21, 1982; also Henry J. Ameral (Harvard assistant treasurer) to Brian P. Murphy, Schuyler Hollingsworth, and George Putnam, April 11, 1979, esp. Exhibit 7, which is an undated memorandum by Robert Wareham. Harvard's shares are only a small fraction of the total shares in the Hutchings Joint Stock Association.

50. Brian P. Murphy to Arthur J. Rosenthal, Feb. 16, 1982.

51. An agreement of the 1930s between Schlesinger and the Press is described in W. W. Smith, memo for the *Harvard Guide* file, Jan. 11, 1951. The terms were 10 percent of list price on the first 2,000 copies and 15 thereafter, and these terms were written into the final contract of Feb. 25, 1952, signed by Wilson and the six professors. On the division of royalties see T. J. Wilson to Harold Bryar (the Press's chief accountant), May 25, 1954.

52. Syndics minutes, March 28, 1950. Houghton Library had approached the Press about publication of the letters even before Roger Scaife left office.

53. Max Hall, "Butterfield to Retire, Taylor Chosen as Successor," in "M.H.S. Miscellany: Published Occasionally by the Massachusetts Historical Society," March 1975. This is a 3,000-word document issued by the Society for release on March 9, 1975.

54. "The Adams Papers: A Ceremony Held at the Massachusetts Historical Society on September 22, 1961" (Boston: Massachusetts Historical Society, 1962), 7–8. The speeches are also in the *Proceedings of the Massachusetts Historical Society* 73 (1961), 119–150.

55. T. J. Wilson, Memorandum for the File, "Re: Adams Family Papers and possible publication," March 17, 1953 (Press, Director's Files).

56. Minutes of meeting Aug. 9, 1952, held in Adams Library, Quincy, Mass.; also memorandum for Rockefeller Foundation written by L. H. Butterfield in 1952 and revised by W. M. Whitehill in March 1954 (both in Massachusetts Historical Society, Adams Papers Archives, General Materials, Box 1, File A2).

57. On historical editing see L. H. Butterfield in *Proceedings of the Massachusetts Historical Society* 78 (1966), 82, 86–87.

58. W. M. Whitehill to L. H. Butterfield, Jan. 8 and Jan. 12, 1954, and subsequent correspondence in File A2 as cited in note 56 above.

59. On governing boards see Syndics minutes, Jan. 19, 1954; Board of Directors minutes, Jan. 22, 1954.

60. T. J. Wilson to N. M. Pusey, Jan. 26, 1954 (carbon in Press's Adams Papers file). The Harvard Corporation acted Feb. 1, 1954. See also exchange

between T. J. Wilson and T. B. Adams, Feb. 16 and Feb. 26, 1954, in Adams Papers Archives, General Materials, Box 1, File A4, and in Press file.

61. W. M. Whitehill to L. H. Butterfield, April 14, May 10, May 12, 1954, and subsequent correspondence (Box 1, File A2).

62. Agreement between Adams Manuscript Trust and Time Inc., Aug. 9, 1954 (Box 1, File A4). The *Life* articles: Oct. 25, 1954; July 2, 1956; June 30 and Nov. 3, 1961; May 25, 1962.

63. Series I, "Diaries"; Series II, "Adams Family Correspondence"; Series III, "General Correspondence and Other Papers of the Adams Statesmen"; Series IV, "Portraits."

64. Calculated for me at the Press from the records of the various Adams Papers volumes. Besides overhead, the cost figure includes manufacture and advertising. Editorial work is done at the Massachusetts Historical Society and financed by them. Production costs were reduced by $40,000 through grants from the National Historical Publications and Records Commission—an unusual occurrence because Belknap books ordinarily do not get publishing subsidies from any outside source. The income figure of $456,000 includes sales receipts of $428,000 and the Belknap Press's share of payments for paperback reprints and for a two-volume collection published by *Newsweek*. Not included in any of these figures is *The Book of Abigail and John* (1975), which grew out of the Adams Papers but was not a part of that series and not a Belknap book. (According to Press records the costs of this book have exceeded the income from sales and subsidiary rights.)

65. Calculated at the Press. Besides the $518,451 transferred to the general funds of Harvard University Press, the John Harvard Library costs include manufacture, the expenses of managing and editing the series, and advertising and promotion.

66. Mark Saxton, interview Nov. 5, 1973.

67. James Parton to T. J. Wilson, June 6, 1962; Wilson to Parton, June 8 (James Parton Papers, Houghton Library, Harvard).

68. Howard M. Jones, interview Oct. 13, 1973.

69. Board of Directors minutes, March 28, 1966, and Oct. 20, 1969.

70. Quotation is from University news release, March 12, 1954. See also Board of Directors minutes, Sept. 25, 1953, and Syndics minutes, Dec. 15, 1953; Jan. 19, Feb. 3, and April 2, 1954; May 3, 1955. Also Press Annual Reports beginning with 1953–54.

71. Mark Carroll to all departments, Aug. 21, 1963.

72. Gene R. Hawes, *To Advance Knowledge* (note 10 above), 109.

8. The Paperback Question, the Double Helix, and Other Stories

1. T. J. Wilson to Board of Directors, "Recommendation Regarding the Editorial Department of Harvard University Press," Sept. 14, 1965 (Donald Scott Papers, Harvard Business School Archives, file labeled "Harvard University Press, Correspondence—Wilson 1964–").

2. Horne's appointment and the other changes that went with it were an-

nounced in a Press news release Dec. 3, 1965, and described in Press Annual Report, 1965–66, pp. 1–2.

3. Press Annual Report, 1965–66, p. 2.

4. Quotations are from Press Annual Report, 1965–66, p. 11. The statistics on paperbacks are my estimates based on examining the Press's card file on books leased to other publishers.

5. Paper *bindings* were not new to University presses. In 1948 some 27 percent of their titles were issued in paper covers, according to Chester Kerr in *A Report on American University Presses* (New York: Association of American University Presses, 1949), 126. These, however, were pamphlets and other publications not aimed at the new paperback market.

6. For a good discussion, see Marshall A. Best, "In Books, They Call It Revolution," in *The American Reading Public* (New York: R. R. Bowker, 1963; based on symposium in *Daedalus,* Winter 1963), 72–75.

7. Gene R. Hawes, *To Advance Knowledge: A Handbook on American University Press Publishing* (New York: American University Press Services, 1967), 6.

8. Typically a quality paperback publisher paid 7½ percent of the book's retail price, which the Press shared fifty-fifty with the author. For clear and concise paperback policy statements by Thomas Wilson, see Press Annual Report, 1963–64, pp. 16–17, and John T. Winterich, "Harvard's Press Marks Half Century of Publishing," *Publishers' Weekly* (April 22, 1963), 21.

9. W. W. Smith to me, Aug. 2, 1982; Grace A. Briggs, interview Jan. 5, 1974.

10. Press's Lovejoy file, correspondence in 1959 including T. J. Wilson to W. W. Smith, Feb. 27; Smith to Wilson, March 4; Melvin Arnold to Wilson, March 9 and 30; Wilson to Arnold, March 11 and 26. The contract is dated March 30.

11. Mark Carroll to T. J. Wilson, "Quality Paperback Publishing," March 16, 1959 (copy in Donald Scott Papers, file labeled "Paperback"), 3, 4, esp. 6.

12. Press contract files and correspondence in file labeled "Atheneum Publishers Project, 1961–March 1962." The agreement as signed for Atheneum by Alfred Knopf, Jr., is dated March 6, 1962; Wilson signed on March 15. After five years the agreement was to be automatically renewed every two years unless canceled. I find no record of cancellation; apparently the arrangement simply became inoperative by tacit consent when the Press decided to enter the paperback field. Atheneum in 1962 made a similar agreement with Princeton University Press, which also entered full-scale paperback publishing later than most.

13. Mark Carroll to T. J. Wilson, Jan. 11, 1962; W. W. Smith to Wilson, Jan. 16, 1962.

14. Board of Directors minutes, Jan. 22, 1962; Donald Scott to T. J. Wilson, Feb. 16, 1962.

15. T. J. Wilson's handwritten notes in the file, undated but obviously in preparation for the Board of Directors; also T. J. Wilson to Alfred Knopf, Jr., March 5, 1962 (carbon in Press file).

16. Board of Directors minutes, March 8, 1965.

17. Mark Carroll to T. J. Wilson, Dec. 13, 1966 (Press file labeled "Harvard

Paperbacks—History"). Carroll told me in a note July 16, 1982, that the "Atheneum arrangement, and the success of others in paperbacks" caused him to change his mind.

18. David Horne to T. J. Wilson and nine others, "The Question of Paperbacks," Nov. 21, 1966. Sales Manager Loring Lincoln, in his memorandum, called for paperbacks with "all possible speed" to enable the Press to compete better in the class-adoption market, in college bookstores, and in general bookstores.

19. T. J. Wilson to W. W. Smith, Mark Carroll, David Horne, and six others, Nov. 25, 1966.

20. David Horne to Mark Carroll, Dec. 13, 1966; Carroll to T. J. Wilson, same date.

21. T. J. Wilson to Ernst Mayr, Sept. 2, 1966; quotation is from T. J. Wilson's typed notes of July 4, 1966 (Press file "Watson, Double Helix, 1966").

22. Oscar M. Shaw, of Ropes & Gray, to T. J. Wilson, Aug. 29, 1966 (Press file, 1966).

23. F. H. C. Crick to T. J. Wilson, Oct. 10, 1966; Wilson to Crick, Oct. 14; M. H. F. Wilkins to Wilson, Oct. 17 (all in Press file, 1966).

24. Pusey's correspondence with Crick in December and January is in University Archives, Nathan M. Pusey Papers, folders on Harvard University Press.

25. M. F. H. Wilkins to N. M. Pusey, Feb. 2, 1967; Pusey to Wilkins, Feb. 20 (Pusey Papers).

26. T. J. Wilson to N. M. Pusey, March 24 and April 14, 1967 (carbons in Press's Watson file of 1967–1968).

27. F. H. C. Crick, letters to J. D. Watson, T. J. Wilson, and N. M. Pusey, April 13, 1967, and M. F. H. Wilkins to T. J. Wilson, May 4, 1967 (Pusey Papers and Press file of 1967–1968); Wilson to Konrad Bloch, John P. Dawson, Manfred Karnovsky, and Ernst Mayr, April 17, 1967; Wilson to O. M. Shaw, April 18 (carbons in Press file).

28. L. C. Pauling to N. M. Pusey, April 25, 1967 (Pusey Papers).

29. Robert H. Montgomery, Jr., to Harvard University Press, May 11, 1967 (Press file).

30. Shaw's letters, dated May 12, 1967, are in Pusey Papers.

31. That Wilson wanted the administration to decide the matter is shown not only by his letters already quoted but also in the Syndics minutes of June 12, 1967, which say that the question of publication "was referred by the Board of Syndics to the President of the University, who placed the matter before the Corporation."

32. Ernst Mayr to Mark Carroll, March 8, 1968; Konrad Bloch to T. J. Wilson, May 19, 1967 (Press file), with a copy to President Pusey.

33. N. M. Pusey to T. J. Wilson, May 23, 1967 (Press file).

34. *New York Times*, Feb. 15, 1968; *Boston Globe*, Feb. 16, 1968. Also of interest: letters in the *Crimson* from T. J. Wilson (Feb. 19), Talcott Parsons (March 2), and J. K. Galbraith (March 9).

35. Board of Directors minutes, Sept. 25, Oct. 30, and Dec. 3, 1953; Syndics minutes, Nov. 4, 1953; Press Annual Report, 1952–53, p. 653. For non-Harvard

sponsors such as the Commonwealth Fund and the Metropolitan Museum of Art, the commission was set at 40 percent of *receipts* plus 5 percent of the manufacturing costs. In 1964 these charges were raised to 45 percent plus 10 percent (Board of Directors minutes, Sept. 28, 1964).

36. Carroll had succeeded Charles C. Pyne, the University Bursar, who had been secretary since 1948.

37. Press Annual Report, 1965–66, p. 9.

38. Jones had six books in the annual "Fifty Books" exhibits of the American Institute of Graphic Arts. Ford had three. Ford remained Senior Designer until he left the Press in 1974, after which he did freelance designing for the Press and other publishers. The Press's production files contain a very sharp memo about jackets from Wilson to Jones and Ford, Sept. 28, 1960.

39. T. J. Wilson to N. M. Pusey, March 13 and March 16, 1967 (Donald Scott Papers, file labeled "H.U. Press—Miscel.").

40. Donald Scott to Pusey, March 31, 1967 (carbon in same file).

41. Same file.

42. The Syndics memo, dated May 23, 1967, and a note about the Corporation's reaction are in Syndics minutes, vol. 4, pp. 154–156.

43. Pusey's message to the Corporation and his notes on his activities of June and July 1967 are in Pusey Papers.

9. Crisis and Reorganization

Epigraphs: L. H. Butterfield, editor-in-chief of the Adams Papers, to Derek C. Bok, Feb. 27, 1972 (carbon copy in Butterfield's files). Derek C. Bok to Butterfield, handwritten letter in Butterfield's files, undated but probably Feb. 28 or 29, 1972.

1. The figure 163 does not include 21 books that were merely distributed on commission for Harvard departments and therefore did not have to be approved by the Syndics. Books in the paperback program, which is described in this chapter, are included in the annual totals (on the ground that they were more like new editions than mere reprints), except that in the few cases of *simultaneous* publication in cloth and paper the title is counted only once.

2. For *A Theory of Justice,* Rawls won the Ralph Waldo Emerson Award of Phi Beta Kappa and the Press's Paine Prize, and he shared the Press's Faculty Prize with I. Bernard Cohen, author of *Introduction to Newton's 'Principia.'* Other prizes awarded for books published in the Carroll years included: Lowell Prize of the Modern Language Association, to Helen Vendler for *On Extended Wings: Wallace Stevens' Longer Poems;* Christian Gauss Award of Phi Beta Kappa, to Walter Jackson Bate for *The Burden of the Past and the English Poet;* and the same prize a year later to Carl Woodring for *Politics in English Romantic Poetry.*

3. Board of Directors minutes, Nov. 20, 1970. See also minutes of May 18, 1970, and Jan. 25, 1971.

4. Mark Carroll, interviews Oct. 24, 1973, and May 7, 1982.

5. D. H. Horne, interview Sept. 21, 1982.

6. Mark Carroll to all departments, Oct. 23, 1967; Nanine K. Hutchinson, interview Sept. 22, 1982.

7. For example, Nanine K. Hutchinson, letter to me Sept. 28, 1982.

8. "Report to the Director and Members of the Harvard University Press," submitted by Bill Allen, Alain Forgeot, Dennis Gallagher, and Patrick McEvoy, March 31, 1970.

9. Some in the editorial department, including the present writer, were surprised and rather scornful at the assertions that the Press lacked a sense of purpose, for we had never doubted that the purpose was to publish good scholarly books. It went without saying that we should do this efficiently.

10. Board of Directors minutes, Oct. 14, 1968; also Mark Carroll to Board of Directors, May 17, 1968. All figures on actual sales, profits, and losses are from Press records provided by Brian Murphy, Associate Director for Operations, and Kathleen Cella, the Press's chief accountant.

11. Board of Directors minutes, March 31, 1969.

12. Ibid., March 2 and May 18, 1970.

13. Ibid., May 7, 1971.

14. William Bentinck-Smith, interview Nov. 13, 1973.

15. On the first budget for 1971–72, see Board of Directors minutes, March 14, 1971. This budget, like the one for 1969–70, was more than half a million dollars off in its sales projection, but this time in the opposite direction. It envisioned sales of slightly over $3 million, whereas in fact they were $3,660,000. But expenses were understated by a much greater margin than sales—hence the actual deficit of $349,900. Carroll achieved the breakeven budget by reducing the "expenses" prediction from $3,172,825 to $3,035,100. Actual expenses turned out to be a little over $4,000,000.

16. Cumulative profit on June 30, 1967, was $312,000. The Press spent $130,647 of this to move the shipping room to the warehouse and remodel the basement of Kittredge Hall for the expanding business staff, also $18,500 for educational or housing loans to two Press officers. The rest of the balance disappeared in the deficit of 1969–70.

17. Not only new books but existing ones were priced higher. A comparison between the annual catalogues of 1967 and 1972 shows that the prices of books already in print in 1967 were increased almost across the board—and by much more than 16 percent. In the four fiscal years beginning in 1967–68, the sales of Press-owned books, making up most of the total, increased hardly at all.

18. Census Bureau figures show a drop in the income which institutions of higher education received from the federal government, from $3.3 billion in 1968 to $2.5 billion in 1969. U.S. Department of Commerce, Bureau of the Census, *Historical Statistics of the United States: Colonial Times to 1970*, pt. 1 (Washington, D.C.: Government Printing Office, 1975), p. 384.

19. *Harvard Crimson*, Feb. 26, 1972.

20. Lybrand, Ross Bros. & Montgomery, "Harvard University Press, Memorandum of Comments, Fiscal Year Ended June 30, 1971," p. 6.

21. On July 11, 1972, with George Hall leading the way, the Board of Directors ordered a change in the policy of calculating inventory costs for write-off pur-

poses. Instead of writing off the entire cost of a book in one lump after six years, the Press began making the write-offs in annual steps during the six-year period, with different schedules for three different kinds of costs.

22. Board of Directors minutes, March 25 and Oct. 14, 1968, and minutes during 1969, passim.

23. John Bishop of the Harvard Business School (interview Nov. 19, 1982) helped me understand the failure of the arrangement between the Press and the Computing Center. For about a year and a half beginning in June 1969, Bishop was director of Harvard's Office for Information Technology; the Computing Center reported to him.

24. Syndics minutes, May 10, 1971.

25. Nanine K. Hutchinson to Press departments, May 21, 1971.

26. Board of Directors minutes, March 29, 1971.

27. Ibid., May 24, 1971; Mark Carroll to all staff, June 2, 1971.

28. Gene R. Hawes, *To Advance Knowledge: A Handbook on American University Press Publishing* (New York: American University Press Services, 1967), 55.

29. Stephen S. J. Hall, interview Oct. 1, 1982.

30. Mark Carroll, talk before the Society of Printers, Boston, March 1, 1972, printed in Christopher Reed, "Trouble at the Harvard Press," *Harvard Bulletin* (April 1972), 28.

31. Board of Directors minutes, Oct. 1 and Oct. 28, 1971.

32. Syndics minutes, Jan. 10, 1972. On joint meeting of Nov. 11, 1971: David Horne to staff, Dec. 1, 1971, and Board of Directors minutes, Dec. 1, 1971.

33. In Mark Carroll's files I have read ninety-one letters which he received. I do not know how many Derek Bok received, but I have seen copies of—or references to—eighteen of them in the files of Carroll and of the late L. H. Butterfield and the late Howard Mumford Jones. Those files also contain Bok's replies to some of the letters. The two headlines were, respectively, in the *Boston Globe* of Feb. 25, 1972, and the *Harvard Crimson* of Feb. 26.

34. The letters to Bok are dated as follows: Butterfield, Feb. 27, 1972; Whitehill, Feb. 26; Jones, Feb. 25. On *Revolution and Romanticism:* Jones to David Horne, April 3, 1972: Horne to Jones, April 7; Maud Wilcox to Jones, April 7 (all in Jones files).

35. David Horne, memo to all staff, March 24, 1972. The meeting took place March 22.

36. Letters of Harvey and Bailey are dated Feb. 28, 1972.

37. All these letters, or copies thereof, are in Carroll files. Carroll's is dated March 30, 1972.

38. Quotations are from official AAUP copies of the two resolutions, dated June 24, 1972. See also *New York Times,* "University Presses Are Struggling to Overcome Fiscal Crisis," June 26, 1972; and *Publishers Weekly,* "AAUP: Coping with Crisis," July 24, 1972, pp. 44–45.

39. Quotations are from "Reciprocal Responsibilities of a University and Its Press," pamphlet, Association of American University Presses, January 1983.

40. David Horne to all staff, March 27, 1972; University news release, March 28, 1972.

Sources and Acknowledgments

GRATEFULLY I thank those who gave me access to collections of documents, those who granted interviews, and those who reviewed what I wrote and helped me improve it.

One indispensable collection of documents was the files of Harvard University Press itself. The Press, headed by Arthur J. Rosenthal, freely opened to me the minutes of the Board of Syndics and Board of Directors, the contract files, the records of individual books, the financial sheets, and anything else I wanted to see. Everyone cooperated in this; I particularly salute Susan Metzger, Maud Wilcox, Brian Murphy, Kathleen Cella, and Joan O'Donnell—and also Grace Briggs, who had recently retired when I began my research in 1973 but who returned to pull out many files and pictures that I might not have found.

Another basic body of primary materials was the Harvard University Archives, headed by Harley Holden. There I found some of the Press's early files, deposited long ago, and large amounts of pertinent information in various kinds of University records. These included Harvard Corporation minutes, Annual Reports of the president (each of which contains the Annual Report of the Press Director), treasurers' statements, catalogues, personnel records, faculty minutes, reports by the Press's visiting committee, anniversary reports of alumni classes, and, most important of all, the presidents' correspondence having to do with the Press and its predecessors. The Eliot and Lowell Papers were open to any bona fide scholar. The Conant and Pusey Papers were not, and I was unable to roam through them at will; but, because they were very necessary to an understanding of Harvard publishing, Robert Shenton, Secretary to the Corporation, and William Bentinck-Smith, who had been President Pusey's assistant, spent a great deal of time making sure that I knew what was in them pertaining to the Press. Without this cooperation my book would have been much less revealing.

I am equally grateful to the late Louise Scott, widow of Donald Scott. She had first met Scott around 1912 when she was secretary to the first dean of the Harvard Business School. In 1973 she gave me Scott's personal files concerning the Press and the Business School, with the understanding that I would eventually deposit them in the Business School Archives. I have done so. The materials Mrs. Scott entrusted to me, now entitled the Donald Scott Papers, contain facts available nowhere else about the founding of the Press and the later administration of Thomas J. Wilson.

Similarly the Paul J. Sachs Archive, in the Fogg Art Museum, was an important source, giving an inside story of the Press's troubles of 1942 and 1943. Discovering the Sachs files was one of the high points of my research, and with the museum's permission I have quoted much from them.

A smaller cache came to light in Greensboro, North Carolina, in the form of letters written by David Pottinger. His daughter, Ann Pottinger Saab, a historian and a Press author, found them among his papers and shared them with me.

Pottinger and Warren Smith were successively second in command at the Press for about forty-five years. I regret having had no chance to interview Pottinger, who died long before I started the project. Smith, who served the Press from 1924 until he retired in 1967 as Associate Director and Business Manager, helped me more than I can adequately express. He gave me his recollections, read drafts of all my chapters as I finished them, and wrote detailed memoranda.

Bentinck-Smith, who is an authority on Harvard history and who worked at the Press for a while in the 1940s, read the whole manuscript with an eye not only for accuracy but also for effectiveness of the writing. Others outside the Press who read the whole thing and commented on it were Oscar Handlin, Rollo Silver, Edward Mason, Mark Carroll, Bessie Zaban Jones, and Robert Shenton. And so did Datus C. Smith, Jr., of Princeton, New Jersey, a senior statesman of scholarly publishing, who was engaged as reader by the Press and who volunteered that he did not mind if I knew his identity. I have acted upon most of his suggestions and have a better book as a result. A number of other people familiar with specific events or periods examined parts of the manuscript at my request.

The "oral history" phase of my work involved a larger group. Some of those whom I interviewed have already been mentioned as readers, but I want to name them again in the paragraphs that follow.

Two people still at the Press added much to my understanding—each in a series of interviews—namely Maud Wilcox, who has been in the organization since 1957, and Brian Murphy, who advised me on the financial tangles of the early seventies. Ann Louise Mc-Laughlin's memories were helpful too.

Former Press employees, in addition to Warren Smith and Grace Briggs, include Dumas Malone, who submitted to two interviews in Charlottesville, Virginia, and wrote me several times in response to my queries. They also include William Bentinck-Smith, Mark Carroll, David Horne, Loring Lincoln, Mark Saxton, Burton Jones, Eleanor Kewer, David Ford, Christopher Reed, Nanine Hutchinson, Lawrence Belden, Christopher Burns, Horace Arnold, Bessie Zaban Jones, Mary Conlan, and Phoebe Wilson.

Besides those Press members, I talked with the following people (some of whom have since died): Howard Mumford Jones, James Bryant Conant, Derek Bok, Oscar Handlin, Stephen Hall, David Bailey, Edward Mason, Marc Friedlaender, Keyes Metcalf, Ernst Mayr, Bertrand Fox, Archibald Cox, James McFarlane, John Bishop, David McCord, Philip Hofer, Rudolph Ruzicka, Dorothy Abbe, and Lyman Butterfield. I corresponded with still others, including Oscar Shaw, Dorothy Greenwald, and Joseph Elder.

Along with all the documents and interviews, another "source" should be mentioned—my own experience as a Press editor from 1960 to 1973.

Most fervently of all, I thank my daughter, Judith A. Hall, herself an author, for generous and time-consuming editorial help at a crucial point of the project.

Harvard University Archives supplied Figures 1, 2, 3, 4, 5, 7, 17, 27, and 31. From the files of the Press came the pictures of Press Directors and various other subjects, and the Press also arranged for the photographing of Press books—as in Figures 12 and 15, for example. The University News Office did the photography for Figures 25, 34, 35, 36, and 43. Figure 8 was provided by George L. Harding, 9 and 11 by Dorothy Abbe, and 18 by Ann Pottinger Saab.

Index

References to illustrations are in italics.

Accounting, 46, 69; mentioned 100–101, 173, 184, 185. *See also* Lybrand, Ross Bros. & Montgomery

Acquisitions. *See* Editorial department

Acting Director: Blanchard, 37; Dwiggins, 37; Pottinger, 61; Scaife, 103, 107; Horne, 200; Handlin, 201

Adams, Charles Francis III, 32, 37–39

Adams, Henry, 11, 135, 153

Adams, John, diary, 144, 147–149

Adams, Thomas Boylston, 144, 148, 149

Adams Papers, 144–148; paperbacks, 164

Administrative vice-president. *See* Vice-president for administration

Allen, B. Sprague, 83

Allen, Frederick Lewis, 120, 141, 148

Aller, Lawrence, 231n17

American Foreign Policy Library: birth, 111, 114–115; flourishing, 134, 137

American Institute of Graphic Arts, 52

Ames, James Barr, 16, 26

Anderson, Elin L., 76

Andrews, Kenneth R., 221n30

Annals of the Astronomical Observatory, 10, 12

Apel, Willi, 82, 111–113

Appleton & Co., 76–77

Arden Editions (Shakespeare), 134

Arnold, Horace: early service, 57–58, 69; and Malone, 96, 98, 99, 225n44; departs, 102; mentioned 72, 81, 92, 243

Art history, books on, 50, 82; Giedion's book on, 79, 80

Assistant Director: Horne, 157; Bishop, 183

Assistant to the Director, 183; Belden, 115, 133; Carroll, 133; Davison, 133; Burns, 183; Hutchinson, 183; Wotherspoon, 183

Associate Director: Pottinger, 65; Smith, 133; Carroll, 134; Horne, 182

Association of American University Presses: forerunner of, 35; Wilson as president of, 133, 232; Cambridge meeting, 169; on Carroll firing, 198; on nature of a university press, 191, 198–199, 202

Atheneum Publishers: paperback agreement, 163–164, 236n12; Adams Papers, 164; *Double Helix,* 168; employs Wilson, 174; mentioned 78, 143, 201–202

Atlantic–Little, Brown, 94, 224n33

Atlantic Migration, 77

"Atlas of History and Literature," 116

Auditors. *See* Lybrand, Ross Bros. & Montgomery

Backman, Joyce, 166

Bacon, Robert, 21; role in founding, 20–24; guarantees loans, 22, 37–39, 41; as Syndic, 23, 27, 28, 31, 32; war and death, 36, 38

Bailey, David W., 99, 214n1

Bailey, Herbert S., Jr., 198

Bailyn, Bernard, 74, 150, 152, 181

Baker, George P., 174, 175

Baker & Taylor, 35

Baldwin, Roger, mentioned 83

Bancroft Prize, 77, 152
Banfield, Edward C., *172*
Bank account of Press, 45, 46, 92
"Bankruptcy," university presses and, 125, 230n1
Barbour, Thomas, 69, 78, 225
Barnard, Chester, 74–75, 107, 181
Bate, W. Jackson, 153, 175, 238n2
Batstone, Fred, 219n69
Bayer, Herbert, 81
Bay Psalm Book, 5
Beale, J. H., mentioned 27
Behavioral Science Editor, 160
Belden, Lawrence P., 115, 118, 133
Belknap, Rey, 140, 142–143, 146
Belknap, Waldron P., Jr., *139*, 139–142, 234n47
Belknap Press, 129, 139–143; books, 143–150 passim, 171, 180, 182; deficit in seventies, 177
Bentinck-Smith, William, 119; on Press, 106–107; on Scaife, 123; *Harvard Book*, 135; acknowledged, 241, 242, 243
Berger, Raoul, 182
Bernstein, Leonard, mentioned 51
Bessie, Simon Michael, 174, 201–202
Bigelow, Jacob, 207n18
Biographies, 82–83, 135, 152–153, 180
Bishop, Costello, 182–183
Bishop, Dimmes, 159, 183
Bishop, John, 240, 243
Blake, Robert Pierpont, 48, 62
Blakiston Co., 132
Blanchard, Charles, 37, 39
Bloch, Konrad, 167, 175
Blum, John M., 138, 164
Board of Directors: created, 122–123; under Wilson, 127, 162–163, 174; and Carroll, 185–187, 195, 196; mentioned 30, 120
Board of Syndics. *See* Syndics, Board of
Bok, Bart J., 132, 231–232
Bok, Derek C., 202; as new president, 61, 191; and Carroll, 195–197; on nature of Press, 176, 197–198, 203; and Press after Carroll, 199–203 passim
Bok, Priscilla F., 232n17
Book-of-the-Month Club, 170
Book prices, 82; raises, 41, 187; protest over, 56; of music dictionary, 112; of

Langer paperback, 117; of paperbacks, 161; mentioned 84, 113, 151–152
Book storage, 58, 121, 129, 131, 193; Press warehouse, 125, 131, 194
Books, number of: cumulative, 2, 169, 177–178; under Rosenthal, 3; under Lane, 24; under Murdock, 43–44; under Malone, 66–67; under Scaife, 107; under Wilson, 125; in print, 175; under Carroll, 177; method of calculating, 211n1, 230n2, 238n1
Books Not Owned (BNO): under Murdock, 43–44; under Malone, 88, 93, 224n29; under Scaife and Wilson, 138, 171, 224n30; commissions raised, 93, 171. *See also* Series books
Boorstin, Daniel, mentioned 83
Boston Museum of Fine Arts, 56
Boston's Immigrants, 78, 201
Bragg, Sir Lawrence, 165
Breed, N. Preston, 119–120
Brewster, William, mentioned 83
Bridgman, Percy, 50, 78
Briggs, Grace, *118*, *158*, 241; early service, 71–72, 119; role in saving press, 123; on paperbacks, 162; retires, 201
Brinton, Crane, 83, 175
Browser (newsletter), 35, 154–155, 190
Bruner, Jerome, 171; book by, *172*
Brzezinski, Zbigniew, 137
Buck, Paul: on zany publishing, 86, 222–223; *General Education*, 111, 113; mentioned 115–116, 134, 143
Budgets, 93, 185–187, 191–192, 239n15
Burns, Christopher, 180, 183, 184, 190
Burr, Allston, 48
Business books, 51, 74–76, 182
Business Manager, 99–102, 173
Butterfield, L. H.: as editor of Adams Papers, 144, 146; on designers, 147; and President Kennedy, 149; on Carroll firing, 176, 197, 238

Cambridge University Press: as model, 8, 13, 19, 40; as oldest publisher, 9; use of "syndic," 23; Bruce Rogers at, 52
Camia, Mildreth, mentioned 219n69
Canfield, Cass, mentioned 230
Cannon, Walter B., 16, 23, 40, 48
Capps, Edward, mentioned 63
Carey-Thomas Award, 144, 145, 148

Carnap, Rudolf, mentioned 83
Carnegie, Andrew, 150
Carrell, Lynn, 131
Carroll, Mark, *177*, *157*, *178*; hired, 133; as Associate Director, 134; manuscripts, 156–159 passim; paperbacks, 162–165 passim, 236n17, 180–181; rises to directorship, 172–175; as Director, 176–195 passim; and staff, 182–184; budgets and deficits, 185–190; and Stephen Hall, 191–193; as standard bearer for university presses, 192, 193; dismissal of, 195–198; later career, 199; aftermath of firing, 202–203
Carver, T. N., mentioned 27
Cary, Austin, 16
Cella, Kathleen, 241
Center for International Affairs, 137
Center for Middle Eastern Studies, 137
Center for the Study of the History of Liberty in America, 169, 185
Chafee, Zechariah, Jr., 69, 78, 92, 101, 108
Chamberlin, E. H., 50, 220n15
Channing, Edward, mentioned 63
Charles Warren Center, 152
Chase, A. H., 233n34
Chase, George Henry, 91
Chastain, Murray, 179
Child, Francis J., mentioned 11
Claflin, William H., Jr., 90–91, 93–98 passim, 103, 107
Clarendon Press, 141
Clark, Grenville, 109, 110, 123
Clemente, Nancy, 180
Club of Odd Volumes, 45, 169
Cochran, Thomas C., mentioned 169
Cohen, I. Bernard, 78–79, 238n2
Cole, Arthur H., mentioned 49
Columbia University Press, 19, 118
Commercial publishers: Press's relation to, 19, 24, 25; and Harvard departments, 89–90. *See also individual firms;* Paperbacks
Commissions. *See* Books Not Owned
Commonwealth Fund, 132, 179, 237n35
Computers, 175, 189–190, 192, 240n23
Conant, James B., *87*, 203; becomes president, 60–61; seeks Director, 61–62, 64–65; replaces Syndics, 69; war years, 85–103 passim; versus Press, 85, 93–

94, 99, 100, 102–103; anniversary toast, 86, 169; on Press as a business, 102, 105; reconciled with Press, 107, 109, 110, 123–124; bans fund raising, 120; and search committee, 121; and science books, 132; mentioned 111, 113, 119, 243
Conkwright, P. J., 147
Contracts, 47
Coolidge, Archibald Cary, 28, 40, 48
Copeland, C. T., mentioned 51
Copeland, Melvin T., mentioned 27
Copland, Aaron, mentioned 51, 170
Copyrights, 47, 201
Cornell University Press, 207n25
Cox, Archibald, 174, 185
Crick, Francis H. C., 165–168
"Croesus": search for, 20, 31; found, 139, 140; mentioned 22, 62
Cross, Frank M., Jr., mentioned 175
Cummings, E. E., 51, 170
Cutler, Carl Gordon, 53, 216n27

Daniel, Ralph T., mentioned 112
David, Donald K., 122, 230
Davison, Archibald T., 82
Davison, Peter, 133
Dawson, John P., mentioned 175
Day, George Parmly, 90
Day, Joseph T., 58–60, 68, 219n10
Day, Matthew, 5
Day, Stephen, 4–5, 8, 30
Dee, Dorothy, 219n69
Dee, Margaret, 219n69
Dee, Mary, 219n69
Deficits: under Malone, 88, 92–93, 95, 101–102, 104; under Wilson, 128; under Carroll, 176, 185–190, 191; after Carroll, 187; hidden factors, 187–190; Stephen Hall on, 192, 193
Depression, 44, 46, 47, 66, 76–77
Design: heyday of, 43, 52–55; of Giedion book, 81; by Jones, 117–118; of Adams Papers, 147; under Wilson, 173, 238n38
DeVoto, Bernard, mentioned 83
Diary and Autobiography of John Adams, 144, *147,* 148–149
Dickinson, Emily, 143–144, 145
Dickson, W. J., mentioned 75

Dictionaries, oriental, 84. *See also Harvard Dictionary of Music*

Dictionary of American Biography, 65, 66, 70

Director. *See* Acting Director; Assistant Director; Assistant to the Director; Associate Director; Board of Directors; Press Director

Display room, 155

Dissertations, Malone on, 68

Distributed books, 211n1, 230n2, 238n1

Dobson, Eleanor. *See* Kewer, Eleanor Dobson

Dorson, Richard M., 116

Doubleday Anchor, 161, 162

Double Helix, 165–168, 174, 237n31

Douglass, Frederick, 150, 151

Dunlop, John T., 51, 171

Dunster, Henry, 4–5, 205n4

Durkee, Clara M., 219n69

Dwiggins, William A., 17–18, 37, *38,* 52–53

East Asian Research Center, 137, 138

Economics, as subject, 10, 15, 79, 181–182. *See also* Harvard Economic Studies

Editing: by proofreaders, 58–60, 70; what editors do, 71; of Barnard book, 75; of historical collections, 146. *See also* Editorial department

Editorial department: forerunner of, 58–60; creation by Malone, 70–71; under Kewer, 70; manuscript editors, 71, 157, 159; expansion under Scaife, 111–112; reorganizations under Wilson, 132–133, 156–159; acquisitions, 133, 156, 159–160; specialist editors, 156–160; under Horne, 157; in Carroll administration, 182; under Wilcox, 201; mentioned 96, 97, 99, 100, 131

Edmund Pendleton, 138–139

Elder, Joseph D., 131–132, *158,* 201; mentioned 159

Eleanor of Aquitaine, 135, 136, 162, 181

Eliot, Charles William, 9, 11, 14, 203; mentioned 13, 116

Eliot, T. S., 51

Elisséeff, Serge, 84

Emerson, Ralph Waldo, 171

Emerson, Rupert, 171

Endowment: sought, 18–21, 31–32, 62,

88; Smith fund, 88; Belknap, 139–142

Executive Editor, 132–133

External conditions, 66, 107, 128; under Carroll, 176, 187, 239n18. *See also* Depression; War, and the Press

Faculty Prize, 153–155

Fainsod, Merle, 137, 174, 175, 185

Fairbank, John K., 127, 134–135, 137–138, 180–181

Fenn, C. H., 84

Ferguson, William S., 48, 50

Festschriften, 136

"Fifty Books," 52, 238n38

Finances, in administrations of: Lane, 37–39, 41; Murdock, 44, 45–47; Malone, 88–96 passim, 104; Scaife, 107; Wilson, 121–122, 125; Carroll, 176–177, 185–196 passim. *See also* Deficits; Loans to Press; Profits; Sales receipts

Finley, John H., Jr., mentioned 83

Fischer, Ruth, 232n26

Fitzhugh, George, 150

Fogg Art Museum, 242. *See also* Sachs, Paul J.

Ford, David, 173, 179, 238n38

Ford Foundation, 129, 138, 173, 187

Foreign affairs, books on. *See* International affairs, books on

Founding of Press, 17–24; the founding fathers, 14, 22–23; Corporation vote on, 23

Fox, Bertrand, 174, 175, 185

Frankfurter, Felix, 78

Franklin Book Programs, 173

Franklin Spier agency, 135, 183

Frederick, Harold, 150

French, Helen L., 219n69

Friedlaender, Marc, 174, 243

Friends of the Press, 141, 233n43

Frisch, Karl von, 179

Frost, Robert, 115

Functions of the Executive, 74–75, 181

Fund raising, 18–21, 31–32, 88–89, 120, 141

Gabriel, Ralph H., 169

Galbraith, John Kenneth, 135

Gay, Edwin F., *18;* role in founding, 17–20, 22–23; as Syndic, 23, 28, 31, 32–33; later career, 36, 39; mentioned 46

General Education in a Free Society, 111, 113

Georgescu-Roegen, Nicholas, 181–182

Giedion, Sigfried, 79, 80–82

Gifford, W. L. R., 20, 21

Gilman, Daniel Coit, 10

Ginn & Co., 11, 14; gives titles to Press, 28, 63, 143; mentioned 12, 23, 35, 58

Glover, Elizabeth, 4, 5

Glover, Josse, 4

Godkin Lectures, 51, 83, 170

Goldberg, Leo, 232n17

Government, books on, 27, 50, 51, 137, 171, 172. *See also* American Foreign Policy Library

Grady, George, 57, 65

Grandgent, Charles H., 49, 51

Gras, N. S. B., 76

Gray, Asa, mentioned 11, 131

Gray Herbarium, 10, 129, 130

Great Chain of Being, 72–73, 74, 162, 181

Green, Samuel, 5

Greenough, James B., 11

Greenwald, Dorothy, 71, 72, 96, 243

Gregson, Walter S., 217n44, 220n10

Grinspoon, Lester, 181

Griswold, Erwin N., 174, 175

Hall, George, 191, 239n21

Hall, Max, 156; publications by, 207n22, 210n58, 234n53

Hall, Samuel, 206n8

Hall, Stephen S. J., 191–197 passim, 203

Hammond, Mason, mentioned 49

Handlin, Mary F., 143

Handlin, Oscar, 78; Press author, 78, 135, 143, 169; on Board of Directors, 174, 185, 203; Acting Director, 200, 200–201; mentioned 242, 243

Hanfmann, George, mentioned 175

Hansen, Marcus Lee, 77

Harbison, F. L., 171

Harman, Eleanor, on editing, 218n51

Harper Torchbooks, 72–73, 161, 162

Harris, Seymour, 50, 232

Hart, Albert Bushnell, 12, 63

Harvard, John, 4, 115. *See also* John Harvard Library

Harvard Alumni Bulletin, 17, 48, 115, 119

Harvard Books on Astronomy, 132

Harvard Business School: role in founding of Press, 17–18; and Press's rise in business field, 74–76; investigation of Press, 184; Donald Scott papers, 242; mentioned 69, 70, 119, 122, 156, 174, 182, 185, 195, 240n23. *See also* Printing and publishing courses

Harvard Case Studies in Experimental Science, 132

Harvard City Planning Studies, 51

Harvard Classics (Collier & Son), 116

Harvard Computing Center, 189, 192, 193, 240n23

Harvard Corporation, defined, 6

Harvard Crimson, 168

Harvard Dictionary of Music, 82, 111–113; mentioned 102, 171; *Brief Dictionary of Music,* 112–113, 162; *Concise Dictionary of Music,* 227

Harvard Divinity School, 23, 48, 129

Harvard East Asian Series, 137–138

Harvard Economic Studies, 15, 28, 50, 135, 171

Harvard Guide to American History, 63, 143

Harvard Health Talks, 27

Harvard Historical Monographs, 50, 171

Harvard Historical Studies, 15, 27, 28, 50, 171

Harvard Law School, 208n33; *Law Review,* 10, 16; casebooks, 15, 16; first Press book, 26; first Law Syndic, 48; mentioned 78, 174, 182, 185, 191

Harvard Medical School, 16, 27, 209n50; mentioned 23, 69, 181

Harvard Monographs in Applied Science, 132

Harvard Observatory, 10, 12

Harvard Oriental Series, 11, 56

Harvard Paperbacks, 180–181; mentioned 28, 49, 72–73, 78, 79, 84, 135, 161, 184, 228n1

Harvard Political Studies, 50

Harvard Semitic Series, 15

Harvard Sociological Studies, 223n12

Harvard Studies in Business History, 51, 76

Harvard Studies in Classical Philology, 11, 12, 28

Harvard Studies in Comparative Literature, 15

Harvard Studies in English, 219n3

Harvard Studies in International Law, 223n12

Harvard Studies in Romance Languages, 211n5

Harvard Studies in Urban History, 182

Harvard Theological Review, 15

Harvard Theological Studies, 211n5

Harvard University Press, nature of: educational versus business, 1, 102, 105, 199, 202–203; and purposes, 25, 184, 239n9; legal status, 32, 47; Malone's view, 68, 91, 94, 102–103; Perry's classic statement on, 109–110; Wilson's view, 125–126

Harvard University Printing Office. *See* Printing office

Harvard-Yenching Institute, 50, 84, 137

Harvey, William B., 198

Haskins, Charles H., 27, 49

Hastings, A. Baird, 69, 78, 225

Hawkes, Marion, 111–112, *118*

Hawthorne effect, 76

Heaton, Herbert, 210, 213

Heinemann (publishers), 63–64, 83

Henderson, L. J., mentioned 27

Henry Holt & Co., mentioned 62, 127, 132, 230n5

Herring, E. Pendleton, mentioned 230

Hilliard, William, 6–8

Hillyer, Robert, 27

History of American Magazines, 76–77

History, books on, 27, 50, 73–83 passim, 134–138 passim, 152; Harvard Historical Studies, 15; legal, 16, 26, 182; science, 78–79, 83, 132; *Harvard Guide to American History,* 143; Adams Papers, 144–148; editing of historical documents, 146; John Harvard Library, 148–152

Hitch, Charles J., 169

Hitchcock, Curtice, 62, 98

Hocking, William Ernest, 80

Hofer, Philip, 141–142

Holcombe, Arthur N., mentioned 49

Holden, Harley, mentioned 241

Holmes, Justice O. W., 78, 153

Homans, George C., mentioned 83

Horne, David H., *160*; editorial department under, 157–159; and paperbacks, 164–165; as Associate Director, 182; as Acting Director, 196, 197, 200

Hough, Jerry F., 137

Houghton Library, 141–142, 144, 171

Houghton Mifflin, mentioned 45, 61, 105, 116, 164, 209n52

Houston, Percy Hazen, 52

How Russia Is Ruled, 137

Howe, Mark Antony DeWolfe, 64–65

Howe, Mark DeWolfe, 78, 153

Humanities Editor, 159, 178, 201

Hutchings, John Henry, 140; joint stock association of, 143, 234n49

Hutchinson, Nanine, 183–184, 239n7

Ideological Origins, 152, 181

Imports, 50, 67, 133–134, 230n2

Inflation, 41, 214n4

Inkeles, Alex, 137

Institute for Comparative Research in Human Culture, 50, 67

Interest payments, 33, 128, 176, 188–189. *See also* Loans

International affairs, books on, 83–85, 134–135, 137–138. *See also* American Foreign Policy Library

International Book Export Group, 173

Jackson, William A., 141–142

Jacques, Herbert, 46, 57, 58, 61, 68, 219n69

James, Edward T., 180

James, Henry (lawyer), 48, 109, 110, 123

James, Janet W., 180

James, William, mentioned 11, 48, 70

Janet, Pierre, mentioned 73

Japanese editions, 75, 76, 79, 135, 137

Jefferson, Thomas, 6, 66, 103, 104

Jewett House, 129, *130*

John Harvard Library, 115, 143, 148–152

John Keats, 153

Johns Hopkins University, mentioned 10, 28, 73; press, 9, 19

Johnson, Herbert H., 216n28

Johnson, Thomas H., 144

Joint Center for Urban Studies, 169

Jones, Bessie Zaban, 114, 242, 243

Jones, Burton J., 117–118, 132, 145, 173, 238n38; mentioned 142, 145

Jones, Howard Mumford, 142, *151*, 240n33; acquires Mott volumes, 76–77; oversees Thackeray project, 114;

Jones, Howard Mumford (*cont.*)
proposes series, 114, 115; as Press author, 116, 135; as Syndic, 120; as head of John Harvard Library, 150–152; on Carroll firing, 197
Jordan, Wilbur K., 49, 83, 120
Journals, 10, 15
Jules, Alfred V., 102, *118*, 132
Jung, C. G., mentioned 73

Kain, John F., 169
Karnofsky, Manfred L., mentioned 175
Kellogg, Christopher C., 173
Kelly, Amy, 135, 181
Kelman, John, 216n27
Kennedy, John F., 149
Kennelly, Arthur E., 23, 40, 48
Kerr, Clark, 170, 171
Kewer, Eleanor Dobson, 70–71, 106–107, *118*, 123, *158*; and Barnard book, 75; on Pottinger, 96; and music dictionary, 111; affected by reorganizations, 133, 157, 159; retirement, 201
Kimball, Theodora, 222n43
Kittredge, George Lyman, 27–29, 29, 47–48, 60; role in founding 19–21 passim; as Syndic, 23, 24; on Murdock, 43; at peak of influence, 61; retirement and death, 69, 220n14; on Lowes, 218n55; mentioned 11, 40, 49, 62, 131
Kittredge Hall: move to, 129–131, *130*; naming of, 131, 231
Kluckhohn, Clyde, 116
Knopf, Alfred, Jr., 174, 236n12
Knopf (publisher), 37
Kuznets, Simon, 175, 181

Lakeman, Curtis E., 57, 68
Lamont Library, 113
Lane, Charles Chester, 26; as publication agent, 14–17; heads printing courses, 17; role in Press founding, 18–19, 22–23; as Press Director, 23, 25–42; in army, 37–39 passim; resignation and later career, 39–40, 41; and Printing Office, 57; mentioned 54, 66, 105
Langdell, C. C., mentioned 16
Langer, Susanne K., 79–80, 116–117; mentioned 81, 161, 181
Langer, William L., 50, 116
Langley, E. F., 211n5

Lanman, Charles R., 11, 217n37
Larsen, Roy E.: heads Visiting Committee, 88, 148; as Syndic, 98, 99, 100; and Adams papers, 148; mentioned, 114, 120, 230n53
Law, as subject, 10, 16, 78, 153; legal history, 26, 182
Lectures published by Press, 16, 28, 73, 75. *See also* Godkin Lectures; Norton Lectures
Legouis, Emile, 216n27
Leichtentritt, Hugo, 82
Leighton, Dorothea C., 116
Leontief, W. W., 79
Leopold, Richard W., mentioned 83
Levinson, Harry, 182, 184
Library of Congress Series in American Civilization, 169
Life magazine, 148, 235n62
Lincoln, Loring B., *118*, 119, 131, *158*, 201; on C. P. Snow, 170; on paperbacks, 237n18
Linotypes, 69, 220n11
Literature and language: series on, 11, 15, 219n3; Kittredge's books on, 27–28; Thackeray project, 114; *Guide to American Literature*, 135; Emily Dickinson projects, 144; Tanselle's *Guide*, 182; mentioned 49, 74, 83. *See also* Loeb Classical Library; Poetry
Little, Brown, 93–94, 103; mentioned 61, 85, 105, 107, 191, 227n10
Loans, to Press: and founding, 22, 23–24; under Lane, 32–33, 39, 41; under Murdock, 45, 46; under Malone, 88, 91; under Wilson, 128; interest payments on, under Carroll, 176, 188–189
Loeb, James: almost a Press founder, 13–14; as fund-raising target, 32; bequest to Harvard, 60, 63–64; mentioned 40, 83, 141
Loeb Classical Library, 14, 63–64, *194*; during wartime, 67, 83; sales growth, 155, 169; mentioned 8, 32, 72, 128, 133
Loos, Melvin, 52
Lorenz, Konrad, 180
Lovejoy, Arthur O., 72–73, 162, 181; mentioned 81, 107
Lowell, A. Lawrence, 21; role in founding, 20–24 passim; Press author, 27; and Lane, 31, 32, 39; and Murdock,

Lowell, A. Lawrence (*cont.*)
  41, 43, 45, 47, 58; mentioned 4, 14,
  60–61, 203
Lowes, John Wilber, 61, 65, 88, 90, 91
Luce, Robert, 51
Lybrand, Ross Bros. & Montgomery
  (auditors), 91, 188, 190, 193
Lybyer, A. H., 27, 28
Lynd, Robert S., 221n33
Lyons, Louis M., book by, *172*

McClurg & Co., 35
McCord, David, 115
McFarland, J. Horace, 17
McFarlane, James W., 91–92, 110
McKay, Donald C., 114
McKean, Roland N., 169
McLaughlin, Ann Louise, 243
MacLeish, Archibald, 62
Macmillan Co., mentioned 15, 19, 155
McNair, Malcolm P., 70, 225n40
Maguire, John M., 48
Makers of Modern Europe, 83
Malone, Dumas, 65, 66, 67; "scholarship
  plus" slogan, 2, 68, 70, 86; biography
  of Jefferson, 66, 103, 104; books published under, 66–85 passim, 111,
  221n40; on nature of Press, 68, 91, 94,
  102–103; starts editorial department,
  70–71; and Conant, 85, 86, 90, 93–94,
  102–103; financial difficulties under,
  86, 88; during wartime crisis, 86–104
  passim; on Lowes and Claflin, 90–91;
  divests Printing Office, 91–92; struggles
  to save Press, 92–96; and Pottinger,
  96–98; and Bailey, 99; and Sachs, 100;
  leaves Harvard, 103–104; mentioned
  107, 114, 120, 127, 171, 199, 243
Management and the Worker, 75–76
Managing Editor, 159
Marichal, Juan, mentioned 175
Mason, Edward S., 69, 174; mentioned
  50, 175, 185, 220n15, 242, 243
Massachusetts Historical Society, 144, 149
Massachusetts Institute of Technology,
  138, 169
Mather, Increase, 5, 49
Mather, Kirtley, mentioned 50
Matheson, Elizabeth M., 138
Maurice and Lula Bradley Smith Memo-
  rial Fund, 88

Mayr, Ernst, 171–172, 179–180; and
  Double Helix, 165, 167; mentioned 175
Mays, David John, 138–139
Maxwell, Donald, 219n69
Melcher, Frederick G., mentioned 230
Mellon Foundation, 187
Melville, Herman, 116
Mentor Books, 117
Merk, Frederick, 50, 143, 224n29
Metcalf, Eliab W., 7, 8
Metcalf, Keyes, 113, 121–123 passim
Metzger, Susan, 241
Meyer, J. Albert, 68–69, 223n22
Meyer, John R., 169
Miller, Perry, 49, 221n41
Modern Color, 53, 216n27
Mongan, Agnes, 82
Monis, Judah, 5
Monotype machines, 15, 33, 220n11
Moore, George F., 23, 28, 40, 48, 49
Morgan, Francesca Copley, 118–119
Morison, Elting E., 138
Morison, Samuel Eliot, 1, 2, 73–74, 143,
  205n1, 205n4, 206n8
Morison, Stanley, 49
Moses, Robert, mentioned 83
Mott, Frank Luther, 76–77, 169
Munn, James B., 69, 225n40
Murdock, Harold, 43–45, *44*, 61, 214n2;
  appointed Director, 41; administration
  of, 43–61; financial reorganization by,
  43, 45–47; typography under, 43, 52–
  54; and Syndics, 47; and Pottinger, 54–
  56, 96; and move to new quarters, 58,
  59; proof room of, 59–60; mentioned
  66, 67, 88, 92, 105, 169, 173
Murdock, Kenneth, 49, 60, 228n32
Murphy, Brian P., 182, 193–194, *194*,
  196, 201; mentioned 243
Murray, Gilbert, 51
Muses' Library, 134, 164
Museum of Comparative Zoology, 10, 69,
  172
Music, books on, 50, 82, 111–113
Myers, Charles A., 171
Myrdal, Gunnar, mentioned 83

Nash, Ray, 209n44
National Historical Publications and Rec-
  ords Commission, 235n64
New American Library, 117, 170

Newsletters, 35, 119, 154, 155, 190
New York Evening Post, 36, 39, 57
New York Metropolitan Region Study, 156
New York Times, 39, 52, 168; mentioned 58, 66, 240n38; *Book Review,* 134, 179
Nieman Fellows, 155, 190
Nilson, John A., 173
Norton, Charles Eliot, 13, 40, 51
Norton, W. W., 62; as publisher, 163
Norton Lectures, 51, 80, 81–82, 115, 169–170
Notable American Women, 180

Observatory, Astronomical, 10, 12
Ochs, Adolph, 66
O'Donnell, Joan, 220n21, 241
Offset printing, 84, 220n11
Oil revenues, 139–143, 177
Operations Manager, 182, 190, 193
Orlov, Ann, 160
Ostrom, John Ward, 232n26
Outside printing by the Press, 32, 45, 46, 215n10
Overhead, as Press expense, 82, 88; for Belknap Press, 140, 148, 150; mentioned 175, 190
Overseers, Board of, 48, 62
Oxford University Press: as model, 8, 13, 19, 40; age of, 9; and Belknap Press, 141; as Press's agent, 173, 213n27; mentioned 23

Packard, Frederick C., Jr., 51
Page, T. E., 63
Paperbacks, 160–165, 180–181; *Philosophy in a New Key,* 79, 116–117; music dictionary, 112–113; rise of, in America, 116–117, 161; in John Harvard Library, 151, 152; prices of, 161; number of leasings of, 161, 163; *Process of Education,* 171; paper bindings, 236n5. *See also* Harvard Paperbacks
Parsons, Talcott, 138
Parton, James, 151–152
Pauling, Linus, 166–167
Payne-Gaposchkin, Cecelia, 232n17
Paz, Octavio, mentioned 51
Peabody Museum, mentioned 18, 120
Pearson, Eliphalet, 6–7

Pease, Arthur Stanley, 64
Penguin Books, 116–117
Pepper, Stephen C., 53, 216n27
Perkins, Dexter, mentioned 50
Perkins, Maxwell, mentioned 65
Perry, Bliss, mentioned 51
Perry, Ralph Barton: as Press author, 49, 85; as Syndic, 70; role in saving Press, 108, 109–110, 123; mentioned 121, 199, 225nn39,40
Personnel. *See* Staff
Peters, James L., 50
Peterson, Eleanor, 219n69
Philanthropy, 41, 89, 141; Lula Smith bequest, 88. *See also* Belknap Press; Ford Foundation; Loeb, James; Mellon Foundation
Phillips, Henry, Jr., 233n34
Phillips, J. D., mentioned 210n64
Phillips Academy, Andover, 7
Philosophy, books on, 72, 79, 171, 178; by Wolfson, 116, 153
Philosophy in a New Key, 74, 79–80, 116–117, 161, 181
Phonograph records, 51–52
Piaget, Jean, mentioned 73
Pocket Books: and music dictionary, 112–113, 162, 227nn20,21; mentioned 116, 231n17
Poetry, 27, 27–28, 51, 144, 153; mentioned 115, 211n5, 238n2
Pollock, Sir Frederick, 78
Post, Chandler Rathfon, 50
Pottinger, David T., 54–56, 97; hired, 37; under Murdock, 43; as designer, 54; and Printing Office, 57; manages Press in interregnum, 61, 63, 219n69; as Associate Director, 65; and Arnold, 69, 96; versus Malone, 96–98, 224n38; resignation of, 96; as Press author, 98; and Bailey, 99; publications by, 214n2, 216n31, 217n48; mentioned 81, 92, 104, 242
Pottle, F. A., 216n28
Pray, J. S., 222n43
President and Fellows, defined, 6
Press anniversaries: twenty-fifth, 68, 86; fiftieth, 9, 169
Press Director, 105; search for, 61–62, 64–65, 121–122, 199–202. *See also* Lane, C. C.; Murdock, Harold; Ma-

Press Director (*cont.*)
   lone, Dumas; Scaife, Roger; Wilson, T.
   J.; Carroll, Mark; Rosenthal, Arthur J.
Press headquarters: University Hall, 4, *12*;
   compared with other presses, 14; Randall Hall, 33, *34*; Quincy Street, 58, *59*;
   Jewett House, 129, *130*; Kittredge Hall,
   129–130, *130*. See also Space problems
Prices. *See* Book prices; Printing prices
Princeton University Press, 14, 35, 178,
   198; mentioned 19, 147
Printing and publishing courses, 17–18;
   mentioned 19, 31, 33, 37, 54
Printing history, 2, 4–5. *See also* Printing
   office
Printing office: Harvard's first, 2, 5; second ("University Press"), 2, 6–8; third,
   9–10; and Publication Office, 11–12;
   profits of, and the Press, 32, 43, 45–46;
   Bruce Rogers at, 52, 54; efficiency of,
   studied, 57, 65; and proof room, 60;
   Malone on, 68; reorganization of, 68–
   69; divorced from Press, 89–92; Syndics on, 95; and Scaife, 114, 120, 121;
   mentioned 31, 100, 102. *See also* Printing prices
Printing prices: early dissatisfaction with,
   9–10; charged by Publication Office,
   15, 209n5; charged by Press's Printing
   Office, 32, 43, 45–46, 89–91
Printing Types, 48–49, 52
Prizes (for Press books): Anisfield Prize,
   76; Bancroft, 77, 152; Carey-Thomas,
   144, 145, 148; Dunning, 78; Emerson,
   238n2; Faculty Prize, 153, 238n2;
   Gauss, 238n2; Loubat, 76; Lowell,
   238n2; Paine, 238n2. *See also* Pulitzer
   Prizes
Process of Education, 171, 172
Production Manager, 69, 102, 132, 173
Profits: under Murdock, 46; under Scaife,
   105, 107, 120; under Wilson, 125,
   239n16; and university presses, 108,
   109. *See also* Printing office
Promotion Manager, 118, 119, 131, 182–
   183; early advertising, 35
Proof room, 58–60, 68, 70
Publication Office, 11–13, 14–17
Publishing: birth of, 5, 8; zany activity in, 86
Pulitzer Prizes: Mott, 76; Hansen, 77;
   Mays, 138; Bailyn, 152; Bate, 153;
   Samuels, 153

Pusey, Nathan M., *151*; on Wilson, 128;
   and *Double Helix,* 166–168; chooses
   Carroll, 175; horrified by deficits, 186;
   mentioned 148, 169, 191, 203
Pyne, Charles C., 238n36

Quarterly Journal of Economics, 10, 15
Quincy Street house, 58–59, 72, 93
Quine, Willard Van Orman, 171
Quinn & Johnson, 183

Radcliffe, 180; publishing course, 133,
   137; mentioned 79, 120
Rand, E. K., 49, 51
Randall Hall, 33, 34, 58, 72, 92
RAND Corporation Research Studies, 169
Randel, Don Michael, 227
Random House, mentioned 162, 163
Rawls, John, 178, 238n2
Ray, Gordon N., 111, 114
Raymond, Percy E., 78, 221n40
Readers (referees), 30, 135–136, 221n33
"Reciprocal Responsibilities of a Univer-
   sity and Its Press," 198–199
Reed, Christopher D., 154, 155
Reischauer, Edwin O., 84, 137
Reisner, George A., 56–57
Reynal & Hitchcock, 62, 98, 127
Reynard Library, 134
Reynolds, Edward, 119, 122, 123, 129
Riverside Press, mentioned 11, 45, 131
Robinson, Fred N., mentioned 51
Robinson, Nelson, 41
Rockefeller, John D., 14
Rockefeller Foundation, 75, 134
Roethlisberger, F. J., 75–76, 107
Rogers, Bruce, 52–54; mentioned 17, 43,
   45, 216n28
Rollins, Hyder E., 49, 216n27, 232n26
Ropes, James Hardy, 48
Roosevelt, Theodore, 16, 21, 138
Root, Elihu, 27, 41
Rosenthal, Arthur J., 3, 201–202; men-
   tioned 183, 193, 241
Rouse, W. H. D., 63
Royalties, 220n23; typical, 49; specific
   books, 73, 82, 211n9, 215n22, 222n41;
   Harvard Guide, 143; paperback, 161–
   162, 236n8; music dictionary, 227n20
Ruffin, Edmund, 150
Rugg, William C., 69, 82, 223n22
Russian Research Center, 137

Ruzicka, Rudolph, 37, 147
Ryder, A. W., 56

Saab, Ann Pottinger, 242
Sachs, Paul J.: appointed Syndic, 40, 69;
  as Press author, 82; Sachs Committee,
  94–99 passim; chairs Syndics, 100; role
  in Malone's departure, 100–103 passim; leaves Syndics, 121; mentioned
  107–108, 242
Sales: efforts under Lane, 35; to bookstores, 35, 54, 119, 170, 180, 186, 187;
  to libraries, 35, 64, 155; Sales Manager,
  56, 119, 131; sales department and paperbacks, 164, 180, 237n18; foreign,
  173. See also individual titles; Sales re-
  ceipts
Sales receipts: under Rosenthal, 3; under
  Lane, 35–36, 41–42; under Murdock,
  44; of Loeb Library, 64, 169; under
  Malone, 67; under Scaife, 107; under
  Wilson, 125; of Belknap Press, 140; of
  John Harvard Library, 150; under Car-
  roll, 185, 186, 187, 195; of Adams Papers, 235n64
Samuels, Ernest, 135, 153
Samuelson, Paul A., 135
Santayana, George, 15
Sarton, George, 83
Sawyer, Ruth H., 219n69
Saxton, Josephine, 131
Saxton, Mark, 131, 151, 158, 183
Scaife, Roger L., 105–107, 106, 118;
  early dealings with Conant, 61, 85, 93–
  94; appointed Syndic, 98; as Acting Di-
  rector, 103, 107–109; writes Malone's
  Annual Report, 104; as Director, 105–
  122 passim; staff of, 106–107, 117–
  119; role in saving Press, 107–109,
  123; versus Printing Office, 114, 121;
  and American Foreign Policy Library,
  114; mentioned 99, 100, 134, 136, 183,
  229n50
Schelling, Thomas C., 171
Schlesinger, Arthur M., Sr., 77, 78, 143,
  180
Schlesinger, Arthur M., Jr., 143
Schofield, W. H., 15, 210n64
"Scholarship plus," 2, 68, 70, 86
Schumpeter, Joseph A., 50
Science and Government, 170
Science, books on, 50, 78–79, 132, 170,

171–172, 179–180; medical, 16, 27,
  83–84, 132, 207n18. See also Elder, Joseph D.
Scott, Catherine S., 118
Scott, Donald, 18, 170; role in founding,
  18–23 passim; seeks funds, 31–32; on
  Scaife, 107; joins Syndics, search committee, and Board of Directors, 120–
  123; role in saving Press, 123; collabo-
  rator of Wilson, 125, 127, 163, 174–
  175; finances Faculty Prize, 153; Don-
  ald Scott Papers, 242; mentioned 36,
  169, 185
Scott, James Brown, 27
Scott, Louise, 153–154, 242
Scribner, Charles, 14
Sears, J. H., 20, 21, 32
Sedgwick, Ellery, mentioned 210n64
Sellers, Charles Coleman, 234n47
Series books, 11, 15, 50–51, 169–171;
  and Syndics, 28, 70, 111. See also par-
  ticular series; Books Not Owned
Sewall, Stephen, 6, 7
Shahn, Ben, mentioned 51, 170
Shapley, Harlow, 132, 231n17
Shattuck, George C., 84
Shaw, A. W., mentioned 210n64
Shaw, Oscar, 167, 237nn22,27
Shenton, Robert, 227n14, 241
Shils, Edward A., 138
Simmons, Ernest J., 82–83
Slocum, Thomas W., 48
Sly, J. F., 50
Smith, Datus C., Jr., 242
Smith, Lula Bradley, 88
Smith, Maurice, 88, 120
Smith, William Warren, 101, 118, 157;
  early service, 43, 56, 72, 219n69; war-
  time action on Loeb Library, 83; as
  Business Manager, 100–102; under
  Scaife, 106–108 passim, 117, 119, 121;
  role in saving Press, 123; as Associate
  Director, 133; influence of, reduced,
  134; retirement, 134, 173, 201; posi-
  tion on paperbacks, 162, 163; acknowl-
  edged, 242; mentioned 102, 132, 201.
  Quoted on: Adam Wilson, 12, 217n40;
  Pottinger, 54, 96; Giedion, 80; Conant
  book, 85; Sachs, 100; promotion, 118
Smithsonian Astrophysical Observatory,
  131
Snow, C. P. 170

Social Science Editor, 156
Society for Scholarly Publishing, 199
Society of Printers, 17, 33, 54, 132, 209n44
Solomon, Arthur K., 78
Space, Time and Architecture, 80–82
Space problems: early moves, 10, 33; under Murdock, 58; under Wilson, 129–131, 174–175. *See also* Book storage
Specialist editors, 156–160, 179, 190
Staff: in WWI, 37; under Murdock, 58, 219n69; under Malone, 70–72; under Scaife, 106–107, 117–119; under Wilson, 125, 127–128, 131–133, 156–160, 174–175; friction among, 127–128, 184; under Carroll, 182–184, 189; morale of, 195, 197–198
Stern, Madeleine, 9, 206n10
Stevens, George, 98
Stillman, Charles Chauncey, 51
Stockton, Philip, 48
Stone, Walter M., 37
Stratton, Burton, 132, 147, 158, 173
Stravinsky, Igor, mentioned 51
Studies and Notes in Philology and Literature, 11, 28, 219n3
Studies in Legal History, 182
Subsidies from authors, 67, 135, 232n30
Sutherland, Arthur E., 208n33
Syndics, Board of: created, 23–24; activities of, 28–30; as Press authors, 27–28 and passim; formal appeals to Corporation, 40 (*1919*), 61–62 (*1934*), 94–95 (*1942*), 108 (*1943*), 175 (*1967*); under Murdock, 47–48; Malone's new board, 69–70; operating rules, 70, 110–111; supports Malone, 90–95 passim; packing of board, 98; supreme authority, 98–102, 122–123; votes no confidence in Malone, 102–103; role in saving Press, 108, 123; under Scaife, 120–121; under Wilson, 127, 175; in *Double Helix* affair, 165, 166, 167; role in 1970s crisis, 190, 195, 197; role in search committee, 199–200

Tanselle, G. Thomas, 182
Taussig, Frank William, 12, 19, 27
Tax-exempt status, 30–31, 161
Technical Impex Corp., 190, 193–194

Tercentennial of Harvard, 73–74
Textbooks, 136–137; prior to founding of Press, 5–6, 7, 16; Japanese, 84; Greek, 233n34; mentioned 27, 108
Thackeray, William Makepeace, 111, 114
Thayer, John Eliot, 10
Theory of Justice, 178, 238n2
Thernstrom, Stephan, mentioned 169
Thompson, Charles M., 219n69
Thornton, Richard H., 62
Thurber, Charles H., 23, 24, 40, 63; mentioned 35, 48, 98
Time Inc. and Adams Papers, 148
Tinker, Chauncey Brewster, 55, 216n28
Torrey, Henry Warren, 209n52
Trilling, Lionel, mentioned 51
Turner, Frederick Jackson, 27, 63
Type metal mystery, 91
Typography, 48–49. *See also* Design

United States and China, 134, 163, 180
United States and Japan, 137, 163
University Hall, 4, 10, 11, 12
University of Chicago Press, 14, 15, 19
University of North Carolina, 121, 127, 169
University Press (the printing organization), 2, 6–8, 9, 10, 30–31
University Press Association, 35
University presses, 1; ages of, compared, 9; Gilman on function of, 10; a zany enterprise, 86; and profits, 108, 109; difficulties of, 119–120, 187, 196–197, 198; Association of American University Presses on nature of, 191, 198–199, 202. *See also* Association of American University Presses; Harvard University Press, nature of
Updike, Daniel Berkeley: as possible Press Director, 13–14, 31; as Harvard teacher, 17; *Printing Types,* 48–49; designer of Press books, 52, 54; mentioned 37, 210n64

Vendler, Helen, 238n2
Vernon, Raymond, 156, 169
Vice-president for administration: creation and functions of, 119, 191; as chairman Board of Directors, 122–123, 191; Press removed from jurisdiction of, 203.

Vice-president for administration (*cont.*) *See also* Hall, Stephen; Reynolds, Edward; Wiggins, Gard

Viking Press, mentioned 135, 137, 163

Vintage Books, 171; mentioned 135, 161, 162, 163

Visiting Committee: created, 48; fund raising by, 88, 120, 141; under Larsen, 88, 148; under Allen, 120; under Cox, 185; under Bessie, 201–202; mentioned 57, 61, 93, 109, 127, 151

War, and the Press: WWI, 25, 36–39; WWII, 66–67, 83–85, 89, 107

Ward, Theodora, 144

Warde, Frederic, 216n28

Warehouse. *See* Book storage

Warner, Sam B., Jr., mentioned 169

Warren, Charles, mentioned 83

Warren, Henry Clarke, 11

Warren, H. Langford, 13

Watson, James D., 165–168

Wedgwood Medallion of Samuel Johnson, 55, 216n23

Weems, Mason, 150

Weidenfeld & Nicolson, 168

Weinschenk, F. L., 208n37

Weinschenk, Gustave, 208nn30,37

Welles, Sumner, 114

Wellesley College, mentioned 133, 135

Wells, David A., 209n52

Wells, Edgar H., 19, 20, 21

Wertheim Publications, 50–51

Western Electric Co., 75–76

Wheeler, William H., 208n30

Whipple, Fred L., 231n17

White House library, 155

Whitehill, Walter, 146–148, 171, 197

Whiting, B. J., mentioned 83

Whiting, John W. M., mentioned 175

Widener Library, 20, 121, 129, 131, 169

Wiggins, Gard, 174, 175, 186, 189, 191

Wilber, Allen S., 62

Wilcox, Maud, *158*; hired and promoted, 133; as Humanities Editor, 159; ac-

quires Rawls book, 178; heads editorial department, 201; acknowledged, 241, 243; mentioned 157, 197

Wilkins, Maurice F. H., 165–167

Willard, Joseph, 6–7

Williams, John Bertram, 11–12, 14

Wilson, Adam K., 11–12, 57, 217n40

Wilson, Edward O., 179

Wilson, James Q., 199–200; mentioned 169, *172*

Wilson, Phoebe, 112

Wilson, Thomas J., 121–175 passim, *126, 149, 157, 170*; paperback policy, 112–113, 160–165; appointed Director, 121–122; as a savior of the Press, 123; expansionism of, 125, 174–175, 176; character and career, 125–128; and Scott, 125, 127, 163, 174–175; and editorial department, 131–132, 133, 156–160; and Smith, 133–134; and Carroll, 133, 134, 172–175 passim; and Belknap Press, 140–142 passim; role in Adams Papers, 144–149; *Double Helix,* 165–168; honorary degrees, 169, 170; international activities, 173; retirement and death, 173–175; mentioned 62, 112, 180, 183, 189, 197

Wohl, Martin, 169

Wolfson, Harry A., 49, 116, 153

Women authors, 79–80

Wood, Henry A., Jr., 122

Woodring, Carl, 238n2

Working capital: need for, 32, 40, 88, 122; under Wilson, 128; interest payments on, under Carroll, 176, 188–189

Wotherspoon, Lois, 183

Write-offs of inventory, 176, 188, 239n21

Wylie, Laurence, 171

Yale University Press, 35, 90, 148; mentioned 19, 65, 66, 157–159, 164, 169, 177

Zinsser, Hans, mentioned 48